Retelling Cinderella

Retelling Cinderella:

Cultural and Creative Transformations

Edited by

Nicola Darwood and Alexis Weedon

Cambridge
Scholars
Publishing

Retelling Cinderella: Cultural and Creative Transformations

Edited by Nicola Darwood and Alexis Weedon

This book first published 2020

Cambridge Scholars Publishing

Lady Stephenson Library, Newcastle upon Tyne, NE6 2PA, UK

British Library Cataloguing in Publication Data
A catalogue record for this book is available from the British Library

ISBN (10): 1-5275-5943-2
ISBN (13): 978-1-5275-5943-1

This book is dedicated to our friend and colleague Giannandrea Poesio whose grand battement jeté led us to this grand allegro, but who did not see our opening night.

TABLE OF CONTENTS

LIST OF ILLUSTRATIONS

ACKNOWLEDGEMENTS

There is a moment when every book has a beginning: a transformation scene. We vividly recall the personalities and excitement, the setting alight of intellectual fireworks and curlicues of imagination. The donation of a collection of Cinderella material sparked an idea over coffee with our friend and research director, Giannandrea Poesio. It was his imagination and enthusiasm for the initial project (an interdisciplinary, international conference) that lit the initial match, but the flames were added to by an excited group of people, all colleagues or former colleagues at the University of Bedfordshire including: Torsten Anders, Elena Caoduro, Luke Hockley, Carlota Larrea, Mark Margaretten, Karen Randell, Paul Rowinksi, Sarah Stenson, Victor Ukaegbu and Clare Walsh. We took this flame of an idea to our colleagues in the library whose care and documentation of the collection and the loan of pieces for the conference made it something different: Karen Davis, our archivist; Sarah Arkle, our Head of Reader Services; and Marcus Woolley, our Head of Learning Resources. The conference attracted many of the scholars whose work you have here and we thank them for their generosity and conviviality at that time and to this. Others have contributed to the event and subsequent discussion and we would like to thank for their support: Professor Mary Malcolm who despite her responsibilities as a senior manager has created the time to join us at the conferences and in discussions of the Research Institute and Mrs Stowe, benefactor of the Cinderella Collection, without whom none of this would have been possible. We are particularly grateful to Elena Caoduro for her involvement throughout this project until the more important task of parenthood took her time. And on that personal note, we would also like to acknowledge the support of our families who, once again, heard that immortal phrase 'just one paragraph to go'.

NOTES ON CONTRIBUTORS

Eleanor Andrews is a retired senior lecturer in Italian and Film Studies at the University of Wolverhampton, UK. She taught French Cinema, including Poetic Realism and the *Nouvelle Vague*, and Italian Cinema, including Neo-Realism and the Spaghetti Western. Her book on Italian director Nanni Moretti's use of narrative space, *Place, Setting, Perspective*, was published in 2014. She is co-editor of *Spaces of the Cinematic Home: Behind the Screen Door* (2015). Her other research interests include the Holocaust and disability in film.

Elena Caoduro is lecturer in Media Analysis at Queen's University Belfast. Her research on memory, nostalgia and European cinema has been published in journals such as *Networking Knowledge, Alphaville Journal of Film and Screen Media* and *NECSUS: European Journal of Media Studies*.

Marta Cola is a principal lecturer in Mass Communications and Postgraduate Portfolio Leader at the University of Bedfordshire, UK. She teaches Television Studies at undergraduate level, and research methods and media institutions at postgraduate level. Her research interests include audience studies, diaspora studies, media and identity.

Nicola Darwood is a senior lecturer at the University of Bedfordshire, UK and leads the undergraduate programme in English Literature, teaching courses on *Ulysses*, modern Irish Literature, the Gothic, and Restoration and Eighteenth Century Literature. Her research focuses mainly on twentieth century women writers and she has published work on Elizabeth Bowen and Stella Benson. She is currently particularly interested in the use of humour in fiction. She is the co-founder and co-chair of the Elizabeth Bowen Society, and the co-editor of *The Elizabeth Bowen Review*.

Nicky Didicher is a lecturer in English literature at Simon Fraser University in British Columbia, Canada, specializing in pedagogy, children's and young adult literature, and eighteenth-century British literature.

Maia Fernández-Lamarque is a full professor at Texas A&M University-Commerce and a Distinguished Global Scholar. She has published extensively in the field of critical theory on comparative cultural studies. She is the author of *Espacios posmodernos en la literatura latinoamericana contemporánea* (Argus-A 2016) and her book, *Cinderella in Spain: Variations of the Story as Socio-Ethical Texts* was published in 2019.

Donna Gilligan is a museum professional, heritage educator, and material culture historian who has worked in in a number of roles in the heritage and museum sectors over the past fourteen years. She specialises in work with historical and archaeological artefacts and museum collections, and has a strong research interest in Irish folklore, legends and mythology. She holds a B.A. and M.A. in English and Archaeology, an M.A. in Museum Practice and Management and an M.A. in Design History and Material Culture.

Sally King is a third-year PhD student at De Montfort University, Leicester, UK. Her thesis examines the representation of the slipper in translations and adaptations of *Cinderella*, and its evolution since the tales of Charles Perrault (1697) and the Brothers Grimm (1812-1857). She is interested in adaptations in film, toys, dance and pantomime.

Vanessa Marr is a senior lecturer in Graphic Design, Illustration and Fashion Communication with the University of Brighton, UK. Her professional experience includes working for Dorling Kindersley as an Art Editor and running her own successful design agency for 8 years. An M.A. in Sequential Design and Illustration refocused her practice, which underpinned by visual design-theory and process, embraces an intuitive and practical approach, facilitating both self-authorship and collaborative investigation.

Lesley McKenna is a senior lecturer in Creative Writing at the University of Bedfordshire, where she teaches specialist modules in Writing Horror and Dark Fantasy Fiction; and Writing Fantasy Fiction. She has a BA first class honours in Creative Writing; and gained a distinction in her Masters by Research degree in 2008. The resulting novel, *Clutching Shadow*, a story of incest, betrayal and death, was long listed for the Cinnamon Press novel prize in 2008. Lesley is also a published prose poet. She is currently working on a Lovecraftian-inspired dark fantasy project that explores dreams, dreamers and the dreamlands.

César Mora Moreo is a student of Social Communication and Journalism in Universidad del Norte, Barranquilla, Colombia. He serves as Research Assistant at the Department of Social Communication in subjects related to cinematographic analysis, literature, journalism and scripts.

Rebecca Morris is a postgraduate student at the University of Hull. She is currently working towards a PhD in children's literature and the working title of her thesis is 'Little Princesses and Schoolgirl Witches: Girl Heroes and the Fairy-tale Tradition in Children's Fiction'. She specialises in children's and young adult literature and has research interests in the Victorian period, early twentieth century fiction and American women's writing.

Enrique Uribe-Jongbloed has been a full professor at Universidad de Bogotá Jorge Tadeo since 2017 and was formerly professor and researcher at the Department of Social Communication in Universidad del Norte, Barranquilla, Colombia. He obtained his PhD from the Department of Theatre, Film and Television Studies at Aberystwyth University, Wales, in 2013. His research interests include identity, language and media production. He edited the book *Social Media and Minority Languages*.

Alexis Weedon is professor of publishing and UNESCO chairholder in New Media Forms of the Book at the University of Bedfordshire, UK. She is the author of *Victorian Publishing: The Economics of Book Production for a Mass Market 1836-1916* (2003) editor of *The History of the Book in the West* (2010), co-editor of *Convergence* (1995-2017) and co-author of *Elinor Glyn as Novelist, Moviemaker, Glamour Icon and Businesswoman* (2014), and writes on publishing, the book as media, and cross-media storytelling.

INTRODUCTION

NICOLA DARWOOD AND ALEXIS WEEDON

In both *Harper's Bazaar* and *Maclean's Magazine* in March 1932 there is a full-page advert for a 'Coach for Cinderella'. The body styling, uses of colour, attention to upholstery, interior trim, fittings and equipment conveniences of this gorgeous concoction, we are told, have 'had the demands of feminine censorship as their standard'. The Coach is in fact a luxury car and the company, Fisher Bodies, is targeting the feminine tastes of the emancipated woman: 'Freed after untold centuries from the narrow restrictions of a purely domestic life, she has emerged, like a radiant Cinderella, into a broader, finer, more beautifying existence'. In this one advert we can see the confluence of themes which surround the Cinderella story: escape from drudgery, wish to travel, the transformation of mundane objects into desirable ones, and joyful pleasure of finery ('A Coach for Cinderella', 51).

The story is so well known that it has become a shorthand for the unexpected success of the disregarded: men as well as women, companies as well as people. Amusingly in the same year as the *Harper's Bazaar* and *Maclean's Magazine* advert, *The Exeter and Plymouth Gazette* reported on the resurgence of fish and chips which was becoming 'a most respectable as well as profitable business', 'ceasing to be Cinderella'. The contrast between American and British cultures in the two publications is diverting, but the meaning of the reference transcends both. Today Cinderella's eclecticism is apparent on social media which provides many examples of cross-cultural use: Instagram's hashtag #reallifecinderella features everything from personal stories to shoe art and the framed motivational quote to 'set my goals and achieve them all'. A similar search on Twitter loads references to dating, weddings, make-overs, party dresses, shoes (lost and found), moments of change in life, and overcoming the odds. Disney .gifs have become digital motifs to communicate feelings of drudgery (cleaning), the pleasure of giving (mice helpers), the doom of deadlines (midnight clock), greed (Lucifer's gambling), and the moment the shoe fits as something comes right. Overall, social media use shows how the term is still being morphed and made relevant in the modern-day.

The essays in this volume reflect on the material and cultural legacy of the tale and how it remains active and relevant in many different societies where social and family relationships are adapting to modern culture. It opens aptly with a wander though one person's collection of Cinderella books, *objet* and ephemera from across the world which has been donated to the University of Bedfordshire. The Collection holds materials ranging from opera and ballet programmes, books and theatre models, to collectable figurines, toys and merchandise which convey the wide variety of adaptations and performances that the story has inspired. These were not simply bought, they were the product of a singular interest in the tale over many years and demonstrate how her passion caused the collector to go to The Royal Ballet and attend a pantomime on the same theme, save the plastic key ring of a crystal shoe and treasure a china figurine. It gathers together contemporary kitsch and original editions of the earliest retellings.

So we took the lead from the collection and structured the book so that the reader moves from contemporary forms of Cinderella back in time. We start with Cinderella as a parodic meme. The frames from the Disney animation have become the creative substrate for mobile memes circulated from phone to phone in Colombia. For comic effect these memes reversed the mild-mannered Cinderella of the children's story, creating a foul-mouthed sassy character. This cultural transduction and appropriation is investigated by Enrique Uribe-Jongbloed and César Mora-Moreo whose research into this phenomena shows how it was localised to specific bus routes and idiomatic dialect. *Cenicienta costeña* parodies the subservience of the traditional character, but also the Disneyfication of the tale. The passivity of Cinderella has been problematised within a more feminist culture. Next in the collection is Marta Cola and Elena Caoduro's inquiry into contemporary online dating through the Tinder app and their discussion of the way the feminine derivative term Tinderella has become meme for women's proactive dating. They lay out for us the array of spin-offs such as advice blogs, multiple newspaper columns, and personal narratives in book form written by women of their experiences of finding a partner online. Such an active role for women can be interpreted differently in different cultures. It is a theme which Nicky Didicher explores in chapter 3 as she takes us into the young adult science fiction world of Marissa Meyer's *Cinder* (2012). The novel challenges both our gender expectations and our moral expectations, enlarging the young readers' spectrum of possibilities. Cinder is a mechanic and a cyborg, more comfortable in coveralls than dresses, and she is incapable of producing tears. The ideology of *The Lunar Chronicles* series promotes diversity and complicates the morality of the traditional Cinderella characters which then have to be assessed afresh by the young reader. Nevertheless, it also employs common romance-novel tropes to re-assert the value of heteronormativity allowing for a conventional happy ending.

Moving from the paratextual use of Cinderella to the transformational narrative itself, Eleanor Andrews investigates differences between the notions of change and transformation across versions of Cinderella and Pygmalion from Ovid's poem to a selection of film representations including *My Fair Lady* (Cukor, 1964), *Educating Rita* (Gilbert, 1983), *Pretty Woman* (Marshall, 1990) and *Nikita* (Besson, 1990). The transformation of Pygmalion objectifies her, creating an object for the male gaze, while *My Fair Lady* and *Educating Rita* dramatise the transformative power of education and its ability to overcome the disadvantages of poverty and class. Filmic and theatrical versions often emphasise Cinderella's transformation through dress and, in the next chapter, Sally King delves into the early English and German translations of *Cendrillon* and *Aschenputtel*, mining these texts for their references to changes in fashion, and ideas of beauty and appearance. She highlights the differences arising from a small variation in word choice, and she reflects on the intertwining of ideology and sartorial detail while considering interlingual and intercultural exchanges which have a significant effect on the way that women are represented in these different editions.

The theatre motif however is never far away and Nicola Darwood's discussion of Nancy Spain's *Cinderella goes to the Morgue: An Entertainment* (1950) draws on a history of pantomime and detective fiction. She considers Spain's appropriation of the Cinderella tale in the post-World War II era, as her characters are embroiled in murder and mayhem in a witty satire on the world of pantomime with all the stock characters a reader could possibly hope to encounter. Moving back into the late nineteenth and early twentieth century Rebecca Morris turns the attention of this collection to the use of the Cinderella motif in the fiction of Anne Thackeray Ritchie and Frances Hodgson Burnett, authors who chose to critique the Victorian ideal of a submissive Cinderella figure and who used their fiction as a vehicle to comment on contemporary attitudes towards gender, particularly in the light of suffrage campaigns in the second half of the nineteenth century.

Underlining the undeniable fact that there is not just one version of the story of Cinderella, Maia Lamarque's essay continues the exploration of the Cinderella tale in a European context as she provides a detailed history of the story within the history of twentieth and twenty-first century Spain. Tracing the history of the Cinderella story in Spain back to the medieval variant, "Estrellita de oro", and then drawing on a considerable body of knowledge of the political history of Spain, she considers how the representation of the Cinderella figure changed in response to societal and political changes over the centuries, from a conservative representation in the 1950s to one of political resistance in the twenty-first century. Donna Gilligan focuses on Irish retellings which draw on a rich tradition of Irish storytelling in both the written and the oral form. Highlighting differences between Perrault and the Grimm Brothers' versions of the tale, she demonstrates how the Irish variants blend Irish mythology and folklore, providing a valuable insight into the native traditions and the contemporary society which enjoyed these tales.

We end with two creative pieces: 'Domestic narratives in Cinderella's cultural translation', which opens with the creative reflections of Vanessa Marr as she considers the tale of Cinderella as 'the ultimate domestic narrative'. Discussing her creative practice of embroidering of yellow dusters, she challenges a dominant motif of the Cinderella tale—that domesticity is the route to marital happiness—and evokes a catalyst for change, not just for Cinderella, but for all women. Her essay embroiders together practice and theory as she explores her own relationship with both the material and the cultural environment needed to effect change. Finally, Lesley McKenna's short story updates the Cinderella tale, setting it within the emotional high-stakes of a high school Prom. Her reflection on the themes of the fairy tale illustrates how the material has limitless flexibility for the creative writer. It is an apt ending to this collection of storytelling transformations of Cinderella.

Modern retellings of the story abound: Kenneth Branagh's live action *Cinderella* (2015) was set the Disney fantasy world of movie stars in ball gowns and crystal shoes, with a little pantomime humour from the transformed animals and the pumpkin coach, but Michael Bourne's ballet touring in 2017–2018 set the story in 1940s wartime Britain, opening with the cry 'do not look at the sky' during air raids: the traditional tale of maidenly coming-out at a ball becomes a wartime affair broken off by a bomb shell falling on Cinderella and her airman-prince who end up hospitalised. Its radical message of broken families and disrupted relationships is emphasised by Cinderella's disabled father, a veteran from the previous war. Nevertheless, the *deus ex machina*, an angel, ensures a fairy tale ending, complete with ball gown and fireworks. These recent versions illustrate the continuing duality of the story. The uplifting message of Cinderella still sells an increasingly problematic conformity to traditional womanhood by persuading you to buy comfort, aspire to be a domestic goddess or reaffirm the myth of a 'happy ever after'. But it's also evident that she can also be the symbol for suffrage, for equality and empowerment. We believe that her story will continue to be reused, reappropriated, and refashioned in a way that continues to highlight changing societal mores and ideologies: always fascinating, for ever changing.

Works cited

Anon. 'A Coach for Cinderella' *Harper's Bazaar* 1932. Print.
—. 'A Coach for Cinderella' *Maclean's Magazine* 1932: 51. Print. http://archive.macleans.ca/article/1932/3/15/a-coach-for-cinderella#!&pid=50 Accessed 20 March 2020.
Bourne, Michael, choreographer. *Cinderella*, 1997, revised and designed for Sadlers Wells and on tour 2017-2018. Ballet.
Branagh, Kenneth, director. *Cinderella*. Performance by Kate Blanchett, Lily James: Allison Shearmur Productions, Beagle Pug Films, Genre Films, Disney, 2015.

CHAPTER ONE

THE MATERIAL CULTURE OF CINDERELLA: INTRODUCING THE CINDERELLA COLLECTION

ALEXIS WEEDON

In August 2012 the University of Bedfordshire was given a collection of items all about Cinderella. It was one person's collection, gathered over a number of years in the 1990s and is an example of a fascination with the fairy tale and its retellings in our culture. It is housed at our library in Bedford and shares its archival lodging with the much larger Hockliffe collection of rare primers, readers and children's books that was donated by a specialist bookseller from the town. On the open shelves in this cool room are the books and alongside are the archive boxes with the *objet* and *ephemera*. There are cuttings, tins, jigsaws, souvenir programmes, figurines, and porcelain collectables. Each are not necessarily unique in themselves, but as a collection it is intriguing. It offers unusual insights into the range of discourses and disciplines that claim the tale of Cinderella.

What was the reason for the acquisition of this material and how can we learn from it? Deposited with the collection is a series of annotated file cards and clearly some of the items were aids to a talk; the laminated copies of illustrations from the famous Opie collection of children's literature for example and the portfolio of front covers of novel adaptations of the Cinderella story for the young adult market. There are numerous clippings from newspapers, sadly for us undated, but the notes say they were the result of 'a year in which she looked for every reference to Cinderella in the news'. Regardless of antiquity or significance, originality or value, the eclectic collection focuses solely on references to Cinderella. Its broad church approach encompasses rare editions and kitsch, collector's items and magazine pages.

Looking through the material some themes emerge. Firstly, there is an interest in education. The owner's decision to donate to the library at Bedford, where the University's history can be traced back to one of the earliest teacher training colleges in Britain, supports this, and it came with a request that the collection was 'put to use' by students. Secondly, it is not a bibliophile's collection and although there are first editions most of the books are not rare or expensive. The material is mostly from the nineteenth and twentieth century, the last acquisition is 2008. Thirdly the collection includes the merchandise that has grown up around the Cinderella characters from key-ring souvenirs to porcelain figurines. And finally there are theatre programmes to professional pantomime, opera, ballet as well as amateur and school performances.

The Collection gives a particular lens through which to view the Cinderella tale. It is not representative, or even a reliable subset, it is necessarily selective and possibly serendipitous, as some items appear to have been gifts to the collector. However it is interesting because of the range of material that has been kept and because it was actively added to in the 1990s, a period of significant change in the media and publishing industries. It therefore provides a glimpse into the history of the tale in children's education and play, specifically in the revisionary retellings following the women's movement in the 1970s and 1980s and the effect of globalisation in the media industries on the representation of the Cinderella character and her alignment with the 'princesses' party dresses and toys marketed to young girls in the 1990s.

Trends and market sectors

To give us some context of the use of the story from the 1800s—the earliest item in the collection is George Cruikshank's chapbook of Cinderella printed in 1814—we can look at the occurrence of Cinderella in Google's text corpus (fig. 1-1). This also provides a clue to the popular use in different linguistic cultures.[1] The analysis of the Google corpus provides, as big data does, alternative ways into a problem. It gives us a glimpse of the use of the Cinderella motif *inside* texts that may not be ostensibly about the fairy tale as we shall see later. The ngrams chart shows a growth trend in its usage in English from the 1790s to the 1920s and after a period of decline, another upward trend from the 1960s to the millennium. In Spanish there is a different pattern, a slow growth from 1890s to 1990s and a third pattern in German and Italian where its use is not significant until after the second world war. There is a suggestion in the chart that the impetus for the retelling of fairy tale and the use of

---

[1] We must treat Google ngrams with caution as it is a limited and unrepresentative corpus and does not have the scholarship of existent bibliographies or bibliographical histories of Cinderella.

Cinderella motif was until the mid-twentieth century dependant on the way the tale was collected by folklorists and retold for the children's market and that translations emphasised the linguistic or national origin. In the second half of the twentieth century, the forces of globalisation came into effect, first through film adaptations and later through 'Disneyfication', franchising of characters and branding.

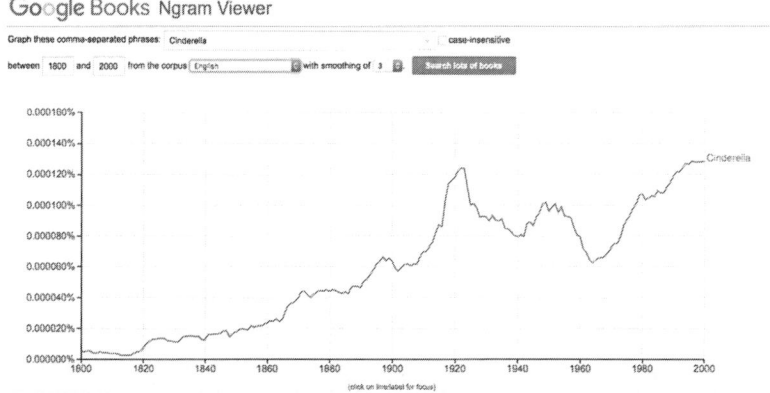

Fig. 1-1. Google ngrams chart of the occurrence of Cinderella in English text corpus. Source: http://books.google.com/ngrams

In the Cinderella collection at the University of Bedfordshire there are a number of books from the 1970s and 1980s about the study of folklore published in Britain and America. It is indicative of a wider resurgence in Anglophone folklore studies; from two women authors in the field there is Katherine M. Briggs, former president of the British Folklore Society's work, *British Folk Tales and Legends: a Sampler*, and the amusingly titled *Field Guide to the Little People* by Nancy Arrowsmith that categorises 79 different types of supernatural creatures, details of which were compiled on her travels through USA, Europe and India. Other trade titles show the appeal of folklore theories to hobbyists such as the controversial proponent of Atlantis, Lewis Spence's work, *British Fairy Origins* and the readable retellings of Cinderella-type stories from across the world gathered by Neil Philip. Alongside these are two University Press titles: Alan Dundas', *Cinderella, a Casebook* and John Martin Ellis', *One Fairy Story Too Many: The Brothers Grimm and Their Tales*. Nevertheless the folk festival revivals and folk studies publications of the 1970s and 1980s are a separate cultural movement.

Reflecting the trends identified in the ngrams, the Cinderella collection has a number of editions in different languages. These date from the 1990s and are indicative of the changes occurring in publishing at that time. The square mini hardbacks of Stephanie Laslett's *Cinderella [Assepoester]* in Dutch and English illustrated by Carole Sharpe (Laslett and Sharpe *Assepoester; Cinderella;* Laslett and Sharpe *Cinderella*) show how transnational the children's sector had become. Audio technology was important in this market as we see with Eva Wenzel-Bürger's picture book *Aschenputtel: ein Märchen der Gebrüder Grimm* [Cinderella: a fairy tale by the Brothers Grimm] that comes with a cassette. For the non-readers Ingrid Buthod-Girard's pop-up panorama book illustrated by Carlos Busquets and published by Hemma foregrounds the continuing and singular importance of the illustrator in children's book market. Busquets's work became global: he is known for his own characters El Conejo Sócrates and Le Petit Lapin Bleu and began his career with the Spanish publisher Editorial Roma. Later he placed his colourful, rich and detailed illustration with Susaeta Publishing, and with Hemma who published children's books in French and Dutch based on the characters from television, film and toys with franchises such as Disney, Barbie, Charlotte aux Fraises, Littlest Petshop and Dora. Hemma are part of Grupo Planeta who have a large stake in the Spanish and Latin American market and are the second largest publishing group in France. Their operation is indicative of the forces of globalisation, the move by many publishers to cheaper printing in Italy, and the reach of character brands.

The Collection also brings up the other uses of the motif: in psychology the Cinderella complex was used to refer to women's fear of independence and wish to be taken care of by men. Colette Dowling described it analytically in her book in the collection. Another application, the Cinderella syndrome, ranges across psychology to self-help books. The Christian author Lee Ezell sees the problem as one of what to do when your dreams don't come true. In psychology it is the name given to dysfunctional relationships between stepmothers and stepchildren: 'A child is one hundred times more likely to be abused or killed by a stepparent than by a genetic parent' warns Martin Daly and Margo Wilson on the cover of *Truth about Cinderella: a Darwinian View of Parental Love* and they examine the destructive power of false accusations made by children of a stepmother or a stepmother over-compensating to gain acceptance by her new family.

Nowadays, the self-help sector has one of largest market shares in Britain and America. The tale of Cinderella deals with family relationships and women's empowerment and offers a short-hand for authors offering help to customers seeking guidance. The titles on Amazon.com show how the story character is read today both as a vindication of womanhood and as an out-dated feminine model: *Simply be Cinderella—the guide to building self esteem, confidence & happiness* reflects positively on the character while *Put the pumpkin down and take yourself to the ball, a fresh fun guide to taking control of your life* implies Cinderella has no agency. Similarly some authors ask: *Would you really want the shoe to fit? Subtle ways women are seduced and socialized into servitude and stereotypes,* while others take issue with the idealised romance: *The real reason you can't find (or keep) a prince.*

In the Collection we see that Cinderella is powerful metonymic in book titles not only in the expected categories of folklore, fiction, children's and education, self-help and psychology, but which also extends into other popular publishing categories in the 1980s and 1990s such as military, sociology, cookery, design history and fashion (Brown; Mazza; Tillett).

Performance and play

Many of the titles in the Collection are from children's fiction and retell the fairy tale for a young audience. There is a strong performance theme in toy books or games, pantomime, plays and songs. These books are aimed at parents and teachers as much as the children themselves. Nineteenth century publishers included it in their series such as Warne's National Nursery Library, Macmillan's The Golden Treasury, Halle's Jack and Jill series, and publishers of children's books kept it on their list: there are examples of T. Nelson & Sons, Blackie & Sons and T. C. & E. C. Jack in the collection. For the slimmer pocket Aldine's penny pamphlets of Tales for Little People catered for the domestic reader. Asking a well-known author to refresh the story is an old publishing tactic: the Victorian writer and poet Dinah Maria Craik known for her novel *John Halifax Gentleman* 'rendered anew' the best popular fairy stories for Macmillan in The Golden Treasury series (*Fairy Book: The Best Popular Fairy Stories Selected and Rendered Anew*). It had a steady stream of repeat print orders for her simple retelling. The language is unimaginative but her name and the pictures sold the book. It was still in print before the First World War when Warwick Goble was the gift book illustrator for Macmillan and produced an edition with thirty-two illustrations.

If Craik's retelling is for reading at the fireside or in a child's bedroom, the later Victorian Florence Bell's is aimed at schools. Although a liberal, her's was no rags to riches story: she was the daughter of the Lord Mayor of London and she married into the steel, colliery and railway industry, but she was a social investigator and educationalist. The Hugh Bell schools in Middlesbrough were named after her husband and the two were involved in the schools' annual activities. *Fairy Tale Plays and How to Act Them* issued by the educational publisher Longman is prefaced by a didactic introduction to rehearsing junior school children, putting together a simple stage, making props and illustrated steps for the different dances that the children perform. Music and songs are included within the play dialogue. Bell dedicated her book to 'Anne Thackeray Ritchie in affection, admiration and gratitude', an author whose own adaption of the Cinderella story is examined in chapter eight of this volume. Bell was not a teacher herself, nor an actor, but she wrote plays and children's books, and staged a costly historical pageant of over 500 people for which she sold her editions of Dickens to fund. Her concern for the community was deep and with stepdaughter Gertrude Bell she researched working class living and reading habits in Middlesbrough published in her book *At The Works*.

Bell's is not the only play in the collection, Eleanor Farjeon's *The Glass Slipper* was originally a collaboration with her brother Herbert in 1944.[2] It was later novelised and this edition is in the collection illustrated by Ernest H. Shepard, especially known for his drawings of Winnie-the-Pooh. Farjeon's love of poetry and lightness of touch captures some of the on-stage moments. Described as 'not a pantomime' the idea was to 'tell the fairy tale for its own sake' and the production was well received by the public (Anon 'Pantomimes'). It was produced by English Academy Award winning theatre and film actor Richard Donat (remembered now for his role in Hitchcock's *The 39 Steps*) and had harlequinade characters, a speaking grandfather clock and music by Clifton Parker. The Ballet Rambert did the dances. In her day, Farjeon won the Carnegie (1955), the Hans Christian Andersen (1956) and the Regina (1959) medals for children's literature and gave her own name to a prize still awarded by publishers. She is recognised now for her poetry and her short story collection *The Little Bookroom* (1955).

The twenty-first century notion that children come to a text after having met the story already through film or television has historical antecedents, as has the engagement of children through participation in the storytelling. Bell's and Farjeon's books show us that many children saw it in a theatrical version, perhaps as a pantomime or a stage play or even an opera before the television era. For example the Collection has Alan Blyth

---

[2] Although MGM had bought the rights to the play, the story differs in the musical film adaption (Walters 1955).

and Emanuele Luzzati's illustrated *La Cenerentola: the Story of Rossini's Opera* for young theatre-goers and theatre programmes from performances as varied as celebrity panto, Royal Ballet, even Cinderella on ice, as well as hand-crafted programmes from school productions. Janet and Alan Ahlberg's amusing *Cinderella Show* derives its humour from such an imagined school production related through graphics and speech bubbles.

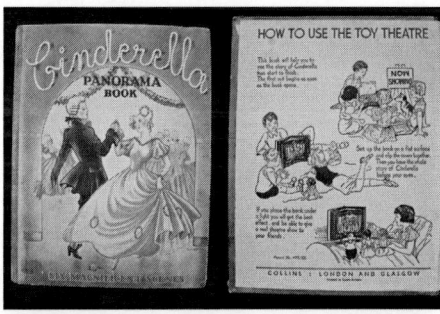

Fig. 1-2. Inside front cover and book opening showing *Cinderella Panorama Book: Six Magnificent Scenes*, Collins c.1950, author's own photographs.

What the children saw on stage could be re-enacted at home and publishers and printers have always been ingenious in how they have used the codex structure and the technology of paper in various forms. Collins's patented panorama book retold Cinderella in 'six magnificent scenes' (c.1950) (fig. 1-2). Instructions on the inside cover showed the children how to use the cut-out characters to dramatise the story. Its board 'pages' are joined and die-cut to fold out as proscenium arches with printed scenes. It was published around the same year as Walt Disney's magic wand book that includes several 3-dimensional plates and glasses to view them with (*Cinderella Magic Wand Book*). Amazingly both have survived childhood and 80 years. More recent interactive publications in the collection include pop-up books, and a crime story version in which Rumplestiltskin is the detective employed by Cinderella's father-in-law-to-be to seek out the truth about her before her marriage, the documentary evidence being hidden in envelopes that the older child can open (Anon *Cinderella: A Mini Pop-up Storybook;* Durant and Collins; Perrault and Mateu). A magic 3-dimensional fairy-tale world by Ronne Randall illustrated by Frances Thatcher also has Richard Jewitt's creative contribution in paper engineering acknowledged. So the collection is about the material culture of Cinderella and as the last accession was made in 2008 and it is exclusively analogue.

Two centuries of lessons from Cinderella

Children's books have always been for education as well as entertainment and Cinderella's story lends itself to a variety of lessons relevant to the period in which they were published. The oldest, George Cruikshank's chapbook, is an early form of what he later issued in his fairy tale library. Cruickshank was a campaigner against the evils of drink due to the fact that his father died early of alcohol poisoning. So at the end of *Cinderella and the Glass Slipper* when the King plans to 'celebrate the marriage of Cinderella and the Prince with "fountains of wine", the Fairy Godmother objects. The King orders all the "wine, beer, and spirits" in the land to be burned in a giant bonfire on the night of the wedding'—a teetotal happy ever after (Scott).

Later in the century the socialist journalist C. Allan Clarke chose the tale for his own retelling. He worked in the cotton mills and then as a teacher, submitting his work to local and national newspapers. His unionism and book *The Effects of the Factory System* brought him into politics, although the reception of his own newspapers convinced him readers wanted entertainment, and he created the comic character Bill Spriggs whose dialogues in Lancashire dialect made his popularity. Clarke lived by his pen and his *Old Tales for Young Folks* issued by the Manchester publisher John Heywood was one of his many publications. The *Old Tales* are 'Jack the Giant Killer', Cinderella and 'Hassan the Rope maker', all stories of the poor bettering themselves through luck, wit and industry; for example in the lesser known tale Hassan loses his gold and yet makes his fortune selling a lump of lead-weight to a fisherman who pays him with a fish containing a diamond. Clarke shares his humour with his young readers calling Cinderella's stepmother 'Raspberry' and stepsisters 'Tart' and 'Spice', while Cinderella's father is 'careless, fond of rich living always in debt'—and is called Bottle. The reference to alcoholism would not be lost the grown-up reader. The wedding draws on the traditional music of northern England when they have fireworks, cannon and a brass band.

Localisation of the tale increases the sense of ownership and identification, as in another regional retelling by folklorist Padraic Colum. *The Girl who sat by the Ashes* was first published in 1919 three years after the Easter Rising armed insurrection against British rule and draws on national Irish myths of enchanted woods, crows and magic cloaks and chatting geese and giants. Colum's Cinderella, called Maid-alone, has her own adventures, but remains steadfast in character and true to her cause. The book was reissued in 1968 with illustrations by Imero Gobbato which is the edition in the Collection. The selection of Cinderella for inclusion is indicative of a broader appeal of the tale to those on the political left: a social revolutionary message can be found in the transformation from rags to riches and the discovery of goodness and beauty among the disregarded and impoverished.

In the 1980s Walt Disney's *Cinderella and her Animal Friends: a Book about Kindness* endorsed the feminine virtues of care and compassion. However by then Disney's perpetuation of old fashioned gender roles was under criticism and authors were writing revisionist tales often employing humour and swapping the gender roles of the main characters. For example in Babette Cole's *Prince Cinders* the big bullying-brothers are punished by becoming House Fairies and do all the house work, while Princess Lovelypenny's true love will fit a pair of lost trousers, not shoes. In Ellen Jackson's American *Cinder Edna*, Cinderella's neighbour Edna shows backbone, saving up her bird-cage cleaning money to go to the ball and travelling in loafers by bus to find her Mr Right. In a swipe at the story itself and its message of finding the ideal partner, Roald Dahl in *Revolting Rhymes* makes Cindy's Prince dumb and vicious and her ugly sister cunning, so she regrets her wish to marry the prince and asks the fairy godmother for a decent man instead. Along similar revisionary lines are James Garner's *Politically Correct Bedtime Stories*, Aislinn O'Loughlin's *Cinderella's Fella*, and the award winning Shirley Hughes' *Ella's Big Chance*.

For the confident reader, the British author Philip Pullman produced a spin-off tale where the hero was one of the rats who the fairy godmother made into a pageboy to accompany her to the ball (Pullman). The boy's adventures were made into a television series in 2001 and the tie-in edition has a flash on the cover announcing this fact, next to the author's Carnegie medal and Smarties prize. For the young teenage group the American author Gregory Maguire's fantasy *Confessions of an Ugly Stepsister* is narrated by her (possibly autistic) older sister. Maguire's tale problematises beauty, making Iris/Cinderella plain and her second stepsister beautiful. It is set in the Netherlands where Iris's stepfather is a tulip grower, her sexually-ambiguous prince is a painter, and it rejects the 'happy-ever-after' ending of the fairy tale. Like Pullman's story, Maguire's too was adapted for television.

While Cinderella has provided creative stimulus for the young adult, teen and older audience, it has long been used in reading schemes. Ann Jungman's *Cinderella and the Hot Air Balloon* illustrated by Russell Ayto is aimed at this market and made 'Suitable for the English [and Scottish] Curriculum'. Similarly Shirley Climo and Loretta Krupinski's *Irish Cinderlad* is recommended for ages 5 to 9. The Collection has a number of Vera Southgate's easy reading Cinderella texts for Ladybird books in editions illustrated first by Eric Winter, then Brian Price-Thomas, then Paul Finn over a period of 40 years.

But perhaps the most telling adaption in the Collection is Anne Sexton's poem 'Cinderella' in her poetry volume *Transformations* (first British edition). Its black humour is not intended for children. It opens with an acknowledgement of the familiar get-lucky, get-rich story of the ordinary person—plumber, the nursemaid, the milkman, the charwoman—who 'makes a pile'. So Cinderella's wishes are made true under the tree on her mother's grave. The Grimm brothers' bloody feet remain in the poem betraying the stepsisters: 'That's the way with amputations. /They just don't heal up like a wish' while Cinderella's shoe fits 'like a love letter into its envelope.' But Sexton asks darkly, what did she wish for? Answering that they lived creepily 'like two dolls in a museum case' never arguing, never aging, preserved like dolls, Sexton shows us through the poem the despair in this loss of idealism.

Collectables and play items

Sexton's dark eerie dolls reflect her imagination not the delight and glamour we see in the iconic objects of the story reproduced as collectables and play items. One such is the godmother and fairy wands which have to sparkle to show magical power. They are a catalyst of the imagination and transform common objects into desirable ones. In childhood play they transform a bucket into a ship, or a cardboard box into a train. Similarly Cinderella's shoes—be they crystal or glass—should be transparent. Toy manufacturers have refined the identifying characteristics and linked them with brands to target specific markets. Dinky toys produced a coach and horses from the movie that displayed images and a description of the film 'The Slipper and the Rose'. There are two Coalport collectable porcelain pumpkins and coaches with mice. Royal Doulton and Disney produced a 'hand made and hand decorated' blond-haired, blue-eyed Cinderella figurine dressed for the ball. Another figurine is the flirtatious flapper cartoon character Betty Boop in a Cinderella dress with puppy carrying the slipper. The dark-haired, large-eyed, curvaceous, shape of Betty Boop is at odds with the innocent and demure Doulton figure. But it is the dress that identifies the character. Cinderella became one of Disney's princess series and has her own merchandise, from wands to the *Disney princess: dreamy dress-up* activity book where readers could 'Look inside for lots of glamorous gowns' to dress a number of card princesses in.

Fig. 1-3. Raphael Tuck's postcard, annotated by sender. In the Cinderella Collection, University of Bedfordshire, author's own photograph.

But before we blame Disney entirely for the commercialisation of the Cinderella tale, it is worth examining Raphael Tuck and Sons' postcards from the 1900s. Tuck encouraged the collecting and sending of his cards with well-publicised competitions (offering £5000 in prizes for the best Christmas postcard design in 1880) and he issued series after series not just of fairy tales but of places, people, drawings and photographs. Ordinary people collected them. One of our Cinderella cards is number 3472 (1904/5) and the sender writes 'I have about 300' (fig. 1-3). Amongst the hundreds of series issued by Tuck are Cinderella cats and slippers and cut-out Cinderella dolls and stills from the Gaumont-British Picture Corp. movie 'Sparva The Modern Cinderella'. Tuck came from Prussia and the firm printed their cards in Germany and Bavaria, but he famously argued with the British Government postmaster to allow a section for writing a message next to the address and so created the design of the modern picture postcard as we know it today.

It is evident from the Collection that Cinderella has come to represent more than the simple folk tale. The newspaper clippings show how the story has been used to question the effectiveness and purpose of our ministers (Will our transport minister be the fairy godmother of the roads and get Cinderella to the Ball?) or ask whether children's rights should be taught in schools (Would you tell your teacher if you knew about the way Cinderella was being treated and living at home?) or questions the role of the state in regulating our lives (Is it a nanny state or should there be a silence curfew during the hours after midnight?). Among the many meanings of the tale, Cinderella has become a signifier for speaking up for rights of those who have not been given a voice.

Lessons from the materiality of the Collection

The Cinderella Collection at the University of Bedfordshire retains the marks of engagement, participation and retelling though marginalia, bookplates, wear and tear of covers as well as the material construction of the form whether it is a panorama theatre, pop-ups or toys and gifts (figs 1.2-3). Such haptic signs build for us an awareness of the depth of imaginative identification. Similarly the diffusion of the Cinderella motif across publishing sectors is indicative of its seemingly boundless capacity for elaboration and amplification. It has become a shorthand for the transformative power of what has been overlooked or considered insignificant and so has been adopted across areas of knowledge from medicine to the military, from economics to psychology.

Thus the Collection's material forms of the story show the inexhaustible capacity for figurative elaboration of the tale—albeit in partial view. Many of these forms are imbued by their owners with currents of feeling, and retain the marks of this through inscription, annotation, and the wear-and-tear of turned down pages, rubbed surfaces and repairs. Library issues, prize bookplates, owners' names or dedications construct for us an awareness of the affectivity of the tale and the desire to hold on to and share the emotion which touched the reader. Cinderella is a perennial story, told in childhood and retold in various guises in our teens and adulthood: its simple romance has many meanings, each applicable to different stages of life. Each cultural generation reflects upon these precariously anchored feelings, re-interrogates them, makes them accessible again by projecting them in new narratives for readers and audiences to internalise reflexively making sense of themselves within their time. Through an examination of its central characters and objects reproduced in book form, as ephemera, collectables and merchandise in the Collection, we have a glimpse, partial though it may be, of the role the story has played through the generations and across cultures.

Works cited

Ahlberg, Janet and Allen Ahlberg. *Cinderella Show.* Viking Kestrel, 1986.
Anon. *Cinderella: A Mini Pop-up Storybook.* 1995.
—. *Cinderella Panorama Book: Six Magnificent Scenes.* Collins, 1950.
—. *Golden Budget of Nursery Stories.* Blackie & Sons, 1931.
—. *Mother Goose and Her Friends in Fairyland.* T. Nelson & Sons, 1920.
—. 'Pantomimes. Cinderellas with a Difference.' *The Stage,* 30 November 1944.
Arrowsmith, Nancy and George Moorse. *Field Guide to the Little People.* Pan, 1977.
Bell, Florence Lady. *At the Works: Study of a Manufacturing Town [Middlesbrough].* 1907.
Bell, Florence and Lancelot Speed. *Fairy Tale Plays and How to Act Them.* Longman, 1896.
Blyth, Alan and Emanuele Luzzati. *Cinderella; La Cenerentola: The Story of Rossini's Opera.* Julia MacRae books, 1981.
Briggs, Katharine Mary. *British Folk Tales and Legends: A Sampler.* Paladin, 1977.
Brown, Debbie. *Debbie Brown's Fairy Tale Cakes.* Hamlyn, 1995.
Buthod-Girard, Ingrid and Carlos Busquets. *Assepoester.* Hemma, 1995.
Clarke, Charles Allen. *The Effects of the Factory System.* G. Richards, 1899.
Clarke, Charles Allen. *Old Tales for Young Folks.* John Heywood, 1895.
Climo, Shirley and Loretta Krupinski. *Irish Cinder Lad.* HarperCollins, 1996.
Cole, Babette. *Prince Cinders* Puffin, 1989.

Craik, Dinah Maria Mulock. *Fairy Book: The Best Popular Fairy Stories Selected and Rendered Anew.* Macmillan, 1863.
—. *John Halifax, Gentleman.* Copyright ed. edition, vol. 1 & 2, Bernhard Tauchnitz, 1857.
Cruikshank, George. *Interesting Story of Cinderella and Her Glass Slipper.* Printed by J.G. Rusher, 1814.
Dahl, Roald and Quentin Blake. *Revolting Rhymes* Puffin, 1984.
Daly, Martin and Margo Wilson. *The Truth About Cinderella: A Darwinian View of Parental Love.* Weidenfeld and Nicolson, 1998.
Disney, Walt. *Cinderella and Her Animal Friends: A Book About Kindness.* Walt Disney Company, 1987.
—. *Cinderella Magic Wand Book.* Walt Disney Company, 1950.
Dowling, Colette. *The Cinderella Complex: Women's Hidden Fear of Independence.* Fontana, 1982.
Dundes, Alan. *Cinderella: A Casebook.* University of Wisconsin, 1988.
Durant, Alan and Ross Collins. *Fairytale Files: Cinderella.* Walker Books, 2008.
Ellis, John M. Bill. *One Fairy Story Too Many: The Brothers Grimm and Their Tales.* Chicago University Press, 1983.
Ezell, Lee. *Cinderella Syndrome: Discovering God's Plan When Your Dreams Don't Come True.* Vince Books, 1994.
Farjeon, Eleanor and Ernest H. Shepard. *Glass Slipper: From the Play of the Same Name by Eleanor and Herbert Farjeon.* Oxford University Press, 1973.
Hughes, Shirley. *Ella's Big Chance: A Fairy Tale Retold.* The Bodley Head, 2003.
Jackson, Ellen and Kevin O'Malley. *Cinder Edna.* Lee Lothrop & Shephard, 1994.
Jungman, Ann and Russell Ayto. *Cinderella and the Hot Air Balloon.* Francis Lincoln, 1995.
Kathleen, Lady. 'Cinderella and the Prince: A Fairy Pantomime with Songs and Music.' *Tales for Little People*, Aldine Publishing, 1910.
Laslett, Stephanie and Caroline Sharpe. *Assepoester.* Librero, 1995.
—. *Cinderella.* Parragon, 1994.
—. *Cinderella.* Parragon, 2001.
Maguire, Gregory. *Confessions of an Ugly Stepsister.* Regan Books, 1999.
Mazza, Samuele. *Cinderella's Revenge.* Chronicle Books, 1994.
O'Loughlin, Aislinn and Marie-Louise Fitzpatrick. *Cinderella's Fella.* Wolfhound Press, 1996.
Perrault, Charles and Francesc Mateu. *Walt Disney: Cendrillon; Un Livre Anime.* 1995.

Philip, Neil. *The Cinderella Story.* Penguin, 1989.

Pullman, Philip. *I Was a Rat! Or the Scarlet Slippers.* Corgi Yearling Books, 2001.

Randall, Ronne et al. *Cinderella: A Magic 3-Dimensional Fairy-Tale World.* Sterling Publishing, 2006.

Reynolds, Leila. *Cinderella's Sisters.* A. Halle Ltd, 1900.

Scott, Martha. 'George Cruikshank at the Osborne Collection.' Online https://torontopubliclibrary.typepad.com/trl/2016/03/curators-choice-george-cruikshank-at-the-osborne-collection.html. Accessed 26 February 2019.

Sexton, Anne. *Transformations.* Oxford University Press, 1972.

Southgate, Vera. *Cinderella.* Ladybird Book, 2008.

Southgate, Vera and Paul Finn. *Cinderella.* Ladybird Book, 2005.

Southgate, Vera and Brian Price-Thomas. *Cinderella: Retold for Easy Reading. Well-Loved Tales.* Ladybird Book, 1981.

Southgate, Vera and Eric Winter. *Cinderella: A Ladybird Easy-Reading Book.* Ladybird Books, 1968.

Spence, Lewis. *British Fairy Origins.* Aquarian, 1981.

Tillett, Iris. *Cinderella Army: The Women's Land Army in Norfolk.* Jim Baldwin Publishing, 1988.

Warne, Frederick. *Warne's National Nursery Library; Comprising Cinderella, the Three Bears, Tom Thumb, Punch and Judy, Jack and the Bean-Stalk.* Frederick Warne, 1870.

Wenzel-Bürger, Eva. *Aschenputtel: Ein Märchen Der Gebrüder Grimm* Carlsen Verlag, 1995.

CHAPTER TWO

THE TRANSFORMATION OF A DISNEY
PRINCESS INTO ITS PARODIC MEME:
A CASE STUDY OF THE CULTURAL
TRANSDUCTION OF THE *CENICIENTA COSTEÑA*

ENRIQUE URIBE-JONGBLOED
AND CÉSAR MORA-MOREO

Once upon a time…

In the Caribbean city of Barranquilla, in the north of Colombia, young
students were often sharing a series of memes through instant messaging
services—be it WhatsApp or Facebook Messenger—which they found
hilarious. The memes were edited stills from the Disney animation film
Cinderella (Geronimi et al.) which included a variety of extras added onto
the images. It could be just a dialogue balloon with some text, or additions
like flowers, hats or similar things[1]. The memes would render themselves
to be manipulated by the users, who would alter the text in the balloon or
add other images onto the stills. Creativity was part of the whole
movement of modifying a famous character, thus generating a variety of
parodic references to the most renowned Disney princess. Basically, the
running gag was that this princess was not what you would expect, her
image and symbolic value as a princess completely erased by the words
that would come out of her mouth. The *Cenicienta costeña* [Cinderella of
the coast] meme would then have an infinity of mutations that expanded
upon that premise and that were added to a Facebook site under the title *La*

---

[1] You can access http://csar2612.wixsite.com/theothercinderella to find a gallery of
the memes with brief notes regarding their local cultural elements.

princesa pupileta, something that could be roughly translated as the 'posh-trashy princess'.

The meme, and its appropriation by youngsters in Barranquilla, provides evidence of two different phenomena that we would like to address here. On the one hand, the pervading influence of U.S. films and television shows—in our case, animations from the 1950s—is a sign of the media dominance that continues in most audiovisual product distribution worldwide, despite the growing number of counter-flows, regional exchanges and geolinguistic markets (Sinclair, 'The Hollywood' and 'Transnationalisation'; Thussu). On the other, these memes are evidence of the culture of participation or convergence culture which sets media consumers as producers and distributors of their own productions (Jenkins et al.; Jenkins). Those two perspectives, the influence of U.S. production and the mythification of its images to imply much more than the stories told, and the creativity that arises from the media distribution and editing tools easily available in contemporary computers and mobile phones, enable new readings of Cinderella as representative of the 'ideal' woman.

The issues regarding the creative transformation of cultural products has been at the centre of international trade in intellectual property and audiovisual products for a while. Academics have addressed this issue from translation to adaptation studies and, as we will present here, cultural transduction. Their academic interest has homed in on understanding how cultural products travel and enter a dialogue with different cultures, and what characteristics or processes enable, hinder, or engender those exchanges. We will present the discussion on how these debates have led to the construction of the cultural transduction framework (Uribe-Jongbloed and Espinosa-Medina), and how the *Cenicienta Costeña* meme fits into the different categories presented by the framework.

Cultural transduction in a nutshell

Transduction, as a concept, has been used in a variety of fields, from biology to literary theory. As is often the case in the social sciences, the term was borrowed from other disciplines and acquired new, specific meanings. Carlos López Charles has presented three different meanings for transduction: 1. the conversion of energy from one medium to another; 2. the way DNA is transferred from one bacteria to another via a viral agent; and, 3. in semiotics, the term refers to the transformation processes of literary works as they become modified (e.g. in translations) (1). The latter is the concept that has been used often in semiotic and literary studies. For instance, transduction refers to the reconstruction of a literary work as it is inscribed in a new context, be that a new cultural construction or a different time frame, and is considered to have begun with the work of Lubomír Doležel (Martínez de Antón), although there are debates from semiology that go as far as 1980 (see Izquierdo Arroyo).

In translation studies, Maria Grazia Sindoni uses a more specific meaning of transduction to address issues of the transformation of the mode or medium of a given work, and presents as an example that 'writing may be remade as drawing or speech-as-action, also involving more than one mode or resource' (28). This definition seems very similar to Lars Elleström's transmediation, which focuses on the transferral of media characteristics between dissimilar media. The interesting thing about this version of transduction—akin to transmediation—is that it is concerned with all possible transferrals from one information element to one that is of a different type or in a different medium. The specificity of transduction for those involved in translation limits the scope of the semiotic meaning described above, whereas Ellestrom's transmediation is a more useful concept, particularly in the case of transformations that may not involve a change in language.

One of such cases is adaptation. It has been considered as a wide-ranging area of studies which is interested in looking at the transformation of any type of product into a different one. For instance, Linda Hutcheon states that:

> in short, adaptation can be described as the following:
> • An acknowledged transposition of a recognizable other work or works
> • A creative and an interpretive act of appropriation/salvaging
> • An extended intertextual engagement with the adapted work
> Therefore, an adaptation is a derivation that is not derivative—a work that is second without being secondary. It is its own palimpsestic thing. (8–9)

The unavoidable idea is the relationship established between a previous work—or works—and the current work under observation. This idea of 'work' as a defined media product is one of the reasons why Elleström argues that adaptation is but one possibility of intermediality, which is in itself only one type of transmediation. He also argues that 'the implicit literature—or theater-to-film formula continues to have a firm grip on adaptation studies' ('Adaptations as Intermediality' 517), obscuring or ignoring that for those processes there was a need of adapting into instrumental media forms (e.g. scripts, storyboards) usually ignored in research on adaptation. This is not to say it has not been taken into account that there are other works that are adapted, and other stages in the process, something that Hutcheon clearly recognises, but rather that we already acknowledge a specificity for the term, and that most academic study of adaptation focuses on the written work to audiovisual work paradigm.

Adaptation studies has taken a look at translation studies and found parallels between the two areas of study which help to understand the process of transformation, for instance the use of a polysystem approach. Film adaptation, and maybe even any film production, could be 'studied as a more or less specific kind of translation (in the broadest sense of the word) of previous discursive practices as well as experiences in real life' (Cattrysse 'Film' 67). This idea works very well with cultural translation. Kyle Conway gives an interesting account of the development of the concept and states that 'cultural translation is a concept with competing definitions coming from two broad fields, anthropology/ethnography* and cultural/postcolonial* studies' ('Cultural Translation' 21 [asterisks in the original]). He points out that the debate between those two approaches seems to be somewhat complementary and that they could benefit from debates on communication studies that have already dealt with the intersection of those two approaches. Conway ('Cultural Translation, Global Television Studies') goes on to apply his definition of cultural translation to the case of the televisual adaptation of *Ugly Betty* (ABC 2006) from the Colombian original, *Yo soy Betty, la fea* (RCN 1999). He uses cultural translation to bridge a gap between adaptation studies and political economy, because he considers that 'the fields have complementary blind spots: adaptation studies provides insight into transformations texts undergo but neglects issues of power, while political economy provides insight into issues of power but neglects textual transformations' (584). Although adaptation studies does not necessarily neglect looking at the influence of power (see Cattrysse 'Cultural Transduction'), the geopolitical approach necessary to understand the transformation, adaptation, translation and reconstruction of a televisual product, requires a more holistic approach to understand the process.

Similar to cultural translation, cultural transduction was developed as a framework to understand the transformation of audiovisual products as they cross cultural and spatial barriers (Uribe-Jongbloed and Espinosa-Medina, 'An Introduction' 'A Clearer Picture'). It took a variety of concepts, refined their meanings and applicability, and framed them around four main tenets: markets, process, people, and products. Patrick Cattrysse is critical of the lack of revision of debates in adaptation studies, and praises the multi-disciplinary approach of cultural transduction and the extension of the analytical scope it provides. The framework has been put to the test with audiovisual products (Espinosa-Medina and Uribe-Jongbloed), videogames and multiple-media products (Uribe-Jongbloed et al.).

The four tenets can be summarised as follows:

- Markets: Looking at the cultural proximity or distance between the market of the original product—or where it was created—and the insertion markets;
- Product: Analysing conditions of the product, which may explain its appeal, or lack thereof, when crossing over cultural borders;
- People: Studying the people involved in the process of recognising, trading and modifying a product to suit specific cultural markets;
- Process: Classifying the mechanism through which the transduction is carried out. (Uribe-Jongbloed et al. 144)

In the process tenet, the cultural transduction framework looks at three possibilities: *Hybridity*, understood as the transformation by organisation or institutions (e.g. a TV studio) of a product, i.e. in TV format adaptations; *Convergence,* where users or end-of-the-line consumers take it upon themselves to create their own versions, modifications or alterations of products (e.g. fandubs); and *Transduction Labs*, where products are only developed for specific markets or cultural conditions despite being created elsewhere. Although originally concerned with the transformation of products by institutions—as defined above under hybridity—Espinosa-Medina and Uribe-Jongbloed ('Latin American Contraflow') have also studied the *planning* prior to the development of a product and the *strategies* designed to overcome market and/or cultural barriers before the product is actually created—as expected of a transduction lab. This case does not seem to fit the case of adaptation, which requires the existence of a previous and a current work, as explained above; nor does it fit remediation, because there is no material transformation. When cultural transduction is recognised before the insertion of a given product into a market, the process of development is already underway without products themselves having been transformed.

Thus far there has been no application of the cultural transduction framework to the study of convergent products. This study of a series of internet memes that have been created with an intertextual reference to an animated movie character therefore helps to expand the understanding and applicability of the framework.

About memes

The concept of *meme* was originally defined by Richard Dawkins in 1976 who extrapolated his reflection on genetic evolution to the field of culture (Trevisan and Goethel). He explained that memes, like genes, are propagated from one generation to another through a process of replication. Dawkins' definition of the meme has remained central to further debates on the fields of adaptation and meme studies (Wiggins and Bowers; Hutcheon). From this initial definition, many authors have ventured to describe internet memes. For Castaño memes are units of information that are replicated through different virtual platforms and can take the form of images, hyperlinks, videos and even phrases (97). This definition seems to summarise another more elaborate one that posits that:

> the label 'Internet meme' applies to any artifact (a film, spoof, rumor, picture, song, etc.) that appears on the Internet and produces countless derivatives by being imitated, remixed, and rapidly diffused by countless participants in technologically mediated communication. Internet memes span various formats, for example videos, GIF files, photographs, and drawings, whether or not accompanied by text. (Dynel 662)

In social networks like Facebook and Instagram, memes are among the most popular content. Such memes can be about anything: celebrities, politicians, even individuals themselves. Memes can be copied with a series of changes, but always maintain a common element that groups them within a specific type of meme. In the case of *Cenicienta Costeña*, the main character of the Disney movie is the element that is kept in all cases. In some images she appears by herself, while in others she is accompanied by the prince, her fairy godmother or her stepsisters.

Although the current popularity of memes would suggest that they are a recent phenomenon that has been possible thanks to the rise of the internet, for Delia Rodríguez these forms of communication go back 'long before the internet existed,' (22) for example the line drawing of the bald headed Kilroy's long nose peeping over a wall, created by the war photographer Robert Capa in 1944 that has been replicated many times in different parts of the world. More generally, Hutcheon argues that:

> Memes are not high-fidelity replicators: they change with time, for meme transmission is subject to constant mutation. Stories too propagate themselves when they catch on; adaptations—as both repetition and variation—are their form of replication. Evolving by cultural selection, traveling stories adapt to local cultures, just as populations of organisms adapt to local environments. (177)

Thus, she considers all forms of adaptation and appropriation to provide evidence of the idea of the meme. Although the internet meme might be only one of such procedures, and it is the one we focus on here, it is by no means the only way memes can be studied. Sergio Roncallo-Dow states that today's media environment has allowed users to 'reinvent what exists, remix it, resemantise it, taking the idea of user-generated content (UGC) to a point that, given the specificity of the current environment, presents itself as something that had not been seen before' (13). Henry Jenkins et al. also discuss how these 'memes serve as themes for ongoing conversations and fodder for creative activity, with each variation demonstrating and requiring particular cultural knowledge' (28).

It is the particular knowledge which becomes fundamental here. In order to understand the humour or criticism embedded in the memes requires a cultural background that represents how certain products have become part of the cultural repertoire of those exchanging the material. Although many memes might exist granting a new value to any given image—even due to ignorance of the source text—some of them actually use the knowledge of the referenced text in order to provide parodic allusions. The spreadability, to use Jenkins' term, of the meme might rest upon its ability to be understood quickly by any given audience, and cultural references play a big role in that process. Wiggins and Bowers argue that memes are a genre, rather than a medium, of participatory culture, characterised by a being spreadable item (yet not everything that is spread is a meme), that is altered or modified—what they call an emergent meme—which finally become cycled in a process of intentional imitation, iteration and rapid diffusion (1897-1899). The intentionality of the process is fundamental, because it represents the participatory nature of those exchanging memes.

This is how the Disney princess became the protagonist of the memes studied here. They became commonplace and their constant cycle of modification and diffusion made them pervasive. Memes based on Cinderella references abound, as a standard internet search would show,[2] presenting evidence of the extent to which the Cinderella story, and especially the *Cinderella* Disney film, are a global cultural commodity. The *Cenicienta Costeña* memes are part of the extended influence of the

---

[2] You can find the Cinderella memes at [accessed 25 March 2020]:
https://www.memedroid.com/memes/tag/cinderella
https://www.memecenter.com/search/cinderella
https://www.pinterest.es/jrtp13/memes-de-cenicienta/
https://me.me/t/cinderella?since=1485686047%2C8506888

Cinderella story and they include a variety of communicational forms which are worth deeper insight.

Methodology

The objective of this research is to analyse the *Cenicienta Costeña* memes which are found on the Facebook humour pages *Aquí se vacila*, with 216,561 followers, and *La Princesa Pupileta*, with 94,452 followers (Facebook, 2018) through the cultural transduction framework presented above. A sample of 100 memes were selected to be the objects of a textual analysis. The memes were those published and available in the Facebook groups mentioned between March and July 2017. The textual analysis included two stages. The first was to read each meme in depth to understand the type of elements that were used as part of the structure of the meme. These elements included panels—in stories that were sequential in nature—and a variety of syntactic elements, including dialogue balloons, over-imposed texts and images. This allowed for the creation of categories that could be analysed for each meme.

The categories developed were:
1. Scene(s) and shot(s) from the Cinderella movie that were used in the meme.
2. References, whether visual or written, of any of the following:
   a. Sex
   b. Alcohol (drinks)
   c. Obscenities
   d. Caribbean coast references (e.g. traditional hats, flowers, etc.)

The memes were classified, and the recurrent themes were studied, both in an interpretive fashion and counting the number of instances. This information was used, alongside the cultural transduction framework, to provide an interpretive analysis of the *Cenicienta costeña* memes.

How Cinderella became 'costeña'

The scene of the *Cinderella* movie most commonly used in the sample, appearing in 56% of the memes, is one in which the princess must leave the prince before midnight and break the charm that allowed her to go to the party in a ball dress. The most used shot, which is part of the same scene, appearing in 39% of the memes, is the frame when Cinderella is standing in front of the prince with arms flexed and with an attitude that seems to oppose the prince (see fig. 1, minute 54:45). However, the Cinderella character created by Disney no longer sports her golden hair which 'is very reminiscent of Grace Kelly' (Míguez 48). On this occasion her hair is black and on top of her head she is wearing a '*vueltiao*' hat, typical of the savannahs of the Caribbean region of Colombia, adorned with a rose mallow, flower of the genus *hibiscus*, symbol for the city and Carnival of Barranquilla (see fig. 2-1). This unlikely damsel holds an *Águila* beer can while facing a prince who questions her decision:

'Princesses do not follow this kind of pages' – says the prince.
'I don't give a damn. I am a fan of the *pupicoleta[3]*, so what (is the problem)?'[4]

Fig. 2-1. Example of one of the many Cinderella of the Coast Memes

That cheeky response of this Cinderella does not correspond to the character of any of the books, series or remakes, but to one of the hundreds of internet memes, shared through social networks like Facebook, that became popular in 2017. The *Cenicienta Costeña*, or princess *pupicoleta*,

---

[3] 'Pupicoleta' is a made-up word in Spanish, comprised of the slang words pupi [posh] and coleta [trashy]. Whereas the former is used in informal Spanish in different areas of the country, the latter is only used in the north of Colombia.
[4] This is our own translation. We have toned down the obscene language, just to use it as a reference.

is the protagonist of these memes and a direct opposite of version of the character created by Disney. Her emergence can be understood thanks to the process of cultural transduction.

In its origins, the female characters presented by Disney have been characterised by submission, obedience and their maiden-in-distress need for a man to rescue them. In this sense, Weston states that 'the most prevalent characteristic of Disney's three original princesses (Snow White, Cinderella and Sleeping Beauty) is that they spend much of their movies as damsels in distress, waiting to be saved by men' (para.1). They portray an ideal of femininity that corresponds to a patriarchal scenario in the construction of the Disney myth (Pop). In fig. 2-1 we can see the opposite is true of the Cinderella of the coast. She is a foul-mouthed princess, who likes to get drunk, leave without requesting permission from her prince and is light years away from the image of damsel in distress shown by Disney in its adaptation of the classic story.   This Cinderella is both evidence of the impact of the tale and Disney's international acclaim, and a parody of the struggles of real women in the Caribbean region in Colombia. *Cenicienta Costeña* mocks the model of a woman proposed by Disney in the 1950s and proposes a contemporary look at Cinderella. More recent adaptations of the story have showed how she 'was liberating and rebelling—almost alongside the women of the twentieth century. In this way, we can glimpse, through the story, the changes suffered by society' (Rodríguez Marroquín 96). According to Susanna Barsotti, in the contemporary rewriting of fairy tales in series and films—and this applies to the meme—many of their classic aspects are criticised as they are aimed at a more adult audience that can identify with them. In this particular case, netizens criticise the obedience of women, represented in the animated classic, and attribute to the main character characteristics unexpected in a princess, which may also be influenced by the feminist movements that have motivated many women to free themselves from the male oppression to which they have historically been subjected.

In 52% of the memes *Cenicienta Costeña* faces the prince and argues with him, a behaviour opposed to the female representation in Disney where every woman was 'submissive, innocent, obedient, passive and under the designs of the father or husband' (Míguez 44). It is interesting that the memes talk about this topic, starting from the characteristic machismo of the city and the high number of cases of domestic violence made public in 2017; Barranquilla has the fourth highest record of this type of violence in Colombia (Instituto Nacional de Medicina Legal y Ciencias Forenses).

The remaining topics in order of relevance are heterosexual sex 28%, parties 21%, and alcohol consumption 13%, and seem to respond the fact that 'memes create an online culture of emancipation and debate in generating political statements by promoting an innovation of awareness and freedom of expression' (Bebić and Volarevic 46). Self-determination and direct opposition to *machismo* are also linked to promiscuity and foul language. In most of the memes, formal and educated language, characteristic of Disney's *Cinderella*, serves as the standard against which profanity provides a clear punchline.

The four tenets of cultural transduction

Cenicienta costeña is an evident case of cultural transformation of a product from one market to another. As the local details of the selected meme (fig. 2-1) highlights, there is a great interest in rendering the contrast between the original reference—the Disney film—and Caribbean contemporary reality. The four tenets of cultural transduction allow us to test the case of the memes.

Markets

According to the conceptualisation and the distinction into three types of flows proposed by Uribe-Jongbloed and Espinosa-Medina, in the case of Cinderella (1950) the flow occurs from core to peripheral market because it is an American film produced by the most hegemonic audiovisual producer which reached the Colombian peripheral market. However, in the reinterpretation of the film that takes place in the memes, the flow occurs within the peripheral market. Although the main audience of the memes would seem to correspond to people living in the Colombian northern coast, who would understand the references and language present in the memes, internet availability renders geographical barriers irrelevant. As a peripheral product, *Cenicienta costeña* can be enjoyed anywhere the Facebook pages can be reached.

People

It is difficult to determine who has played any of the possible roles in the process of transforming Cinderella into *Cenicienta costeña* since Internet memes seldom include authorial information. In this case, the websites (distributors) disseminate the product. However, among the categories proposed by the cultural transduction framework, the concept of the alchemist is represented in the Internet users, which are those that transform the frames of Disney's Cinderella, eliminate the cultural gaps of the product and carry out the process of re-culturalisation so that it can be understood for the local public.

Product

Disney's *Cinderella* (1950) can be considered a universal product due to its worldwide exhibition, repeated broadcast and sales on DVD. The classic tale of the young woman oppressed by her stepmother and stepsisters who finally meets a prince, a metaphor of social promotion in the version written by Charles Perrault, is one of the most famous thanks to this film adaptation. It is not the only one (as this volume so clearly demonstrates). There are also modern reinventions like *Tinderella: A Modern Fairy Tale* where the protagonist 'does not wait for a fairy godmother to fix her up, she uses Tinder' (CollegeHumor) or the novel *Ash* (2009) by Malinda Lo, starring a lesbian Cinderella. They are examples of the universality of the story that allow us to understand how a product, in this case the Disney film, transcends the place where the original idea or product was designed and ends up becoming a meme that makes fun of gender conventions and the subjection of women in South America.

Not only is the story universal, the visual elements are considerably universal as well, at least to the expected target audience. From the 100 memes analysed, nineteen corresponded to single shots of the animated film (like the one shown in fig. 2-1), whereas eighty-one included a variety of shots making up a sequential narrative (as in fig. 2-2). They display the use of the comic strip conventions in the memes, using panels and dialogue balloons. It is curious that only one of the memes in the selection use over-imposed text divided into the upper and lower part in single image memes, something that is quite common for other memes, and almost a fundamental characteristic of the genre.

Processes

In every process of cultural transduction there are elements that are modified to suit the local culture. Cinderella is an American film that is the adaptation of a German fairy tale, and the memes located on the Caribbean coast of Colombia were also reinvented by users with particularities of the region, including colloquial expressions such as 'que plan chevere' [What a cool plan!], 'y esa vaina que es?' [What's that crap?], 'Haces que mis dias

Fig. 2-2 Cenicienta costeña's Sobusa line bus travels[5] image by #QuilleraVaciladora from https://goo.gl/6V5qJW

---

[5] A simplified translation into English could be:
1: Fuck, this ain't no double-decker!
2: Get on, get on, we can fit 10 more people.
3: Step on it, are you going to stretch the bus or what?

sean más la monda' [You make my days cooler than fuck], phrases whose use is associated with the region. Those obscenities serve the dual purpose of locating the product, while also showing irreverence and the counter-cultural aspect of the meme. Although the language used would be hardly translatable because the memes use slang profanity exclusive to the Colombian Caribbean region which has a blatant disregard for the formal rules of written Spanish—in 85% of the memes the dialogues of the characters contain vulgarities that are widely used in Barranquilla, yet unknown in most other parts of the country, to reinforce the location of the stories—the graphic elements could be easily altered to be understood in other latitudes. An example is the meme in which *Cenicienta costeña* complains about the discomfort she experiences when riding a full bus of the Sobusa company (the second panel fig. 2-2). Although the type and visual elements of the bus are only relevant to locals of Barranquilla, a similar situation could be understood elsewhere. For instance, if the bus were changed for a London double-decker or a peak-hour Underground wagon, the joke would be understood in Britain, and the situation could be considered to be universally shareable.

Conclusion

The memes are clearly evidence of the convergence process. They are created, modified and shared through Facebook pages, Twitter lists and WhatsApp groups. Users create their own versions of the memes and share them through their social networks, a very usual feature in the memes. Clearly, these exchanges evince that 'internet memes—remixed images and videos circulated online, inviting participation through creation of derivatives—may be viewed as a form of subversive communication in a participatory media culture' (Huntington 1). This subversive role allows for the humour to be made more explicit, by drawing on the shift of expectation and the use of obscene language. The convergence process implies that there is little to no censorship regarding the content, which allows for counterhegemonic discourses that do not conform to normative

---

4: Lady, shut up and move to the back, you are blocking the entrance. The exit is on the back.
5: I'm not going to move in this shit, step on it. Leave passengers for the next bus.
6: Get off, please, or you'll make me lose it.
7: Fuck you, dickface, you are always flying. One goes with the balls stuck in the throat because you'd rive with a flaming hot rod up the ass. It is very hot in here and you fill this cock up, pull up now.

requirements. Shareable media has overcome some of the usual barriers that create cultural icons following a pattern of cultural dominance.

The animated movie *Cinderella* (1950) produced by Walt Disney is one of the most popular versions of the story and has served as input for memes, but the universality and relevance of the story is something that this whole book clearly exemplifies. Cinderella has travelled far and wide, becoming a contemporary trope even for cultural products as disposable as internet memes. Its appeal and continuous influence cannot be underscored enough, for the classic Disney image is fundamental to understand the humour, critique and rebellious nature of the *Cenicienta costeña* memes. We concur with Barsotti, who claims that 'contemporary artists have dealt with the usual themes of the fairy tale under a critical, sceptical perspective, with the intent to cause a disturbance in the viewer and to remind him that fairy tales do not offer any alternative to reality' (77).

In this trip the princess not only moved from the United States to Colombia. She has gone from being a submissive servant who hopes to be rescued by a prince charming, to an independent and politically incorrect woman who confronts the prince, drinks beer and leaves parties with her friends, providing a reinterpretation of gender roles that have been made possible thanks to the creativity of internet users and that lends itself to be interpreted by the cultural transduction framework. The memes are at once evidence of the pervasive power of American cultural products, and also of the possibilities for criticism, parody and political disruption which are enabled by current social media platforms and software. The story of Cinderella is so pervasive and culturally shareable, that it also lends itself to the most common form of contemporary social subversion and criticism: the meme.

Works cited

Barsotti, Susanna. 'The Fairy Tale: Recent Interpretations, Female Characters and Contemporary Rewriting. Considerations about an 'Irresistible' Genre.' *Journal of Theories and Research in Education*, vol. 10, no. 2, 2015, pp. 69–80.

Bebić, Domagoj, and Marija Volarevic. 'Do Not Mess with a Meme: The Use of Viral Content in Communicating Politics.' *Communication & Society*, vol. 31, no. 3, 2018, pp. 43–56.

Castaño Díaz, Carlos Mauricio. 'Defining and Characterizing The Concept of Internet Meme.' *Revista CES Psicología*, vol. 6, no. 1, 2013, pp. 82–104.

Cattrysse, Patrick. 'Cultural Transduction and Adaptation Studies: The Concept of Cultural Proximity.' *Palabra Clave*, vol. 20, no. 3, 2017, pp. 645–62.

—. 'Film (Adaptation) as Translation: Some Methodological Proposals.' *TARGET: International Journal of Translation Studies*, vol. 4, no. 1, 1992, pp. 53–70.

Cinderella. Directed by Clyde Geronimi, Hamilton Luske, Wilfred Jackson, Walt Disney Productions, 1950.

CollegeHumor. Tinderella: A Modern Fairy Tale. CollegeHumor, 2014.

Conway, Kyle. 'Cultural Translation, Global Television Studies, and the Circulation of Telenovelas in the United States.' *International Journal of Cultural Studies*, vol. 15, no. 6, Oct. 2012, pp. 583–98.

—. 'Cultural Translation.' *Handbook of Translation Studies*, vol. 3, John Benjamins, 2012.

Dynel, Marta. ' "I Has Seen Image Macros!" Advice Animals Memes as Visual-Verbal Jokes.' *International Journal of Communication*, vol. 10, 2016, pp. 660–88.

Elleström, Lars. 'Adaptations as Intermediality.' *The Oxford Handbook of Adaptation Studies,* edited by Thomas Leitch, Oxford University Press, 2017, pp. 509–26.

—. *Media Transformation: The Transfer of Media Characteristics among Media.* Palgrave MacMillan, 2014.

Espinosa-Medina, Hernán David, and Enrique Uribe-Jongbloed. ' "Do It, but Do It Dancing!": Television and Format Adaptations in Colombia in the 1980s and Early 1990s.' *New Patterns in Global Television Formats,* edited by Karina Aveyard and Albert Moran, Intellect, 2016, pp. 125–39.

—. 'Latin American Contraflow in Global Entertainment Media: Kingdom Rush Series and Zambo Dende as de-Localised Media Products.' *Media International Australia*, 2017, pp. 1–15.

Huntington, Heidi E. 'Subversive Memes: Internet Memes as a Form of Visual Rhetoric.' *Selected Papers of Internet Research*, no. 2009, 2013, pp. 2002–05.

Hutcheon, Linda. *A Theory of Adaptation*. Routledge, 2012.

Instituto Nacional de Medicina Legal y Ciencias Forenses. '2017 Forensis: Datos Para La Vida.' *Forensis: Datos Para La Vida*, vol. 19, no. 1, 2018, pp. 255–301.

Izquierdo Arroyo, José María. 'Sobre La Transduccion (Mediaciones Semiológicas).' *Boletín Millares Carlo*, no. 1, 1980, pp. 179–218, http://mdc.ulpgc.es/cdm/ref/collection/bolmc/id/9 Accessed 25 March 2020.

Jenkins, Henry. *Convergence Culture: Where Old and New Media Collide.* New York University Press, 2006.

Jenkins, Henry. Sam Ford and Joshua Green. *Spreadable Media: Creating Value and Meaning in a Network Culture.* New York University Press, 2013.

López Charles, Carlos. 'Transduction between Image and Sound in Compositional Processes.' *Perception,* no. 485, 2008, pp. 1–5.

Martínez de Antón, David. *La Teoría de La Transducción Literaria. Hacia Una Teoría Dialógica de La Obra Literaria.* Universidad Autónoma de Madrid, 2015.

Míguez, María. 'De Blancanieves, Cenicienta y Aurora a Tiana, Rapunzel y Elsa: ¿qué Imagen de La Mujer Transmite Disney?' *Revista Internacional de Comunicación y Desarrollo,* no. 2, 2015, pp. 41–58.

Pop, Doru. 'Mythology Amalgamated. The Transformation of the Mythological and the Re-Appropriation of Myths in Contemporary Cinema.' *Ekphrasis,* no. 2, 2013, pp. 10–25.

Rodríguez, Delia. Memecracia: Los Virales Que Nos Gobiernan. Gestión 2000, 2013.

Rodríguez Marroquín, Ángela María. 'Érase Una Vez Muchas Cenicientas: Cómo Leer El Modelo Femenino Del Siglo Xx Desde Las Películas Norteamericanas de La Cenicienta.' *Memoria y Sociedad,* vol. 16, no. 33, 2012, pp. 84–98.

Roncallo-Dow, Sergio. 'Confused Travolta o El Placer de Lo Simple.' *Palabra Clave —Revista de Comunicación,* vol. 19, no. 1, 2016, pp. 8–14.

Sinclair, John. ' "The Hollywood of Latin America", Miami as Regional Center.' *Television & New Media,* 2003.

—. 'Transnationalisation of Television Programming in the Iberoamerican Region.' *MATRIZes,* vol. 8, no. 2, 2014, pp. 63–77.

Sindoni, Maria Grazia. '"The Semantics of Migration". Translation as Transduction: Remaking Meanings Across Modes.' *Hermes —Journal of Language and Communication in Business,* no. 55, 2016, pp. 27–44.

Thussu, Daya Kishan. 'Mapping Global Media Flow and Contra-Flow.' *Media on the Move: Global Flow and Contra-Flow,* edited by Daya Kishan Thussu, Routledge, 2007, pp. 221–38.

Trevisan, Michele Kapp, Eduardo Biscayno De Prá and Mariana Fagundes Goethel. *Meme: Intertextualidades e Apropriações Na Internet.* Revista Observatório vol 2 no. 1 May 2016, pp. 277–98.

Uribe-Jongbloed, Enrique, et al. 'Cultural Transduction and Intertextuality in Video Games: An Analysis of Three International Case Studies.' *Contemporary Research on Intertextuality in Video Games,* edited by

Christophe Duret and Christian-Marie Pons, IGI Glopal, 2016, pp. 143–61.

Uribe-Jongbloed, Enrique, and Hernán David Espinosa-Medina. 'A Clearer Picture: Towards a New Framework for the Study of Cultural Transduction in Audiovisual Market Trades.' *OBSERVATORIO (OBS*)*, vol. 8, no. 1, 2014, pp. 23–48, http://obs.obercom.pt/index.php/obs/article/view/707/642 Accessed 25 March 2020.

—. 'An Introduction to Cultural Transduction.' *Palabra Clave*, vol. 20, no. 3, 2017, pp. 615–21.

Weston, Tamara. 'The Problem with Princesses.' *TIME*, 2009, http://entertainment.time.com/2009/12/09/top-10-disney-controversies/slide/the-problem-with-princesses/ Accessed 25 March 2020.

Wiggins, Bradley E., and G. Bret Bowers. 'Memes as Genre: A Structurational Analysis of the Memescape.' *New Media and Society*, vol. 17, no. 11, 2015, pp. 1886–906.

CHAPTER THREE

TINDERELLA, A MODERN FAIRY TALE OF ONLINE DATING AND POST-FEMINIST MEDIA CULTURE

MARTA COLA AND ELENA CAODURO

When the American romantic comedy *You've Got M@il* (Nora Ephron) came out in 1998, online dating seemed a bizarre activity belonging only to trendy Manhattan professionals, played in the film by Hollywood A-stars Meg Ryan and Tom Hanks. Since then many things have changed: online dating has become mainstream and a growing number of individuals have started using dating websites and more recently mobile apps. According to Giulia Ranzini and Christoph Lutz the level of stigma associated with online dating is now fast shrinking as this new way of meeting people becomes more common (81). Due to a plethora of different reasons, such as the flexibility between online and offline identities, the accessibility provided by smart phones and a change in public opinion towards alternative methods of dating, dating sites and apps represent revolutionary tools for individuals to meet new romantic partners. In fact, research carried out in 2013 by the dating site eHarmony UK predicted that by the year 2031 thirty-eight per cent of couples will meet through a form of online dating, and twelve per cent will meet through social media or other social websites. These figures indicate that within the next fifteen years half of all couples will have met online. The study also forecasts that 'by the year 2040, 70% of relationships will be able to attribute their coming-together to either online dating or online communication' (eHarmony UK).

In recent years, Tinder has emerged among the different platforms for online dating as one of the most popular. As an LBRTD (location-based real-time dating) app Tinder thrust into prominence for its algorithm, which employs geographical proximity between users to identify potential dates. It allows users to like or dislike other users' photos through a swiping motion (left for no interest, right for like), and interact via chat if both parties like each other. Mansoor Iqbal reports that as of February 2019 Tinder has fifty-seven million users around the world, of which 4.1 million subscribe to one of the premium versions, it is available in forty languages and used in more than 190 countries. With over twenty billion matches made since its launch, Tinder users go on one million dates per week. Sean Rad and Justin Madteen, cofounders of Tinder, chose a stylised flame as the app icon, and the name itself, which denotes the incendiary material used to light a fire, plays on the possible fires of passion that users could experience online. The global success of Tinder is so widespread that it brought about the introduction of new jargon related to online dating, including the term 'Tinderella'. Generally indicating a female app user, the term plays with the Cinderella fairy tale and has generated a diverse collection of paraphernalia that reflects the complexities of dating in the twenty-first century.

In this chapter, we aim to engage with the contemporary phenomenon of online dating, in particular with the mobile app Tinder, and its relationship with the Cinderella fairy tale, ultimately exploring how the emergence of Tinderella paraphernalia (books, video, photo projects, theatre) functions as re-narration in light of cultural and social change. Tinderella can be seen as the modern Cinderella, even if her date ends in one-night stand or in a fairy tale romance. In the following we discuss dating advice addressed to modern-day Tinderellas which displays discourses of aspirational transformation and selfhood, typical of postfeminist media texts. In fact, the figure of the female dating-app user has become the focus of so many advice columns in magazines and entire chick lit novels that on the one hand it shows the success of the dating app, on the other it implies the required professionalism of the modern day 'wannabe' girlfriend. The dating zeitgeist seems steeped in a neoliberal mind-set that demands agility, branding (a business mentality) and self-reliance. Aspiring partners must fend for themselves in a competitive marketplace and leverage their best assets. Thus, advice articles jump in to impart guidance on the best strategies to master online dating as contemporary fairy godmothers. Discussion will focus in particular on the postfeminist ethos of the advice, the transforming self-narratives and the effort to regulate every aspect of women's conduct.

Tinder, how it works and how it is perceived

The rise and development of the Internet gave new opportunities for individuals to connect socially and also romantically. While in the early

1990s online chat rooms enabled users to communicate, the first online dating websites, such as eHarmony and Match.com, were created with an emphasis on matching interests. The mobile dating app evolution was initiated by the advancement of smartphones and satellite geolocation which increased opportunities for relationship initiation. Following the revolutionary features of Grindr, a gay, bisexual and curious men app, Tinder replicated its GPS capabilities, and as reported by Vanessa Grigoriadis on *The Rolling Stone Magazine*, it was produced as a 'simplified dating app with the focus on images'. Tinder users have their own space where they can upload pictures, a short text bio, and links with other social media accounts. As Mansoor Iqbal explains in his study published by BusinessofApps.com 'The Tinder app is built around the idea of the double opt-in—taking out the element of embarrassment and unwanted attention'. This feature allows communication between the two parties only if both of them access the visible information (picture, bio and social media accounts if publicly visible), like each other and initiate a conversation. There is a second level of gate keeping: geographical proximity. Tinder displays the available users only within a certain radius and if both swipe the profile image right then a 'match' has been made, thus allowing them to engage in instant messaging and private communication. According to Jessica James, the dating app operates through digital embodied self-presentations which 'rely on first impressions, snap judgment or initial attraction'. Because of this interactive design, the left or right swiping becomes an entertainment element; the spontaneity and immediacy of the movement on the touchscreen is seen as a fast, informal and relaxed approach to choosing a possible partner.[1] Therefore, the swipe logic of left and right gives Tinder a gamified approach to dating. This is confirmed by opinions of users interviewed by Bianca Bosker for *The Huffington Post*. While for one student, 'People don't think of [Tinder] as online dating, they think of it as a game [...] a beauty context plus messaging', others consider it 'a judging app'.

After being tested initially in some U.S. college campuses in 2012, Tinder shortly became very popular all over the world, and, as reported by J.J. Colao for *Forbes.com* in November 2013, it rapidly expanded in countries such as Brazil and the United Kingdom, which 'have each added over a million users in the last two months. Both are growing at around 2% per day according to the company. On the low end that translates to

---

[1] There is now a new feature: swiping up, which means to 'super like'. Individuals can use it every 12 hours and once activated it informs users that their pictures have been 'super liked'.

about 20,000 users in each market each day'. The use of Tinder also grows in unexpected places such as Dubai, Turkey, Egypt and Morocco. Data collected by Iqbal indicate that by late 2013, Tinder recorded 350 million swipes per day, which means 4000 per second. The app, originally free-to-use, has also developed subscription options (Tinder Plus, in 2015 and Tinder Gold in 2017). The success was so vast that Tinder has also become the focus of many blogs, articles and even Instagram accounts. Writing for the dating service of *The Guardian*, David Cox correctly explains the phenomenon, he argues 'There used to be a stigma against online dating, but when you get a certain critical mass of people doing it, the social norms shift'.

Research conducted among young adults in the United Kingdom by Hannah Gurney in 2018 interestingly shows that all participants had a good level of awareness of Tinder, despite the variable factor that not every participant had first-hand experience of using the app. As the number of downloads and users show, the wide usage makes Tinder one of the most used and popular dating apps of all time. The major, international scale of Tinder and its popularity are contributing factors as to why individuals who have not personally used the app have a fundamental understanding of how the app works. Moreover, Tinder has received a large amount of media coverage, with blogs and articles on nightmare Tinder dates, in addition to books and references in TV series. This media exposure along with the amount of users are factors to consider and reasons why the participants who have not personally used Tinder are still familiar with the app and its nuances. When comparing the responses of the participants who have not used Tinder to the participants who have, Gurney proves a clear correlation to the level of understanding of the app and how it works. The research also highlights two main ways of describing and perceiving Tinder: as an app that is heavily based on appearance and as a platform for meeting new people.

As predicated by several media theorists, among them McLuhan, McQuail, Gurevitch, Coleman and Blumler, the introduction of new technologies into society can have repercussions, both negative or positive. It turns out that Tinder is an immense contender in contemporary mediated dating culture: it has the potential to re-shape online and offline dating and has monopolised its market and changed the stigma against online dating. In the context of dating, the theory of 'disruptive technologies' does bear relevance in relation to Tinder and interpersonal relationship formation. Coined by Professor Clayton M. Christensen in his 1997 book titled *The Innovator's Dilemma*, the notion of disruptive technologies is distinguished from another category, 'sustaining technology', which relies on incremental improvements to an already established technology. For Christensen, disruptive technology when first introduced, lacks refinement, often has performance problems because it is new, appeals to a limited audience and may not yet have a proven practical application. Online dating apps have, in terms of applying this theory, disrupted the traditional ways in which dating and romantic interpersonal relationship formation takes place. It is more obvious to note how new technological advancements have changed or disrupted behaviours. For example, sending an email or text message has disrupted the sending of a letter. However, as interpersonal relationship formation is not as clear-cut as sending a letter or an email it is harder to pinpoint the change in its discourse. Despite this, one can fairly and logically suggest that the trends in addition to the societal normalisation and acceptance of online dating do have the capabilities to change the landscape of traditional dating by offering easily accessible platforms that are not restricted by geographical locations. This means therefore that online dating has become a disruptive technology to traditional dating habits.

The origins of Tinderella

The term 'Tinderella' first appeared in February 2013 in the University of Illinois's student newspaper as a play on words between the classic fairy tale, Cinderella, and the popular mobile dating app, Tinder, in order to describe female Tinder users. In the same year the term appeared in Urban Dictionary.com, an online resource updated by users which collects neologisms and slangs; here Tinderella is defined as 'a really hot girl on Tinder', 'an attractive female discovered through the Tinder dating application'. Other entries define Tinderella as 'your dream girl that you see on Tinder', or 'when a Tinder Date inexplicably turns into a fairytale romance'. More recent Urban Dictionary definitions draw links to the classic fairy tale:

> Hello I saw you on Tinder yesterday and decided to find and add you on Facebook. It took me a quite while. But, hey, it is just like the Cinderella tale when the prince is searching for Cinderella. I am glad that our story might have a similar ending.

The neologism, however, came to the fore in January 2014 when CollegeHumor.com released a video online: *Tinderella: A Modern Fairy Tale*, a two-minute animated short, claiming that 'present day Cinderella doesn't wait for a fairy godmother to fix her up, she uses Tinder'. The video, also available on YouTube, reached more than eleven million views and features an innocent and gentle young woman called Cindy who browses away at her phone until her charming Princeton appears on her screen. Located less than a mile from her position, Cindy swipes left and after a positive reply from Princeton, arranges a meeting at a local club called The Ball. Then, Cindy's phone batteries die in the midst of her pursuit and she seems unable to locate her prince in the chaos of the club. The video presents a happy ending with Cindy having a one-night stand, enjoying the liberty of finding a casual lover and avoiding commitment. CollegeHumor takes the classic tale of Cinderella and moves it into the world of iPhones, dating apps and hookup culture parodying the version of the story. *Tinderella: A Modern Fairy Tale* employs a Disneyesque animation style characterised by soft lines, large round doe eyes, outlines in colours rather than black, and smooth movements. The video also chooses to avoid a traditional ending, namely Cindy and Princeton starting a relationship, and instead prefers to give Cindy the freedom of not needing a long-term partner.

The sexual undertones are not a foreign departure from the classic Cinderella fairy tale as *Tinderella* borrows the slipper symbolism, which can be seen having a sexual connotation. As Bruno Bettelheim argues there is a strong sexual symbolism linked to the slipper:

> The shoe must be a slipper that does not stretch, or it would fit some other girl, such as the stepsisters. [...] A tiny receptacle into which some part of the body can slip fit tightly can be seen as a symbol of the vagina. Something that is brittle and must not be stretched because it would break reminds us of the hymen; and something that is easily lost at the end of a ball when one's lover tries to keep his hold on his beloved seems an appropriate image for virginity (264-5).

Within the several versions of Cinderella, the slipper always played a role no matter its material: from the glass of Perrault, to the gold of the ancient Chinese tale and in Brothers Grimm version. As Cinderella's foot fits into the slipper held by the prince, the two find each other, and it similarly works for the Tinder match: if one fits into the 'desire' of the other, swiping right, the match happens and Tinderella finds, as in the CollegeHumor video, not a fairy tale but a one-night stand.

The tale of Cinderella, as the poor passive girl, needing the help of a fairy godmother to transform her into a glowing princess, is in a way overturned by the figure of Cindy, our Tinderella who might not wait for Prince Charming to turn her life around, but decides to hunt for a prince herself. As a Tinder user, and being a user implies being active, she looks for possible partners, she is a free agent: single and childless and able to enjoy herself in restaurants, clubs and other social places thanks to her city lifestyle and being capable of earning a good salary. Cindy embodies the new young woman, confident and free who can brazenly enjoy her sexuality without fear of judgement, but also displays anxiety for what the future holds for her. As such, the video encapsulates a postfeminist ethos proclaiming that women can gain empowerment and agency through an insistent emphasis on individualism and consumerism.[2] While in the past sexualised representations of women in the media presented them as passive mute objects, such as in the animated Disney version of Cinderella, today postfeminist sensibility presents women not as straightforwardly objectified but as active desiring sexual subjects.

Tinderella and postfeminist media culture

The concept of Tinderella has gained popularity and become the central topic of several productions. From books to photo projects, from theatre performances to blogs, and regular columns in newspapers, Tinderella is embedded with different aspects of the Cinderella metaphor and symbolism, and is used to represent modern fairy tales in light of cultural and social change.

Among them it is worth mentioning *Confession of a Tinderella: The laugh-out-loud true story of one girl's experience of life on Tinder*, the memoir of Rosy Edwards, who recounts the difficulties of being single in the twenty-first century. Presenting herself as a career-minded woman, in reality Edwards does not know which career to have in mind, and although she is apparently happy being single, a part of her desires a boyfriend. She recounts how, after a few unsuccessful dates with friends of friends, she put herself on Tinder, where she falls for the wrong guys, ditches the nice ones, and ponders the possibility of finding her happy ending. Described on the back cover as 'Brilliantly honest and hilariously funny, Rosy's story shows us all that the key to a successful love life could just be a swipe away', *Confession of a Tinderella* recuperates some tropes of *Bridget Jones's Diary* such as awful dates, the anxiety of singlehood and social pressure about women's alleged biological clock.

---

[2] The tenets of postfeminism remain a subject of much discussion. By considering *Tinderella: A Modern Fairy Tale* as part of postfeminist culture, we follow Yvonne Tasker and Diane Negra's understanding of postfeminism as 'a more complex relationship between culture, politics, and feminism' than the surpassed second-wave of feminism (1).

My Quest to Become Tinderella deals with similar themes: as an autobiographical collection of short stories the author, Piper Graham, retells episodes that she had personally experienced over the course of three years of online dating. 'As a 33 year old female, with an insatiable desire to find love, I have compiled some of my most entertaining and heart wrenching tales into this book and I am excited to share them with you' says Graham' (back cover).

These books draw together so many of the themes developed from the highly debated notion of postfeminism.[3] Rosalind Gill considers the notion as a sensibility, namely that postfeminism is a cultural phenomenon that encapsulates the contradictory nature of postfeminist discourses, feminist and anti-feminist themes. She has explored in great depth its features, among them:

> femininity as a bodily property, the shift from objectification to subjectification; the emphasis upon self-surveillance, monitoring and self-discipline; a focus on individualism, choice and empowerment; the dominance of a makeover paradigm; a resurgence in ideas of natural sexual difference; a marked sexualization of culture; and an emphasis upon consumerism and the commodification of difference (147).

One of the most striking aspects of the Tinderella phenomenon is its obsession and preoccupation with the body, given that the profile picture plays such a pivotal role in securing matches on the application. In both novels the body is presented as source of power, but also in need of constant monitoring, discipline and remodelling. We can witness how the discourse has shifted from the objectivisation of the female body to making it an active subject and yet, the female body is still under scrutiny. The protagonists are aware of the power of their look: they are young, attractive white middle-class professionals who, in order to conform to even narrower canon of female beauty, are prone to dieting, fitness regimes and beauty treatments. Moreover, the lengthy descriptions of fashion accessories and garments, as well as gadgets and technology stress the crucial role of consumerism within the postfeminist discourse.

These Tinderellas are presented as women who, even though they have a liberated approach, are constantly in search of the right man, very similarly to the female characters in TV shows such as *Sex and the City*

---

[3] There is little agreement about what postfeminism is, as the term is often contradictorily used to signify a break with second wave feminism, a third wave or a backlash. We follow Rosalind Gill's attempt to frame it as a sensibility made up of a number of interrelated themes.

and *Ally McBeal*. They claim to be liberated and clearly enjoy their sexuality, but placate their anxieties with consumerism and constantly searching for their other half. As Angela McRobbie discusses: 'post-feminism positively draws on and invokes feminism as that which can be taken into account, to suggest that equality is achieved, in order to install a whole repertoire of new meanings which emphasise that it is no longer needed, it is a spent force' (255).

In addition to individuals creating social media accounts or blogs to share and discuss personal Tinder experiences under the label of Tinderella, press and magazine articles in the form of sex and relationship advice abound. For example, 'Is "Tinderella syndrome" ruining YOUR love life? Women are so dependent upon dating websites they're unable to approach men in real life' by Bianca London published by the *Daily Mail online,* 'Meet "Tinderella"—The 27-Year-Old Queen Of Online Dating' by Caroline Moss on the *Business Insider India,* and 'She's gotta have it: diary of a Tinderella, aged 23' by Hannah Rogers published by *The Times*, articles which are representative of popular press discourses which treat relationships as work. Using analogies from finance, marketing and management the articles provide advice on how to find 'Mr Right'. The articles suggest putting the same effort to tailor the Tinder profile (photo and bio) as the effort made for work CVs. Women are advised to build checklists of what they want in a partner, thus encouraging them to take control of their intimate lives and attain their goals. Moreover, a weekly column by Tinderella, Fabulous Columnist featured in *The Sun* newspaper during 2017 traced weekly adventures and presented the process of dating as a military campaign. Interestingly fate and fairy-tale stories are treated with derision, finding a partner is a job that requires research, planning and strategy. Nevertheless, a happy ending is possible for those prepared to become an entrepreneur of the self. This entrepreneurship discourse uses a language of empowerment, agency and equality and yet the ultimate goal is very traditional rather than feminist: namely find and keep a man.

However, this trend of postfeminist media texts developed around the figure of Tinderella seems to be countered by more critical examples which attempt to highlight the issues of online dating. For example, Tinderella is also the title of a photo project, firstly presented in 2016 by Kirra Cheers, an Australian photographer based in New York City. Cheers curated and presented in a group show depicting 'Modern Romance' and decided to take a more personal approach to the theme, documenting her personal experience of online dating with Tinder. She went on a whirlwind seventeen first dates over the course of two months with men she met on the dating app. Out of the seventeen dates she went on, eleven men allowed Cheers to photograph them; the photographic show was then titled Tinderella. As Jenna Garrett reports, Cheers' black-and-white portraits are featured alongside screen captures of crude messages she received. 'I wanted to document my own experience so that people can compare it to their own', Cheers tells Jonathan Storm for *Business Insider* and 'the resulting series shows what it's like to navigate modern dating, on both a personal and universal level'. The project allowed the photographer also to reflect on traditional gender roles:

> Most people wanted me to confirm my interest in them as a person and not simply as an art project. In this way, I saw it as a swapping of traditional gender roles—posing the question that perhaps men and women aren't all that different. Change the power dynamic and you achieve the same result. I found the role reversal to be empowering. A mentor suggested that this process of objectifying men was similar to collecting butterflies—a comparison I greatly enjoy. (Brooks)

This process of reflecting on the widespread phenomenon of sexual harassment via Tinder has been subject to much media attention. A plethora of social media accounts have been created to discuss Tinder, for example the Instagram account 'ByeFelipe'. Set up in October 2014 this account aimed to socially and publicly call out or shame male users of Tinder for sending rude, misogynist and inappropriate messages to women. 'ByeFelipe' gained many followers and became a platform for women to discuss serious issues about sexual harassment and misogynist behaviour on Tinder in a light-hearted manner. Run by Alexandra Tweten, 'ByeFelipe' exposes the sexism women experience online by publishing examples of verbal abuse, unwanted graphic pictures and crude sexual solicitations. The Instagram account expanded into a feminist campaign which included a website, a podcast, a petition for implementing anti-harassment policies in social media (Thompson 70). A much more entertaining and heart-warming account emerges from Melissa Brenzinger's blog titled '30 Days of Tinder'. The blog is about her personal experiences with dating through Tinder and is exemplary of the numerous bloggers writing about Tinder. Started as a fun experiment, Brenzinger suggests using the app with a pinch of salt in order to avoid tarnishing your sense of self.

A quite different point of view is the one used in the performance *Tinderella! Cinders Slips It In*, presented by Above the Stag Theatre, known for performances targeting LGBTQ audiences, between the end of 2015 and beginning of 2016. In this Christmas pantomime reworking of the ugly duckling becoming swan, Cinders is a young man living in the imaginary Eastern European kingdom of Slutvia, the Prince is an online-dating-addicted singleton and the Fairy Godmother is an American lesbian trying to settle in this new fantastic land. The story tells how once upon a time, a slave boy called Cinders lived with his murderous stepmother and her daughters in a little landlocked kingdom. Now although this kingdom lacked democracy and had been banned from Eurovision on behavioural grounds, it boasted a Prince whose balls were the envy of the world. After a chance encounter between the Prince and Cinders, the two have to face many obstacles, in particular changing the law that prohibit gay marriage. The camp version of Tinderella is full of gay jokes and slapstick comedic episodes but is peculiar for mixing education and entertainment. In fact, with references to homophobia, sexism, Syria and civil rights it provides an antidote to the harshness of the world with laughter and happiness. This performance is in stark contrast to the vast literature on Tinderella which claims the absolute invisibility of any sexualities outside the heterosexual norm.

Conclusions

For all the advice to be sexually open when dating on Tinder, lesbian desire is completely absent and books and blogs reinforce the heteronormative paradigm. This might simply suggest that Tinder is not perceived as a queer-friendly app; there exist in fact specifically lesbian and queer-friendly apps, for example Her, which has around 4 million users, Fem a predominantly video-based app, Lesly or Scissr. However, it is also proof that in postfeminist media culture there is an erasure of lesbian desire, because queerness unsettles normative constructions of female sexuality. Online dating apps such as Tinder have soared in popularity over the past few years, but at the same time they have exposed how women and sexual minorities are becoming the subject of aggressive behaviour and language in these digital spaces. These performances of toxic masculinity online and misogyny could be read as a response to perceived increases in women's power and agency. Although Tinder and other dating apps are not solely used for casual encounters, they have often been defined as 'hookup apps'. Modern Tinderellas, young attractive and single women, who engage in casual sex are the ultimate expression of feminist sexual liberation. And yet double standards continue: women who appear in these digital sexualised spaces may face aggression and abuse for not living up to the impossible demand to be available but 'not too prudish' or 'not slutty'.

As McRobbie maintains, memoirs, social media accounts, blogs and articles in the press 'normalise post-feminist gender anxieties so as to re-regulate young women by means of the language of personal choice. But even "well regulated liberty" can backfire (the source of comic effect), and this in turn gives rise to demarcated pathologies' (262). Online dating offers women an increased level of choice and control in finding partners but ultimately the risk of harassment on apps such as Tinder functions as a form of discipline. It is interesting to note how the modernisation of romance narratives has changed the attributes of the romantic heroine. Whereas the classical figure, a traditional Cinderella, offered goodness, innocence and simplicity to the prospective partner/husband, modern Tinderellas are required to be skilled in a variety of practices: from marketing to sexual behaviours, and their 'worth' in the online dating marketplace seems to be rooted in patriarchal ideals of feminine beauty. Overall, the Tinderella paraphernalia are enjoyed by users and viewed as self-help guides enabling them to be their own fairy godmothers and transform themselves, but this act of transformation is also a way to regulate the self. Nonetheless, there are instances of feminist resistance and activism on this issue in blogs, Instagram accounts and performances such as 'ByeFelipe' and *Tinderella! Cinders Slips It In* which draw attention to sexism, harassment and inconsistencies and counter postfeminist logics with derisive laughter.

Works cited

Ally McBeal. Created by David E. Kelley. 20th Century Fox Television, 1997-2002.

Bettelheim, Bruno. *The Uses of Enchantment: The Meaning and Importance of Fairy Tales*. Vintage Books Edition, 2010.

Brooks, Katherine. '"Cinderella" Is The Tale Of One Artist And The 17 First Dates She Found Online.' *HuffPost*, 19 September 2014 https://www.huffingtonpost.co.uk/entry/tinderella_n_5825920? Accessed 21 June 2019.

Brenzinger, Melissa. '30 Days of Tinder.' 2016, https://30daysoftinder.com/author/melissaluxuriates/ Accessed 21 June 2019.

Bridget Jones's Diary. Directed by Sharon Maguire, Little Bird, Studio canal and Working Title Film, 2001.

Cheers, Kierra. Tinderella, New York Photo Series, 2014, https://www.refinery29.com/en-us/2014/10/75934/a-search-for-prince-charming-on-tinder#slide-1 Accessed 21 June 2019.

Christensen, Clayton. *The Innovator's Dilemma: When New Technologies Cause Great Firms to Fail.* Harvard Business School Press, 1997.

Cinderella. Directed by Clyde Geronimi, Hamilton Luske, Wilfred Jackson, Walt Disney productions, 1950.

Colao, J. J. 'Not Just For Hookups: Tinder Looks To Conquer Business Networking.' *Forbes*, 8 April 2013 https://www.forbes.com/sites/jjcolao/2013/04/08/tinder-for-business-dating-app-looks-to-conquer-other-matchmaking-verticals/#2de117935dbd Accessed 21 June 2019.

CollegeHumor. 'Tinderella: A Modern Fairy Tale.' 2016 Available at http://www.collegehumor.com/video/6948903/tinderella-a-modern-fairy-tale Accessed 21 June 2019.

Cox, David. 'Online Dating – What's driving the popularity boom?' *The Guardian Soulmates*, undated, https://soulmates.theguardian.com/blog/dating-locations/dating/online-dating-what-s-driving-the-popularity-boom#.W0TDUdhKgb0. Accessed: 21 June 2019.

Edwards, Rosy. *Confession of a Tinderella: The laugh-out-loud true story of one girl's experience of life on Tinder.* Century, 2015.

eHarmony UK. 'Over 50% of couples will meet online by 2031.' *Eharmony.com* 2013, https://www.eharmony.co.uk/dating-advice/%20 online-dating-unplugged/over-50-of-couples-will-meet-online-by-2031#. Accessed 21 June 2019.

Garrett, Jenna. '"Tinderella": the story of one NYC photographer and her many Tinder dates.' Feature shoot. 8 September, 2014, https://www.featureshoot.com/2014/09/tinderella-the-story-of-one-nyc-photographer-and-her-many-tinder-dates/. Accessed 21 June 2019.

Gill, Rosalind. 'Postfeminism Media Culture: Elements of a Sensibility.' *European Journal of Cultural Studies*, vol.10, no. 2, 2007, pp.147-66.

Graham, Piper. *My Quest to Become Tinderella.* BookBaby, 2016.

Grigoriadis, Vanessa. 'Inside the hookup factory.' *Rolling Stone Magazine,* 27 October 2014, http://www.rollingstone.com/ culture/ features/inside-tinders-hookup-factory-20141027. Accessed 21 June 2019.

Gurevitch, Michael, Coleman, Stephen and Blumler, Jay G. 'Political Communication – Old and New Media Relationships.' *The ANNALS of the American Academy of Political and Social Science.* Vol. 625, Issue 1, 2009, pp. 164-81.

Gurney, Hannah. 'Online Dating and Mating: Tinder and its Effects on Interpersonal Relationship Formation in the Modern Age.' Master's Dissertation. University of Bedfordshire, 2018.

Iqbal, Mansoor. 'Tinder Revenue and Usage Statistics.' *Business of Apps*, 27 February 2019 http://www.businessofapps.com/data/tinder-statistics/ Accessed 21 June 2019.

James, Jessica L. 'Mobile dating in the digital age: Computer-mediated communication and relationship building on Tinder.' Master's Dissertation. Texas State University, 2015. https://digital.library.txstate.edu/handle/10877/5529 Accessed, 21 June 2019.

London, Bianca. 'Is "Tinderella syndrome" ruining YOUR love life? Women are so dependent upon dating websites they're unable to approach men in real life.' *Daily Mail Online*, 11 August 2014, https://www.dailymail.co.uk/femail/article-2721700/Is-Tinderella-syndrome-ruining-YOUR-love-life-Women-dependent-communicating-online-unable-approach-men-real-life.html   Accessed 21 June 2019.

McLuhan, Marshal. *Understanding Media: The Extensions of Man*. MIT Press, 1994.

McQuail, Denis. *Mass Communication Theory. An Introduction*. London: Sage, 1983.

McRobbie, Angela. 'Post-Feminism and Popular Culture.' *Feminist Media Studies*, vol. 4, no. 3, 2004, pp. 255-64.

Moss, Caroline. 'Meet 'Tinderella'—The 27-Year-Old Queen Of Online Dating.' *Business Insider India*, 6 November 2014, https://www.businessinsider.in/Meet-Tinderella--The-27-Year-Old-Queen-Of-Online-Dating/articleshow/45061117.cms Accessed 21 June 2019.

Ranzini, Giulia and Christoph Lutz. 'Love at first swipe? Explaining Tinder self-presentation and motives.' *Mobile Media & Communication*, vol.5, issue 1, 2016, pp.80-101.

Rogers, Hannah. 'She's gotta have it: diary of a Tinderella, aged 23.' *The Times*, 11 February 2017. https://www.thetimes.co.uk/article/shes-gotta-have-it-diary-of-a-tinderella-aged-23-pqz6wtwvf Accessed 21 June 2019.

Sex and the City, TV series. Darren Star, creator. HBO, 1998-2004.

Storm, Christian. 'This Photographer's Pictures Of Her Tinder Dates Say A Lot About Modern Dating.' *Business Insider*, 23 September 2014, https://www.businessinsider.com/tinder-date-portraits-2014-9?IR=T Accessed 21 June 2019.

Tasker, Yvonne and Diane Negra. 'Introduction.' *Interrogating Postfeminism: Gender and the Politics of Popular Culture*, edited by Yvonne Tasker and Diane Negra, Duke University Press, 2007, pp. 1-26.

'Tinderella.' *Urban Dictionary*, 2019,
    http://www.urbandictionary.com/define.php?term=tinderella Accessed
    21 June 2019.
'Tinderella, Fabulous Columnist.' *The Sun*, 22 December 2017,
    https://www.thesun.co.uk/fabulous/5193793/tinderella-xmas-party-
    hook-up/ Accessed 21 June 2019.
Thompson, Laura. '"I can be your Tinder nightmare": Harassment and
    misogyny in the online sexual market.' *Feminism & Psychology*, vol.
    28, no. 1, 2018, pp. 69-89.
You've Got M@il. Directed by Nora Ephron, performances by Tom Hanks
    and Meg Ryan, Warner Brothers, 1998.

CHAPTER FOUR

LOSING YOUR FOOTING:
THE TRANSFORMATION OF GENDER ROLES
AND GENDER IDEOLOGY IN MARISSA MEYER'S
CINDER

NICKY DIDICHER

Fairy tale retellings and adaptations will naturally reflect the ideologies of the culture that produces them.[1] It is not surprising that Western Cinderellas from the past fifty years have tended to be strong, brave, and independent, what in North America is called the 'spunky' girl, rather than what we now perceive as the old-fashioned passive princess who weeps and needs assistance from her fairy godmother or the spirit of her dead mother, 'as feminist writers pushed for new sets of narrative models for young girl readers' (Bottigheimer 29). In her Young Adult science fiction fairy tale romance series *The Lunar Chronicles*, beginning with *Cinder* (2012), American novelist Marissa Meyer attempts to challenge both our gender expectations and our moral expectations, pushing readers toward a larger spectrum of possibilities. Through a textual analysis based in the field of literature studies, I find that, while Meyer's novels do more than perform the now-expected feminist transformation of the passive princess into the spunky girl, and Prince Charming into the sensitive guy, she is more successful in challenging moral expectations than gender ones and does so in a way that illuminates current Western ethics. Linh Cinder (protagonist of book one) and the *Lunar Chronicles* series complicate the morality and the moral choices of traditional fairy tale characters in a way

---

[1] This chapter derives from two separate papers delivered at the All about Cinderella Conference, one by Nicky Didicher and one co-authored by Nicky Didicher and Emily Seitz. Nicky Didicher combined and substantially revised them. She would like to thank Linda Peters for her feedback and suggestions.

that challenges Meyer's readers to consider more possibilities for the behaviour of good people. However, although she appears to be reversing Perrault's and the Grimms' motifs of femininity in order to produce a postmodern Western version of femaleness, Meyer still uses common romance novel tropes which reassert the values of heteronormativity and weakness, and the books routinely omit any characters who are not cisgendered and heterosexual.

Femininity is always a performance (whether it matches one's inner self or not), and tellings of the Cinderella tale often draw our attention to those performances, either as a reflection of current sociopolitical gender ideology, as a reinscription of an older version of femininity, or as a combination of those functions. Meyer combines them, without much in the way of decolonising or queering, in contrast to recent politicised fairy tale retellings by Nalo Hopkinson, Emma Donoghue, and Dan Taulapapa McMullin that Cristina Bacchilega has analysed for the ways in which they 'affect a form of queering, one that troubles sex/gender/sexuality normative categories *and* relocates the genre geopolitically, socially, and generically' (*Transforming* 71, italics in original). While Meyer's *Cinder* relocates 'Cinderella' to New Beijing geographically and to science fiction generically, her Eastern Commonwealth feels mainly Western with the occasional mention of chopsticks, her science fiction tropes are standard ones, and socially *Cinder* reproduces the class structures inherent in traditional European Cinderella stories without doing much to critique their oppressive nature: she decries tyranny but approves benevolent class hierarchies. In spite of Jennifer Mitchell's reading of the book as queer (2014), *Cinder* does little to trouble sex/gender/sexuality normative categories. Meyer may be using the relocations of her series as a way to shake up her readers' thinking about traditional European fairy tales when it comes to ideas of what actions and people are 'good', but she is still well grounded in traditional attitudes to gender and sexuality, and her books form a less political strand in what Bacchilega identifies as the current 'fairy-tale web' (*Transforming* 1 & passim).

The heroine of *Cinder* is a cyborg mechanic living in New Beijing. Her cybernetic left hand and leg, as well as the central processing unit attached to her spine, helped her survive a devastating fire when she was a toddler, but mark her as a second-class citizen in her society. She lives with and has to give her earnings to her cruel and selfish guardian Linh Adri, her kindlier adoptive father having died. Although one of her adoptive sisters is more affectionate than the other, Cinder's closest relationship is with the house droid Iko, whose defective personality chip makes her long for lipstick and going to dances. Cinder seems at first to be against the sorts of feminine attributes and behaviours that Iko longs to embody, preferring coveralls to dresses and repairing droids to dancing.

Performing femininity

We can usefully compare Cinder to Cendrillon and Aschenputtel with regard to their markers of femininity and moral goodness.[2] Many traditional Cinderella stories such as those by Perrault and the Grimms inscribe the protagonist's femininity in her body, especially in her small feet encased in unusual footwear, and in her magnificent clothing, which marks her as marriageable and noble. Meyer undercuts these traditions and offers us a more culturally comfortable feminist version of Cinderella's female body and clothing, but we see also Cinder longing to conform to traditional expectations, which gives these value. Cendrillon's markers of moral goodness include her ability to cry and her kindness to her nasty stepsisters, while Aschenputtel's include her capacity to cry and to pray. Cinder is unable to cry (her tear ducts having been surgically removed), she does not pray, and she is only kind to one of her adopted sisters. Just as she has one smaller foot at the beginning and end of the novel, an outdated child-sized prosthetic foot, so *Cinder* has a foot in both camps when it comes to her being a traditional or revisionist Cinderella.

In Perrault's *Cendrillon*, successfully performing femininity means giving visual signals of aristocratic grandeur: Cendrillon is beautiful, moves and dances well, behaves politely, and dresses in ostentatious good taste. While Perrault specifies that she is peerlessly good, 'd'une bonté sans exemple' (245), this quality in itself does not help her win the prince. Rather, it is her tears that invoke her godmother's assistance that lead to her marriage: 'sa Maraine, qui la vit toute en pleurs, luy demanda ce qu'elle avoit : Je voudrois bien... Je voudrois bien... elle pleuroit si fort qu'elle ne put achever'; her godmother, who saw her all in tears, asked her what was the matter. 'I would like... I would like...'. She was crying so hard she could not finish (247, my translation). As Marina Warner points out, the earliest illustration of the European Cinderella character features her crying on the hearth (204): that tears are so essential to Cinderella says something about the value of tears, with their implied weakness and lack of emotional control, in identifying feminine goodness. It is not until

---

[2] I focus on these two traditional Cinderellas not only because they are well known, but because Meyer appears to have them in mind: she uses epigraphs from an English translation of *Aschenputtel* and details, such as the pumpkin coach, from *Cendrillon*.

Cendrillon cries that her fairy godmother appears, and she knows what the inarticulate girl needs to succeed: magnificent clothing. At the ball, Cendrillon demonstrates kindness to her stepsisters by sharing with them the citrus fruits the prince has given her, and after her own marriage she arranges for them to marry great lords—Bottigheimer calls her 'a paragon of early modern virtues' (34)—but this kindness is not the reason the prince marries her. In the second 'morale' at the end of the text, Perrault specifies humorously that what she needs to succeed is in fact not 'bonté' but 'sa Maraine':

> It is no doubt a great advantage to have lively spirits, courage, good birth, good sense, and other similar talents that Heaven gives you, but, although you may have them, they will not get you far if you do not also have godfathers and godmothers [i.e. mentors] to make them effective in society. (253, my translation)

For Perrault, a successful performance of feminine goodness requires social graces, social support, being overwhelmed by tears, and sexual purity. The Maraine encases Cendrillon's feet in glass slippers, the only object she does not transform from another. For centuries, glass and crystal have been associated with 'purity, especially female purity, and with marvelous states between life and death' (Hoffman 57). In her act of encasement, the fairy godmother symbolically preserves Cendrillon's chastity, an important part of female virtue in the late 1600s.

In the Grimms' *Aschenputtel*, similarly, it is the heroine's tears that ensure magical help from the birds who represent the spirit of her dead mother and that, in the end, mark her as successfully feminine and marriageable. As in Perrault, there is an emphasis on visual splendour, but much less so in comparison, and more emphasis on her crying: Aschenputtel 'ging jeden Tag hinaus zu dem Grabe der Mutter und weinte, und blieb fromm und gut'; she went every day out to her mother's grave and cried, and stayed pious and good (1857 version, p. 119, my translation). Aschenputtel is cleverer than Cendrillon, getting away from the chasing prince through a dovecote and up a tree, but she also weeps and prays for what she wants, and the birds give it to her. As readers of these older versions, we assume that the heroines' performance of what society deems valuable in women matches their inner nature, because the Cinderella characters appear to lack their stepsisters' hypocrisy and their stepmother's scheming. Aschenputtel is a lower middle-class heroine, walking to the ball on her tiny feet and climbing trees, unlike Cendrillon's natural upper-class abilities to dance and design beautiful hairstyles, which reflects the Grimms' more middle-class readership rather than Perrault's implied female readers from the gentry.

Nevertheless, in both these versions it is the heroines' key moments of feeling helpless and being overwhelmed by emotion, the times that they lose their footing on the hearth, grave, or palace steps, that set their lives on a stable footing, ensuring their success in marriage and stable futures. It is also these key moments of feeling helpless and overwhelmed that let their readers know how to be successfully feminine and good. The *Oxford English Dictionary*'s definitions of the noun 'footing' include 'the action or an act of positioning the feet so as not to slip or stumble; stable positioning of the feet' ('Footing' 1a) and 'a firm or secure position from which further progress may be made' ('Footing' 15). Traditional femininity offers stability through weakness: Cinderella falls to the ground/hearth, losing her footing, and thereby secures help from another woman, a mother figure, which will give her a secure position from which to progress.[3]

Cinder's body

Cinder is a cyborg (part organic, part mechanical) in a society that demeans and enslaves both cyborgs and androids (human-shaped robots), but she is also an accomplished mechanic, the breadwinner for her adoptive family: practical, self sufficient, and determined. She builds her own carriage from a vehicle resembling an old orange VW beetle and tries to avoid going to the ball, only doing so to save the prince's life from his evil fiancée. Unbeknownst to her, she is also the lost Lunar princess Selene. Like many recent spunky heroines, Meyer's version of Cinderella does not have the graceful femininity of Perrault's or Disney's characters, but Cinder's bodily awkwardness becomes a key and permanent part of her character rather than merely something to overcome by the ball scene.[4] Although Cinder is thin, angular, and awkward, her body is both female and marriageable. In particular, Meyer emphasises that Cinder's

---

[3] It is interesting and ironic that the two most recent quotations in the *OED* to illustrate losing one's footing both involve a female subject: '1983 Canberra *Times* 22 Jan. 6 She climbed a tree to get a better view and lost her footing. 2004 J. MANSELL *One you really Want* xx. 108 Nancy promptly lost her footing and went over backwards'.

[4] Even in book four at her coronation, Cinder is awkward and gets a stain on her dress. Her droid friend Iko says 'It was inevitable. […] It's part of your charm' (*Winter* 813).

sexual/reproductive organs were kept during the procedure that made her a cyborg. Donna Haraway in the 'Cyborg Manifesto' posits that:

> organisms and organismic, holistic politics depend on metaphors of rebirth and invariably call on the resources of reproductive sex. I would suggest that cyborgs have more to do with regeneration and are suspicious of the reproductive matrix and of most birthing. (181)

For Haraway, cyborgs are aligned with regeneration rather than reproduction, which reflects her belief that cyborgs are creatures of 'a post-gendered world' (150). Meyer, however, explicitly gives Cinder both female gender and reproductive organs; after scanning Cinder's body, Dr. Erland notes, 'your reproductive system is almost untouched. You know, lots of female cyborgs are left infertile because of the invasive procedures, but from the look of it, I don't suspect you will have any problems' (116). Meyer's cyborg is not Haraway's postgendered creature, since, as a princess, Cinder is expected to produce an heir. Cinder's body is female and fertile, even if not voluptuous, which helps Meyer to resubscribe to an older version of femininity and establish Cinder as marriageable, in spite of her lack of grace and her low-class status as cyborg.

In the events leading up to and during the ball, Cinder's clothing changes from gender-neutral cargo pants and work gloves to something more emblematic of traditional femininity and marriageability, as both Prince Kai and Cinder attempt to make her cyborg body conform to traditional femininity. Kai feminises Cinder's body by giving her a pair of silk gloves. Cinder's perception of the gloves as 'fit for a princess' (299) is ironic because she is in fact a princess although she does not know it yet. However, Cinder is not performing the feminine role of the princess when she receives the gift; she is performing as a mechanic and a (cyborg passing as fully) human. Prince Kai is unaware of Cinder's cyborg identity, but he does know that she is a mechanic who does not wear silk gloves. He wants to encourage her to attend the ball as his special guest, and perhaps in a small way he is shaping Cinder into a more feminine figure. The silk gloves are a feminised version of the garment Cinder usually wears, her work gloves. By offering a gift, Kai signals his romantic interest in Cinder, and by accepting the gloves as a gift, Cinder signals, in romance novel fashion, that she may return his interest.

When Cinder decides she must go to the ball after all, because she finds out that Kai's fiancée, Levana the evil Lunar queen, is planning to murder Kai after their marriage, she dresses herself in the ballgown of her recently deceased stepsister Peony (who was the kinder sister and the one to whom Cinder was kind), Kai's gloves, and white dress boots she takes from her remaining stepsister Pearl's closet.[5] Cinder moves from a more feminist gender-neutral type of clothing, equivalent to the traditional Cinderella's rags, to a more traditionally feminine ballgown and long silk gloves. It is not a look she is used to, but one that she wants to make work for Kai's sake.

Cinder arrives at the ball dishevelled and sore from walking on her dilapidated too-small child foot—Linh Adri, her stepmother/legal guardian has confiscated her adult foot—but she urges her body to conform to traditional femininity: '[h]er leg was beginning to ache from carrying it, but she resisted the urge to limp, picturing ever-graceful Pearl in her ball gown and heels, and wished her body into conformity' (342). Cinder is embodying, or attempting to embody, Peony's and Pearl's femininity. By wearing Peony's dress and Pearl's boots, and by wishing her body to conform to Pearl's gracefulness, Cinder is emulating their femininity: the stepsisters have become figures for natural grace and taste in *Cinder*, instead of Cendrillon. Here, Meyer seems to be both rejecting and re-enforcing traditional notions of grace and appearance as markers of femininity and morality, in that the garments belong to the stepsisters, traditionally villainous, but Cinder desires them as more than a disguise to get her into the palace: she wants to be magnificent and graceful.

Cinder is upset because her pretty silk gloves and stolen gown have been stained by oil and rain before she arrives at the ball. The garments now reflect Cinder's identity as both princess and cyborg mechanic; however, Cinder wants to look elegantly feminine. Prince Kai finds her failure to be elegant amusing but endearing:

> Kai's lips twitched, and though he still looked baffled, he did not look angry or disgusted. Cinder gulped. As she got nearer, her arms burned to wrap around herself, to cover her filthy, wrinkled, water-stained dress as best she could, but she didn't allow them. It would have been futile, and Kai didn't care about her dress.
>
> If anything, he was probably trying to discern how much of her was metal and silicon. [Cinder believes incorrectly that Kai is now aware of her cyborg status.]
>
> She kept her head high, even as her eyes stung, even as panic filled her [computer-interfaced] vision with warnings and precautions. (338)

---

[5] The cover of *Cinder* features an inaccurate representation of both Cinder's leg—it is hollow and metal, not flesh with metal bones as pictured—and her footwear, which appears on the cover as a red stiletto. This makes both the shoe and foot appear more traditionally feminine and is presumably designed to attract more purchasers in that way.

The apparent lesson about performing femininity in this scene is that a good postmodern feminist girl may be awkward when dressed elegantly, but still needs the comfort of social standards of feminine appearance; meanwhile, the good postmodern feminist boy will not care about traditional standards of dress and grace but love her for who she is. Three pages later, they are dancing, Cinder's heart is 'hammering', and 'before she could apologise [for the stained gloves], she felt herself being gently pushed away and spun beneath his arm. She gasped, for a moment feeling light as a butterfly, before she stumbled on her undersized cyborg foot and fell back into his embrace' (341-42). Under Kai's lead 'her body seemed to be memorising the pattern of the dance steps, making each movement slightly more fluid than the last, until she almost felt as if she knew what she were doing. Of course, the tender pressure of Kai's hand on her waist didn't hurt' (342). Not every chapter of *Cinder* contains a scene that so clearly signals the genre of romance novel, but this one does, the one in which the worldly man makes the awkward girl feel more womanly, and it gains extra power from its placement in the key ballroom scene. Meyer creates a standard heteronormative scene of attraction, one in which a woman relies on a man, reassuring her readers that dancing in a ballgown with a handsome boy is a source of excitement and social value.

In spite of this scene and others that are similar, Jennifer Mitchell defines Cinder as queer by using an expanded definition of 'queerness' that includes 'fragmented, composite selves as well as cross-species selfhoods and sexualized desire' (54). While Mitchell acknowledges that Cinder is feminised and Kai masculinised, she feels that their true characters are 'masked by superficial heteronormative traits' (53). Mitchell argues that because Cinder is less curvy than her stepsisters, because her family defines her as nonhuman, and because she tries to pass as non-cyborg, that she cannot signify monolithically and is therefore queer (54-55). However, Meyer makes it clear to us that Cinder is fertile, that Cinder's family and society are incorrect to Other her, and that Cinder has a valid claim on Kai because the perceived class gap between them does not actually exist. What seems to be a fragmented self is in fact fully human, in spite of those who would make her less so because of her artificial parts or make her unnatural because of her emerging Lunar mental powers—Lunars, especially those from the royal family, have the ability to change how others perceive them and to force others' bodies to move against their will. By the end of the novel Cinder knows who she is, and her selfhood is no longer fragmented or unstable. She may not signify monolithically in that she is both princess and cyborg, both Lunar by birth and Earthen by culture, but she is monolithically a cisgendered heterosexual heroine. Femininity is not a superficial mask for Cinder, but physically who she is as a reproductive female destined fairy-tale-fashion to be Luna's queen and the Commonwealth's empress.

Cinder's moral goodness (and her fairy godfather)

Meyer presents Cinder's moral goodness differently from traditional Cinderellas, who rely on tears and prayers to better their situations. Cinder's understanding of her situation is connected to her identity as a cyborg and how people perceive her in her hybrid body. In Meyer's novel, Cinder is incapable of producing tears, which subverts the feminine performance of crying in traditional Cinderellas, as her tear ducts were removed during the procedure that made her a cyborg. Cinder herself feels sometimes relieved at not lapsing into tears, so that she will not appear weak. For example, when her stepmother sells her as a test subject for research into the deadly disease that killed Peony, and Cinder has just been metaphorically raped by a med-droid—'someone was in her head. Inside her. An invasion. A violation. She tried to jerk away but the android held her firm' (81)—the narrator tells us 'it was one of those rare moments she was glad to have no tear ducts, otherwise she was sure she'd be a snivelling disaster, and she would have hated herself all the more for it' (81). It is interesting to note that this sentence implies that most of the time Cinder wants to be able to cry, though not to be weak. When she suspects she is responsible for Peony's illness, the narrator specifically mentions 'the painful dryness of her eyes' (52) as Cinder cradles Peony in her arms. Later in the novel, Adri insists '"You aren't even *human* anymore'. 'I am human," said Cinder…. 'No, Cinder. Humans cry'" (279, italics in original). Crying, for Adri, is part of the human identity, and she categorises Cinder as nonhuman. Because crying is part of the traditional performance of goodness and femininity, Cinder's inability to cry contrasts with the reactions of Cendrillon and Aschenputtel when they are feeling helpless and overwhelmed. Cinder has her own ways to react to being overwhelmed, but they do not involve Cinderella's tears.

Although Cinder is the protagonist of her novel and she is oppressed by her family in similar ways to traditional Cinderellas, she is not 'd'une bonté sans exemple' (peerlessly good). Her actions are a mixture of kindness to others, for example taking Peony with her to the junk yard, and self centeredness, for example sneaking away from the letumosis outbreak in the market in Chapter 1 rather than being quarantined by the medical authorities, which she only feels badly about when she thinks that may be how Peony contracts the disease. After Peony's death, Cinder prepares to flee New Beijing in her rebuilt ground car and rescue her droid friend Iko from her stepmother's wrath, but then is willing to give up their chance at escape in order to try to warn Kai about Levana's plans, which is an act of noble self-sacrifice. This leads to the climactic scene of the novel, which Meyer orchestrates to include justifiable attempted murder on Cinder's part.

During the ball, Levana reveals to Kai and the assembled crowd that Cinder is a Lunar escaped illegally from Luna and orders her arrest. Levana's taunting leads to Cinder's mechanical systems overheating and 'her jaw aching with hatred. She was glad that no tears would betray her humiliation' (355). When Cinder publicly declares that Levana is not beautiful, but using mental powers to appear so, Levana takes mental control of Cinder's body, has her grab a guard's gun, and tries to force Cinder to commit suicide. This attempt, however, triggers Cinder's latent Lunar mental powers into full force, and she is able to break Levana's control and fire instead at the ceiling. At this moment Levana looks 'almost afraid', and Cinder 'point[s] the gun at the queen. She pull[s] the trigger' (364). Cinder's life is no longer in danger from Levana's control of her body, though of course Levana is still her enemy. Cinder's attempt to kill Levana is thwarted by a guard interposing his body, and Cinder only then flees from the ballroom. Meyer could have had Cinder drop the gun and run, rather than attempt to murder the queen. Readers may applaud or at least acknowledge the justice of replying to attempted murder by trying to murder the would-be killer, but Cinder is not a guard, a police officer, or in any other way legally justified in shooting at Levana. Cinder has been raised on Earth with what the novel's readers will recognise as ethical standards of honesty, integrity, and not harming others except in self defence, but, being related to villains (Levana is her aunt) and having inherited Lunar mental powers and perhaps the tendency toward the megalomania that those powers encourage in their wielders, Cinder is pulled toward both good and evil. For example, at the end of book one when Cinder thinks about using mind control on others, 'the thought both sickened and frightened her, but the resolve [to control others] made her calm again' (387).

Meyer's narrator calls the Lunar mental abilities 'magic' (e.g. *Cinder* 170, 354), but in these science fiction fairy tales she codes magic as evil, while technology is mostly good but misunderstood/misused. Both the Maraine in Perrault's version of *Cendrillon* and the birds who act on behalf of the dead mother in the Grimms' version of *Aschenputtel* support the heroine's efforts to attend the ball and use their magical powers for good, mostly without hurting others (the birds do peck out the eyes of the stepsisters in the later version of the Grimms' story), and the Cinderella character never says to herself 'perhaps these are devilish powers and I should resist them'. But in Meyer's novel, magic is clearly something that the evil characters have and use. Good characters who have the 'gift', including Princess Winter (Snow White) and Dr. Erland (Rapunzel's father and Cinder's fairy godmother) refuse to use it but go slowly insane from that refusal. Winter remains purely good until the end of book four, when she attempts to use her gift to save her beloved Jacin and becomes deranged because of it, but Dr. Erland is always willing to compromise his morality for a good cause: getting Cinder on the Lunar throne. During the series, Cinder will also follow the path of compromise: as she develops her mind control abilities, Cinder will control her friends' minds and bodies with their consent and take over those of enemies without their consent. In book two, when she controls three innocent dock workers without their consent, she does it 'hating this gift that was too unnatural, too powerful, too unfair. But the thought to release her control over them never crossed her mind' (*Scarlet* 61). The feeling that using her mental powers gives her reminds her of when Dr. Erland overwhelmed her systems to release her gift, but now it is 'almost comforting—almost pleasant' (61). In book three she uses her gift to torture the evil witch from the Rapunzel story to prevent her from killing Cinder and her friends, leading to the witch's deranged suicide. Readers may justify this as self-defence (similarly to her attack on Levana), but her actions are in excess of self-defence: Sybil gives out 'not just a scream, but a scream made up of pain and delirium, torture and agony' (*Cress* 487). It is difficult to imagine Cendrillon, who cares for her nasty sisters, or Aschenputtel, who is pious and good, taking such actions. Traditional Cinderellas are happy to benefit from magic, but do not actively use it themselves. Cinder's use of magic will corrupt her, but she needs to use it in order to win against Queen Levana. In this way, Cinder's story promotes an 'ends justify the means' morality, rather than the strict 'turn the other cheek' morality of Perrault and the Grimms.

This push against traditional morality, showing that sometimes it is necessary for good people to perform unethical acts, is something that Meyer already makes clear in book one of the series, in the climax and also in the denouement. At the very end of the novel, Cinder is in jail awaiting trial and return to Luna (effectively a death sentence), with her prosthetic hand damaged and missing the small foot she lost fleeing the ball. Dr. Erland is a refugee Lunar working undercover in the New Beijing imperial palace trying to find a cure for letumosis, which Luna's scientists developed as a biological weapon to attack Earth. Erland visits Cinder in her cell to inform her that she is Princess Selene and tell her to break out of jail and join him in Africa and also reveals that he invented the cyborg draft to find Selene. Like Cendrillon's godmother, he knows what Cinder needs to succeed without her asking him, and he provides the support she needs, including a new adult-sized foot instead of small slippers.

Dr. Dmitri Erland is an interesting character in the *Lunar Chronicles* and a complement to Cinder when it comes to moral behaviour. Readers first encounter him in *Cinder* when Adri sells Cinder to the government as a test subject supposedly 'volunteering' for the cyborg draft (chapter 7). The narrator describes him as short, aging, balding, and sexist: he cannot remember female assistants' names, seems to be targeting teenaged girls as test subjects, and puts male cyborgs in a placebo group. Meyer sets up her female teen readers to dislike him intensely, and the fact that his med-droid then virtually rapes Cinder by inserting metal probes into her control panel makes Erland appear to be a villain. Gradually, though, Meyer makes readers reconsider their prejudgment of Dr. Erland's morality. He discovers that Cinder is Lunar, creates an antidote for letumosis from her blood, and allows her to use part of it to try to save Peony (Cinder is too late, and instead she uses the antidote to cure the child who sickened in the market). He tries to prevent Cinder going to the ball, because he knows Levana will recognise her; promotes Cinder's blossoming relationship with Prince Kai; and, when he visits her in jail, he brings her a splendid new hand with inset tools and weaponry and the new foot, both of which he has commissioned and paid for and both of which will give Cinder strength and self-sufficiency. All of these help to redeem him in the readers' eyes. On the other hand, he delays telling Cinder he suspects her to be Selene; he uses his mind control powers on her and overwhelms her computer system, which allows her to access her Lunar gift; and, in order to get into the jail to see her, he uses mind control on the guard. In some ways he is an inversion of the Maraine character in *Cendrillon*, particularly in being of male sex and gender and in forbidding Cinder to go to the ball. It is not until the denouement of the novel that Meyer makes him more clearly into the fairy godfather. Dr. Erland says to her, 'funny, isn't it? So much advancement, so much technology. But even the most complicated security systems aren't designed with Lunar cyborgs in mind. […] you *must* escape' (378, italics in original). His emphasis on Lunar cyborgs points to the fact that Cinder in her own body combines technology and magic, and that she will need both to escape her prison cell. Dr. Erland is the *deus ex machina* who basically waves his wand, supplying her with socially bad but useful extra parts from an Earthen point of view and helping her regain her dangerous but useful missing Lunar parts. Although he does not actually rescue her, he provides the spunky girl with the means to rescue herself. His assistance involves both technology and magic, both good moral actions and questionable ones—readers may be uncertain whether he should be using his evil mind control powers to help the heroine. He tells Cinder to meet him in Africa and disappears, but should she trust this benefactor who evidently has mental health issues and who has just revealed to her that he invented the cyborg draft in order to find her, putting hundreds of deaths on her conscience?

Dr. Erland represents two kinds of power, technology as a doctor and magic as a Lunar, 'a witch doctor as much as an acclaimed royal scientist' (*Cinder* 162), enhancing Cinder's technological and magical abilities. In book four of the *Lunar Chronicles*, Dr. Erland's daughter Cress thinks of him, '[s]o many things he'd done—some good, some terrible. And all, Cinder had told her, because he was determined to end Levana's rule. To avenge his daughter. To avenge *her*' (*Winter* 54-55, italics in original). Dr. Erland may be Cinder's fairy godmother analogue, but he is ambiguously good by traditional standards and his magic is double-edged. Warner reminds us that 'Cinderella's goodness changes character; even her colouring reflects canons of virtue and standards in beauty according to circumstances' (204). Presuming that Meyer's portrayal of Cinder's and Dr. Erland's goodness reflects current Western moral ideologies, I conclude that modern Western societies are willing to use dangerous tools to achieve their goals—which can include vengeance—and feel themselves justified in doing so.

In contrast, Princess Winter, the other good Lunar character with the gift of magic, is both a traditional passive princess character, and clearly and consistently good. She refuses to use her gift on moral grounds, because an early attempt to use her gift to help a servant led to the woman's suicide. However, her choice to refuse the gift gives her hallucinations that immobilise her, make her weak, and make her need constant rescue. She is an attractive and positive character; but, in showing that such a firm moral choice to do no harm to others leads to crippling mental instability, Meyer says to her readers that they need to move away from traditional ideas of goodness and moral behaviour and toward the compromised position of Cinder and Dr. Erland if they are to succeed in life, to keep their lives on a solid footing.

Cinder's moments of being overwhelmed

Just as Cendrillon and Aschenputtel have moments when they are overwhelmed by emotion, so, too, does Cinder. However, where Cendrillon's and Aschenputtel's times of weakness, despair, and tears lead to magical assistance and clothing, Meyer treats Cinder's moments of paralysing weakness in rather different ways. Instead of one main scene of overwhelming emotion that instigates help from the godmother or dead mother, Cinder has multiple scenes of overwhelming emotion that render her computer systems immobile and make her lose consciousness. In these cases, she is in need of assistance, usually from male characters not mother figures. In book one, this happens first when she is in Dr. Erland's lab in chapters 13-14, but also in the elevator with Kai (chapter 24) and at the ball (chapter 36). In book two, her system is overwhelmed by plugging into Thorne's stolen spaceship (Carswell Thorne is the prince character from the 'Rapunzel' story), and she only survives because he finds her control panel in the back of her head and attaches her to an external power source (*Scarlet*, chapter 10). Cinder's mental torture of Sybil Mira in book three occurs as a result of being under attack from her friend Wolf (from the 'Red Riding Hood' story) while he is under Sybil's control, and afterward she appears 'corpse-like' (*Cress* 487). Thorne knows to push her reset button and, although she needs his help to revive, Cinder is angry that he has done so and says 'Don't. Open. My control panel', to which Thorne replies 'Then stop going comatose on me!' (488).

Even though she cannot cry, and even though she finds her moments of being overwhelmed embarrassing and debilitating, it is nevertheless exactly these key scenes that demonstrate Cinder developing the strength of character and of magic she can use to defeat the evil queen, which she does at the end of book four in another murder in self defence scene. When Cinder is overwhelmed, it is not usually from internal emotional responses to an outward situation, although this is the case in the elevator scene, but most often internal biotechnical responses to a physical or mental violation (for example, the med-droid's prongs, the spaceship's system, Levana's and Sybil's attacks). This tells *Cinder*'s readers of the importance of being a survivor not a victim, doing whatever it takes to protect yourself and save those you love when you are violated; however, there is also an implication that the times of weakness are key in triggering Cinder's success by releasing and/or enhancing her mental powers and spurring her to action. For example, it is not until Cinder feels overwhelmed at the ball that she feels powerful enough to break Levana's mental control and point the gun at her enemy's head. Disturbingly, this appears to suggest that it is necessary she be violated. It is also disturbing that she usually needs to be rebooted by men, and, if we consider that the Lunar ability to control others' perceptions and actions is also a violation, as a result, Cinder becomes willing to mentally rape others.

By the end of the series, Cinder still has a foot in both camps when it comes to being both a traditional and a revisionist Cinderella: she emerges from her times of weakness as the strong spunky heroine, but the times of weakness allow her to perform as a traditional female needing rescue by a man. This presents a dichotomy in that Meyer appears to be telling her female identifying teen readers that our society still deems weakness and vulnerability to be valuable, while, at the same time, promoting female agency and action. Meyer tells her readers they are dominated by emotion and need to be overwhelmed, but also that they should let neither their weakness nor their integrity prevent them from taking action in the defence of themselves or those they love.

Conclusions

While Meyer has not, in Bacchilega's terms, 'trouble[d] sex/gender/sexuality normative categories', she has to a certain extent 'relocate[d] the [fairy tale] genre geopolitically, socially, and generically' (71). In relocating the Cinderella story to a Pan-Asian science fiction setting, Meyer presents us with a possible future that maintains a lot of Western cultures' pasts. We still have a class-based society, binary and heteronormative gender ideology, and an oppressed young woman who falls and transforms in order to rise and marry. Two of the key changes Meyer makes are the denotation of magic as evil and the lesson that good people need to use evil means to succeed. She also explores the ways in which we incorporate technology into our lives, particularly through Cinder's cyborg and hybrid identity. Technology is another double-edged sword in Meyer's series: with it we have an oppressed subclass of androids and cyborgs, but without it we would not have Cinder's best friend Iko or Kai's right-hand droid Nainsi; with technology Cinder survives the fire that Levana intended her to die in as a small child, but technology also creates letumosis. Victoria Flanagan, in *Technology and Identity in Young Adult Fiction* (2014) argues that Meyer, in making her protagonist a cyborg, is writing a posthumanist novel. However, the novel *Cinder* does not have the narrative experimentation Flanagan identifies as significant to her definition, and neither does it seem to me that Meyer 'rejects the idea that consciousness is at the heart of human subjectivity' (57). Rather, consciousness is key to subjectivity in *The Lunar Chronicles*, and only those androids who have consciousness are humanised. I cannot see Cinder as posthuman in the way Flanagan defines it; neither would I say that Meyer is either a trans-humanist with a utopian view of improving the human race physically and mentally via technology, or a dystopian

Luddite. What I believe she is saying by means of the morality of her series is that both the old powers in fairy tales, magic, and the new powers in science fiction, technology, are implicated in moral dangers and possible corruption—we use them at our peril, but we are right to use them to protect ourselves and our loved ones.

Meyer does widen the scope of gender expectations in the *Lunar Chronicles*: the series ends up with two spunky girl protagonists, Cinder and Scarlet, and two from the passive princess mould, Cress and Winter. Likewise, their male love interests come in a variety of stereotypes: Kai is the sensitive guy, Wolf the tough guy, Thorne the rogue underdog, and Jacin the knight in shining armour. She also switches her fairy godmother character's sex and gender to male and gives gender to android characters. However, the expansion of gender roles is mainly adding traditional stereotypes back into the spectrum of possibilities, not adding characters with genders and sexual orientations beyond the cisgendered and heterosexual binaries. Even the android characters tend to be gendered female and heterosexual.

Where for Perrault a successful performance of feminine goodness requires social graces, social support, sexual purity, and tears, for Meyer's Cinder performing feminine goodness means lacking social graces but longing for them, having peer-group support and male assistance, having fertility, and being overwhelmed/violated as a catalyst for agency and action. For this postmodern Cinderella, performing feminine goodness requires both taking action as the feminist spunky girl and being weak and overwhelmed. She requires both the moments of weakness and the agency to take action for herself; she requires both the desire to help those people she loves and the willingness to hurt people she does not love.

Cinder may lose her foot at the ball, but that losing of her footing on the palace steps is the catalyst for her eventual success. This Cinderella has moved from a glass slipper to a metal foot, from female fragility to feminist strength. The cyborg foot, though, denotes unstable footing as well as strength, and Meyer's portrayal of femininity and morality is worrying. Meyer's readers, presumably mainly female identifying teenagers, will look to the novels for models of ways to perform femininity. We need to be careful not to lock young readers into the small footwear of a binary system, whether they fit into the binaries or not, and it should be possible to expand the range of behaviour of good characters without justifying vengeance. Cinder may be a Cinderella who reflects today's American gender and ethical ideologies, but I personally would prefer the Cinderella for tomorrow to have a wider range of options. She/he/they should not have to cling to outdated ways of performing femininity, should not have to cry, collapse, or need rescue. Nor should the Cinderella of tomorrow be forced either to the extremes of purity and self-sacrifice on the one hand or to the willingness to torture, rape, and murder for the sake of righteous vengeance on the other.

Works cited

Bacchilega, Cristina. *Fairy Tales Transformed? Twenty-First Century Adaptations and the Politics of Wonder*. Wayne State University Press, 2013. Project Muse Ebooks Literature.

Bottigheimer, Ruth. 'Cinderella: The People's Princess.' *Cinderella Across Cultures: New Directions and Interdisciplinary Perspectives*, edited by Martine Hennard Dutheil de la Rochère, Gillian Lathey, and Monika Woźniak, Wayne State University Press, 2016, pp. 27-51.

Flanagan, Victoria. *Technology and Identity in Young Adult Fiction: The Posthuman Subject*. Palgrave Macmillan, 2014. Springer Ebook.

'Footing, n.' *Oxford English Dictionary*. Oxford English Dictionary Online, 2018.

Grimm, Jacob, and Wilhelm Grimm. *'Aschenputtel.' Kinder und Haus-Märchen gesammelt durch die Brüder Grimm*, 7th edition, volume 1 of 2, Verlag der Dieterichschen Buchhandlung, 1857.

Haraway, Donna J. 'A Cyborg Manifesto: Science, Technology, and Socialist Feminism in the Late Twentieth Century.' *Simians, Cyborgs, and Women: The Reinvention of Nature*, Free Association Books, 1991, pp. 149-82.

Hoffmann, Kathryn A. 'Perrault's 'Cendrillon' among the Glass Tales: Crystal Fantasies and Glassworks in Seventeenth-Century France and Italy.' *Cinderella Across Cultures: New Directions and Interdisciplinary Perspectives*, edited by Martine Hennard Dutheil de la Rochère, Gillian Lathey, and Monika Woźniak, Wayne State University Press, 2016, pp. 52-80.

Meyer, Marissa. *Cinder*. Square Fish, Feiwel & Friends, 2012.

—. *Cress*. Feiwel & Friends, 2014.

—. *Scarlet*. Square Fish, Feiwel & Friends, 2013.

—. *Winter*. Feiwel & Friends, 2015.

Mitchell, Jennifer. ''A Girl. A Machine. A Freak.': A Consideration of Contemporary Queer Composites.' *Bookbird: A Journal of International Children's Literature*, vol. 52, no. 1, January 2014, pp. 51-62. Project Muse.

Perrault, Charles. 'Cendrillon, ou la Petite Pantoufle de Verre.' *Contes* (1698), edited by Catherine Magnien. Livre de Poche, 1990, pp. 245-53.

Warner, Marina. *From the Beast to the Blonde: On Fairy Tales and their Tellers*. Chatto & Windus, 1994.

CHAPTER FIVE

MYTHIC TRANSFORMATIONS ON SCREEN: CINDERELLA MEETS GALATEA

ELEANOR ANDREWS

The tale of *Cinderella* is part of the plentiful and hugely popular 'rags to riches' theme which Christopher Booker describes as one of the seven basic plots in literature (5) where someone lowly is transformed into something splendid. Although the myth of *Pygmalion* follows a different trajectory, the transformation from a simple object into a beautiful living person is the essential part of the plot. The many re-interpretations of the ways in which these narratives are interwoven has been a fruitful area of study and one that has been explored to a considerable extent in recent years (Berst, Block, James, Joshua, McDonald, Singer and Wartenberg). The film world has developed these stories into many narratives, frequently combining the primary myth with the fairy tale. Some of these include: *Sabrina* (Wilder 1954; Pollack 1995), *A Star is Born* (Wellman and Conway 1937; Cukor 1954; Pierson 1976 Cooper 2018) and *She's All That* (Iscove 1999), where a female is elevated from someone modest, simple and possibly plain into someone confident, impressive and beautiful, usually through the agency of a male.

Cinderella

At the heart of the fairy tale of Cinderella, a young woman of humble status is magically transformed into a more desirable person of higher social class, is accepted into this class and the story ends in marriage. The tale of Cinderella dates back to a ninth century Chinese story, in which a lowly girl marries a prince, after being identified because she is able to fit into particularly small and delicate shoes, small feet being part of the Chinese traditional notions of beauty (Jameson 71–97). The story has five hundred variants in Europe alone, including the gory account (*Aschenputtel*) first published by Jacob and Wilhelm Grimm in 1812 and Charles Perrault's better-known version published in 1697, which includes the Fairy Godmother, the coach made from a pumpkin and the controversial glass slipper,[1] as well as alternatives from Asia and Latin America (see Dundes *passim*; Bettelheim 236–277; Booker 53). The Cinderella story has been an influence on literary works including William Shakespeare's *King Lear* (Dundes 229–244) and Charlotte Brontë's *Jane Eyre* (Davies xi-xxxiv). The film world has retold this tale numerous times, from the earliest version *Cendrillon* (Méliès 1899), through the Disney cartoon of 1950 (Geronimi, Jackson and Luske) to the contemporary perspective seen in *Cinderella* (Branagh 2015). There have also been a couple of versions where the maligned character is male: *Mr Cinders*, a musical (1929) and film (Zelnik 1934) and *Cinderfella* (Tashlin 1960), a comedy vehicle for Jerry Lewis.

Pygmalion

Several versions of the Pygmalion myth were written in Cyprus before Ovid's more well-known account, completed in 8 AD. In Ovid's poem, *Pygmalion* (Book X: Fable VII), the eponymous character is a lonely sculptor who rejects the women of his island because of their low morals, and carves a beautiful, ideal woman from ivory.[2] He falls in love with the statue which is brought to life when Pygmalion prays to Venus. In later literature, from the eighteenth century, the woman comes to be known as Galatea.[3] The now living statue becomes his wife and bears a child, Paphos. The structure of the myth reveals the metamorphosis of a man's created work into a longed-for human form through supernatural agency, and ends in the social convention of marriage. Essaka Joshua's study of the Pygmalion myth notes in detail the variations of the story which appears in numerous formats. The tale has been retold, reinvented or subverted in many ways over the last two thousand years with forms of the

---

[1] There has long been discussion of whether there was a mistranslation in the English version of Perrault's story so that the slippers worn by Cinderella to the Prince's ball were in fact made of fur ('vair' in Old French) and not glass ('verre'). (Sedden-Ralston 38) Other scholars have shown that 'pantoufles de verre' were in the original version, so that it is not an error of translation.

[2] In some versions of the story the statue is made from beeswax.

[3] For further discussion on the naming of Pygmalion's statue see Helen H. Law's essay 'The name Galatea in the Pygmalion myth', and Meyer Reinhold's essay 'The Naming of Pygmalion's Animated Statue'.

story appearing in literature, painting, sculpture and music, including a large number of nineteenth century retellings of the tale where it is a person and not a statue who is altered.[4] Examples of this widespread use of the myth include the plays *The Winter's Tale* (Shakespeare 1623), *Grimaldi, or, The Life of an Actress* (Dion Boucicault 1855) and *Pygmalion* (Shaw 1913), the novel *Trilby* (George Du Maurier 1894), the children's story *Pinocchio* (Carlo Collodi 1883), the ballet *Coppélia* (1870), with music by Léo Delibes, and the films *Vertigo* (Hitchcock 1958), *Weird Science* (Hughes 1985), *Mannequin* (Gottlieb 1987), *Lars and the Real Girl* (Gillespie 2007) and *Ruby Sparks* (Dayton and Faris 2012).

Scope

This chapter investigates the connections and variability between a selection of films in which a transformation occurs, and relates this to the myth and the fairy tale: *Pygmalion* (Asquith and Howard 1938), *My Fair Lady* (Cukor 1964), *Educating Rita* (Gilbert 1983), *Pretty Woman* (Marshall 1990) and *Nikita* (Besson 1990). George Bernard Shaw's play, *Pygmalion,* both delighted and scandalised its first audiences when it was produced in 1913. A brilliantly witty reworking of the classical tale of the sculptor Pygmalion, it is also a barbed attack on the British class system and a statement of Shaw's feminist views. As Joshua maintains, Shaw used elements of the 'rags to riches' story which is a feature of both *Cinderella* and Shaw's *Pygmalion* (97). In the subsequent films, *Pygmalion* and *My Fair Lady,* which closely follow the play's structure, flower seller Eliza Doolittle (Wendy Hiller 1938; Audrey Hepburn 1964) is educated in elocution and social niceties by the linguistic expert, Professor Henry Higgins (Leslie Howard 1938; Rex Harrison 1964), so that she can briefly appear to pass into the aristocracy as a duchess and then more permanently join the English middle classes.

Educating Rita was originally a stage play by former teacher Willy Russell and was first performed in 1981. Both play and film have a theme about instruction, where Rita (Julie Walters), a working-class hairdresser, takes an Open University Course under the tutorship of Dr. Frank Bryant (Michael Caine), an alcoholic with matrimonial problems. Through the instruction she receives she widens her horizons and changes her marital status and aspirations. Vivian (Julia Roberts), in *Pretty Woman* is

---

[4] Joshua (2001) notes that as well as the twenty mentions of the myth in Latin and Greek literature, including Ovid, there were over 150 re-narrations in European fiction, of which 100 were in English literature from 1390 to 1999.

transformed from prostitute to society hostess by her wealthy employer, Edward Lewis (Richard Gere). Initially, he employs her as an escort for important social occasions, but as the narrative progresses the couple become romantically involved with each other. At the start of *Nikita*, the eponymous heroine (Anne Parillaud) is a dishevelled, destitute murderer and drug addict. She is forced by the French government to be transformed over a period of three years into a secret assassin.

This chapter foregrounds the common threads in the two narratives of *Cinderella* and *Pygmalion* as well as the variances between them, identifying in particular notions of change and transformation, together with certain recurring motifs, and the historical and social perspectives of these re-interpretations of the source narratives. Several points of comparison in the source narratives can be identified from the outset:

1. the physical transformation of the female protagonist;
2. the alteration of her status and name;
3. the magical/divine intervention in the metamorphosis, with the creator not being the transformer;
4. the lack of the female character's mother;
5. the conclusion of the tale in marriage.

These points will then be compared to the films under investigation to examine where there are any similarities or connections.

The physical transformation of the female protagonist

At the centre of both basic narratives there is the transformation from one state into another, generally an enhanced one. In Timothy Vesonder's opinion, '[t]he core of the Pygmalion myth and the Cinderella folk tale is the transformation, not the marriage' (44). The transformation is something which, in the case of *Cinderella*, is often the most longed-for scene in any pantomime production of the tale. A positive transformation, whether of people or places, is always well-received: witness the popularity of makeover programs on television, which play to notions of discontent with the self which are frequent nowadays (O'Dea 41–47). Tamar Jeffers McDonald argues:

> Transformation television may be very prevalent right now but, […]. despite the currency of the up-to-the minute fashions draped on the transformed woman, such programmes still reach back to much earlier folklore and fairytales to evoke the magic of the exterior revolution. (26)

A positive transformation introduces the idea of novelty and anticipated success. These are almost always exciting, with a before and an after, and the hope that things in the future will be brighter, better, more attractive and enriched because of a significant, positive change. Indeed, few people would expect failure to occur after such a transformation. On the other hand, human beings reduced to plants, animals and insects—as in some myths and fairy tales—are perhaps less exhilarating. In these cases, the character's trajectory is seen in a downward social path, with less power, control and (probably) no voice.

Transformation through costume

In both the literary and filmic texts examined here, clothes are used as symbolic markers, first of the subject's original lowly standing: the statue is naked; Cinderella and Eliza are clothed in rags and Rita, Vivian and Nikita are all dressed in clothes as appropriate indicators of their social situation at the start of each narrative. As part of the metamorphosis to human female, princess or acceptable middle-class lady there is a change of outward appearance. Thus, ivory becomes human tissue and the already human women are attired in beautiful, more expensive garments. McDonald notes that Eliza's transformation through costume is 'incremental' (57) as her original ragged costume is burned by Higgins' maids, to be replaced by clothes which are 'all neat, clean and becoming' (56). As she moves into society these everyday outfits are exchanged for the glamorous ensemble she is dressed in for the Ascot races and the striking gown which she wears to the Embassy ball; in the musical version, *My Fair Lady*, these are both created by the noted designer Cecil Beaton. Stella Bruzzi argues that the fairy tale dream of *Pretty Woman* 'is expressed through clothes' (14). She adds that the appropriation of the new wardrobe that Vivian purchases on Rodeo Drive in Beverly Hills, using Edward's credit card, shows that a 'woman is at her most alluring when wearing clothes that do not belong to or are new to her' (14). Bruzzi continues:

> The slippage between personality and clothes ensures that, on their own count, the clothes are not particularly 'special', but rather function as a symbolic visual shorthand for desirable femininity, volume (the number of options, changes, bags and boxes) being of far greater significance than style. (15)

More importantly, Vivian succeeds not only in wearing the new clothes, but in truly taking on the persona of the sophisticated woman that Edward wants and needs.

Nikita begins her journey of transformation as wild haired, unkempt drug addict who has been sentenced to life in prison for her role in an armed robbery where a policeman is killed. Her captors fake her death, and she is given the choice of becoming an assassin, or being killed. In the key transformation scene, Nikita learns from the experienced Amande (Jeanne Moreau) how to make herself physically attractive. The image of the two of them is captured in a mirror[5] as Amande shows the younger woman how to apply lipstick, while commending 'pleasure as a woman' and the 'two things which have no limit: femininity and the means of taking advantage of it' (subtitles in English). Through the magic of a lap-dissolve, the audience witnesses, again in the mirror's reflection, the metamorphosis of Nikita from a 'malnourished, badly dressed, unattractive, and angry woman to a poised, chic, graceful and gracious one' (McDonald 10).

There is a scene early in *Educating Rita* where the protagonist has been invited to a social occasion at her tutor's house. Uncertain of herself at the start of her education, and unsure how to behave amongst the educated middle-class academics, she tries on several different outfits, each one a trial at a different persona. In the end, she fails to attend the party: she is not yet ready for her new world. Like Eliza, her physical transformation is gradual, and she experiments with several different styles until she has the confidence to be herself. By the end of the film her bleached-blonde hair is its natural colour, and her mini-skirts and tight blouses have been replaced by casual student-like wear. Her tutor, Frank, is however not impressed with the changes he has, to some extent, wrought in his pupil. When faced with the self-assured Rita, who analyses his poetry and repeats the intellectual jargon he has taught her, he is horrified that her freshness and wit seem to have disappeared. He likens himself to Mary Shelley, author of *Frankenstein,* suggesting that Rita is a monster of his creation.

The essential part of a transformation is referred to in television circles as 'the reveal'—the moment when the metamorphised subject is presented to the outside world. The displaying of the newly transformed Eliza at the Ambassador's reception is a direct parallel of the revealing of the finely dressed Cinderella at the Prince's ball. Paula James comments on Shaw's combining of the two narratives in the ball scene in *Pygmalion* and *My Fair Lady*, in what she calls the 'Cinderella filter'. This physical representation

---

[5] As Riccardo Basso (2016) maintains, 'Mirrors are reflections and duplications of reality, which can be said of cinema itself; the introduction of this "meta" element between reality, cinema and reflection is often the very reason why filmmakers choose to use mirrors as part of their works' (2).

of the scene, which does not occur in the original play, is a 'spectacular visual feast' in both films (70). Nikita dresses elegantly for her first official assassination which starts off as a birthday celebration in a beautiful restaurant, 'Le Train Bleu' in Paris. Vivian is publicly displayed when she goes to the opera to watch Verdi's *La Traviata*,[6] a work which parallels, to some extent, Vivian's own life, wearing a stunning red evening gown and jewels. Only in *Educating Rita* is there no such scene of spectacle; Rita does change physically, but it is more a case of trying to find her natural self and being comfortable in her surroundings rather than a search for dazzling beauty.

Change of status and name

As well as the development and education of the various characters there is a subsequent rise through the social ranks. This follows the *Cinderella* and *Pygmalion* pattern, where the maligned skivvy marries a prince and becomes a princess, and the inanimate statue comes to life and marries the sculptor. Eliza becomes a member of the bourgeoisie and (probably) marries Freddy Eynsford Hill (David Tree, 1938; Jeremy Brett, 1964). Vivian relinquishes her former profession as a prostitute and (probably) marries the wealthy and powerful Edward. The audience never witnesses the wedding scenes in these films, so it has to be speculative, but a happy ending is required. On the other hand, Rita, once educated and into middle-class intellectual life, leaves her marriage behind and seeks to 'sing a better song' (Russell 50) or at least 'a different song' (77)—a reference to her dissatisfaction with her original life which is shared by her mother. Susan Hayward (1998) describes a very different outcome for Nikita. At the beginning of the narrative she is 'the embodiment and the site of inscription of violence: she starts out as a punk-junkie who uses violence to fulfil her needs and subsequently becomes the agent of State violence' (20). However, by the end of the film, instead of a happy ending with either marriage or personal satisfaction, Nikita is 'inexorably forced out of the picture—erased, punished for her earlier transgressive self' (20).

With the alteration of status there is also a significant change of name or way of being addressed. H. Edward Deluzain comments, '[r]egardless of when, why, or how often it happens, though, the giving and receiving of a name is an event of major importance'. He adds, '[t]he sense of personal

---

[6] *La Traviata* (*The Fallen Woman*, Giuseppe Verdi, 1853) tells the story of a courtesan, Violetta, who has rival lovers: Alfredo, a young bourgeois from a provincial family and Baron Douphol, an aristocrat.

identity and uniqueness that a name gives us is at the heart of why names interest us and why they are important to us as individuals and to our society as a whole' (np). While it is true that the original statue has no name at all in Ovid's poem and is only later named Galatea, and Cinderella is the cruel soubriquet for the mistreated and never named heroine (in Perrault's version), on the other hand, Eliza is addressed both more politely and formally during and after her transformation, especially by Professor Higgins' friend, Colonel Pickering (Scott Sunderland, 1938; Wilfrid Hyde-White, 1964). She says, 'the difference between a lady and a flower girl is not the way she behaves, but how she's treated' (Shaw 80). Vivian is also treated with more respect once she has abandoned the skinny tops and miniskirts for a more elegant wardrobe. On her second visit to Rodeo Drive, dressed so smartly that she is unrecognisable as the girl who had tried to shop there before, she is fawned over by the staff who had been so rude to her previously. Rita returns to her original name of Susan. She had chosen the name 'Rita' because the American writer, Rita Mae Brown, was the author of one of her favourite novels, *Rubyfruit Jungle*, where the heroine, like Rita, strives to educate herself. On its publication in 1973, the novel was controversial for its explicit portrayal of lesbianism. This book is a marker of Rita's complex taste even before she is 'educated' and it is noteworthy that Frank, an academic specialist in English literature, has never read this novel. After her metamorphosis, Nikita is given two new names, which reflect the two sides of the constructed persona given to her by Amande and Bob (Tcheky Karyo): Marie for every day, in her 'normal' role as a woman, and Joséphine as a code name for the times she is called upon to be a killer.

Primary creation versus magical/divine transformation

In the myth, Pygmalion is the creator and original transformer, however, the ultimate metamorphosis, from one substance to another, as well as from an inanimate object into a living one, is carried out by the goddess Venus. Arguably, Pygmalion's creation of the statue, as his epitome of the perfect woman, is as important as the final transformation. Nonetheless, the woman, Galatea, who has been fashioned following Pygmalion's overwhelming longing for a faultless female, has no say in her altered state. The Galatea of the original myth, as well as having no name, also has no voice. In the end she is coupled with Pygmalion, at his desire, but it is unknown from the original poem whether she is happy with her lot.[7]

Unlike Galatea, Cinderella is not created by an equivalent of the Pygmalion character, but is an animate person at the start of the narrative. When the transformation occurs in *Cinderella*, at least as far as Perrault's version is concerned, it is the Fairy Godmother who instigates the change, but warns that it is at first only temporary. However, the fantasy of the change in *Cinderella*, as with *Pygmalion,* revolves around a female as object of desire, in this case on the part of the Prince, and by extension the desire emitted by the male reader/spectator.[8] Another difference is that, unlike Galatea, the object of transformation here appears to be a willing participant.

The missing mother

Neither Cinderella nor Galatea has a mother: Cinderella, because her mother has died prior to the beginning of the story; Galatea, because she was not human to begin with. The trope of the absent mother who is supplanted by a wicked stepmother is a common one in fairy tales: in *Snow White* or *Beauty and the Beast*, for example, as well as *Cinderella.* Marina Warner notes that the Grimm brothers 'could not bear a maternal presence to be equivocal, or dangerous' (212). They preferred to replace the bad mothers of the original tales 'in order for the ideal to survive and allow Mother to flourish as symbol of the eternal feminine, the motherland, and the family itself as the highest social desideratum' (212). Bruno Bettelheim suggests a Freudian analysis of the situation, splitting the notion of the Mother into good and evil, arguing:

> The fantasy of the wicked stepmother not only preserves the good mother intact, it also prevents having to feel guilty about one's angry thoughts and wishes about her—a guilt which would seriously interfere with the good relation to Mother. (69)

Although there is a Fairy Godmother figure in the Pygmalion myth in the form of the goddess Venus, and Pygmalion himself fills the role of Prince

---

[7] In her poem 'Pygmalion's Bride', Carol Ann Duffy (51-52) speculates on the negative outcome of the union between Pygmalion and Galatea and gives the heroine a voice.

[8] For further discussion of the male gaze see Laura Mulvey 'Visual Pleasure and Narrative Cinema', pp. 6-18.

Charming,[9] there seems to be no parallel for the wicked stepmother. In all the films under consideration, the object of transformation already exists as a human being, with a life, and sometimes a family and back-story. Eliza, like Cinderella, does not have a mother and her father, Alfred Doolittle (Wilfrid Lawson 1938; Stanley Holloway 1964), has little concern for her well-being, treating the education of his daughter as an opportunity to make some money for himself. Eliza emphasises continually that, despite living a poverty-stricken life, she is respectable and not someone prepared to sell herself ('I'm a good girl, I am' 34). Indeed, she pays Higgins for her lessons. Nevertheless, she is still seen as being a chattel in the control of the patriarchy, as her father, intervening in the negotiations, receives five pounds when he hands over his daughter. The audience learns nothing about Vivian's mother and no character in *Pretty Woman* fills the role of wicked stepmother. The 'wild-child', Nikita, cries out to her mother when she believes she is being given a lethal injection, but otherwise her mother is absent and her past life as 'Marie' is all a fiction. Rita's mother, on the other hand, is prominent in some scenes. Feeling at first alienated from the world of academia, Rita goes back to her roots and visits a pub with her family, and they appear to have a jolly time drinking and singing together. However, Rita notices that her mother is crying and her explanation for this is that they 'could sing better songs', i.e. improve on their current life. This behaviour spurs Rita on to realise that she cannot now return to her old life but must seek out a better song for herself (Russell 50) in continuing with her education.

The role of education

A major difference between the original stories and the films under examination is that there is no divine or magical intervention which brings about the change. The transformer in the films, who could be seen in the role of Fairy Godmother, is generally an educator of some sort, either academic or social. There may also be additional helpers, like Colonel Pickering, Henry's mother, Mrs. Higgins (Marie Lohr 1938; Gladys Cooper 1964) and the housekeeper, Mrs. Pearce (Jean Cadell 1938; Mona Washbourne 1964), in Shaw's *Pygmalion*, the hotel manager, Barney

---

[9] Prince Charming is first mentioned in 1837 and is from the French 'Le Roi Charmant' name of the hero of Comtesse d'Aulnoy's 'L'Oiseau Bleu' ('The Blue Bird') (1697). An English translation was included in *The Green Fairy Book*, 1892, collected by Andrew Lang. In English he was adopted into native fairy tales including *Sleeping Beauty* and *Cinderella*.

Thompson (Hector Elizondo), in *Pretty Woman* or Amande in *Nikita*. This type of hierarchical relationship has in more recent times been named within education circles 'the Pygmalion effect', where a teacher's positive or negative expectations can influence pupil performance proportionally (Rosenthal and Jacobsen). *Educating Rita* is also based on a theme of education where the male tutor's influence over his student causes her life and her prospects to change totally. Vivian in *Pretty Woman* is changed under the guidance of her employer, Edward. Like Higgins, he fashions someone he deems to be of lowly status into someone worthy of being his consort. Nikita also experiences an educational change in certain aspects. She has two mentors for the two sides of her persona that she must develop as a government murderer. The male mentor, Bob trains her as a professional contract killer, while the female trainer, Amande, re-educates her as a *femme fatale*.

In the original Pygmalion myth, the object of alteration has a completely passive role, and in the fairy tale, Cinderella wishes to go to the Prince's Ball, but has no particular requests for transformation. Equally, Nikita is not changed through her own volition and the metamorphosis is only on the outside, as she remains dangerous within, hence the two names and two distinct personas. However, in contrast to this, in Shaw's *Pygmalion* and *Educating Rita*, the object of transformation puts herself forward for the purpose. Both Eliza and Rita desire to change their lives and successfully transform themselves through hard work using their intelligence. Vivian is also willing to change, and enjoys the opulent trappings that surround her in her new position. However, although she is changed externally, perhaps she is not entirely altered inside, as she is prepared to go back to her previous role once the contract with Edward has been fulfilled.

Changes to the male protagonist

Pygmalion and the Prince in the original narratives, although central to the plot, remain unchanged by the end of the story. This is not the case for the male protagonists of the films. Higgins, who is a gifted man in his field, is an egocentric, confirmed bachelor, with few genuine social graces and no empathy whatsoever.[10] In Shaw's hands, Higgins is the Pygmalion figure,

---

[10] Rodelle Weintraub suggests that Higgins has Asperger's disorder in his essay 'Bernard Shaw's Henry Higgins: A Classic Aspergen', p. 389.

but he is not her Prince Charming.[11] Unlike Pygmalion, who treasures his statue, decorating it with flowers and jewels, Higgins has no such respect for Eliza. In fact, possibly only Eliza's admirer, Freddy, comes close to the original Pygmalion in his devotion to Eliza. In the end, she is more an experiment to Higgins and the focus of a wager between him and Pickering, than a person with emotions. However, without him realising it, Eliza has become almost indispensable to him and therefore he has also been changed and has become, if only mildly, more aware of other people's concerns. In the original play Shaw makes it clear that romance will never be possible between the two protagonists. In a parallel to *Cinderella,* it is Freddy who emerges as a version of Prince Charming. However, the unpopular finale to the original version of the play, which runs counter to audience expectations of a romantic happy ending, is subtly changed in the 1938 film version of the play, as well as in *My Fair Lady,* so as to remain ambiguous. In these later works Eliza and Higgins are reunited at the end of the film at his home, and the outcome of their relationship is left open-ended.

Frank in *Educating Rita,* Edward in *Pretty Woman* and Bob in *Nikita,* are also all flawed males with large egos and a certain amount of paranoia. Although Frank and Bob do not end up romantically attached to their Galateas, they certainly have strong feelings for them which leads to a certain amount of jealousy when they see their *protégée* in the arms of another man. Both men are changed by the experience of being with these women. Frank eventually sobers up before his two-year sabbatical in Australia and, at the end of *Nikita* the usually undemonstrative Bob feels nostalgia for Nikita now that she has gone into hiding. Edward is transformed from someone ruthless into a more caring individual as a result of knowing Vivian. In typical Hollywood/fairy tale fashion, he gets the girl and goes off with her in a parody of the knight on a white charger (here, a white limousine) who scales the tower (with the help of a fire escape ladder) to rescue the princess.

Staircase Motif

The staircase in both literature and film is a symbol of the way the lives of the characters can go up and down the social scale.[12] This is a trope in *film*

---

[11] Hisashi Morikawa likens Higgins to Sherlock Holmes, as scientist and detective, and Dr Frankenstein and Dr Jekyll who assume the God's role as Creator (2).

[12] See Eleanor Andrews 'Whither Shall I Wander? Up and Down the Staircase in Film.' *Spaces of the Cinematic Home: Behind the Screen Door.* Editors Eleanor

noir and the gangster genre where the narrative arc of the protagonist rises and falls in success. Although this motif does not appear in the *Pygmalion* myth, this image plays a significant role in *Cinderella* where it is also about change. In the films under discussion, the heroine is mostly seen on her way up the stairs, implying her ascent of the social scale.[13] In the case of *Educating Rita,* the heroine is at first unable to ascend the steps to Frank's house for a social occasion, and she stands watching the dinner party through the transparent barrier of a window. A later sequence, when she is both educationally and socially more confident, sees her run up the steps to his front door. In contrast, at the nadir of his academic career, when alcoholism has led to his exclusion from the university, the audience witnesses Frank descending the staircase, as Rita watches him. In *Pretty Woman,* after a quarrel, Edward and Vivian stand outside a lift, the modern method of ascending and descending. When the liftman enquires whether she wants to move down, she declines, the lift doors shut, and she then stays with Edward. Subsequently, her upward trajectory is further emphasised when Edward takes her on an airplane ride to the opera. Nikita enters the room where her physical transformation will take place, by ascending a spiral staircase, which implies the complex and twisted nature of her metamorphosis.

The concept of attempted social climbing is emphasised by the prominent appearance of a poster for Disney's *Cinderella* (1950) in the *mise-en-scène* early in the Italian film *Roma, Ore 11 / Rome, 11.00* (De Santis 1952). The film is based on an actual event which occurred in Rome on January 15 1951. Two hundred young women queued on a stairway in Via Savoia to apply for a single post as a typist in an accountant's office. In the fictional representation, as the women queue on the stairs, an argument breaks out about the fairness of the interview procedure, and the disturbance triggers off the collapse of the staircase, causing all the women to fall. As a result, many of them are injured and one of them dies. The scenes on the staircase are initially about upward progress as the applicants line up for the interview. Antonio Vitti argues that 'the stairway stands for the dreams and aspirations of the women—an image reinforced by the women's upwards stares towards the office door' (64).

Andrews, Stella Hockenhull and Fran Pheasant-Kelly. Routledge, 2016, pp.137-151.
[13] Scenes with the protagonist fleeing downstairs, such as at the end of Prince's ball in *Cinderella,* often mark the return of the character to her original state.

Historical and social influences

In all these narratives the stories and their retellings are products of the age in which they appeared. For instance, the original Pygmalion story comes from a time when ivory figurines were revered, when the gods were deemed to intervene with the lives of humankind in a very direct and visible way, when statues were honoured with jewels and flowers and when women were in a passive role *vis-à-vis* their men folk. As Pygmalion kisses his newly awoken Galatea she blushes and, 'raising her timorous eyes towards the light of day, she sees at once her lover and the heavens' (Ovid 324, lines 243-297). Equally, the seventeenth century Cinderella is a reserved, bashful girl who submissively does as she is told by her stepmother, stepsisters and Fairy Godmother. By 1913, when Shaw's play was first presented, the status and representation of women had advanced a little and the Suffragette movement was at its height.[14] However, even after her transformation, Higgins can only see matrimony, although not with him, as a way forward for her.

Rita's family in the 1980s is an example of certain un-aspirational working-class families of the period who still see marriage and child-bearing as the obvious choice for most working-class girls. Rita is harassed by her relations for not having produced a child by the age of twenty-six. Her new-found education frees her, not only intellectually, but also socially and, as an incomer to the lower middle classes, she can consider theatre visits, discussion groups and trips abroad. The main thing that she emphasises in her final scene with Frank is that now, through education, she has a multitude of choices, including the possibility of having a baby. As James notes:

> Towards the end of the film they have a confrontation in Frank's study, which has distinct echoes of Higgins and Eliza batting back and forth in Shaw's play. Rita is able to combine her old feisty tone with her new-found eloquence and fight back in the painful exchange she has with Frank. (85)

Vivian, a decade later, lives by her looks and the original set-up with Edward is purely business. As they discover more about each other's background the romance develops, and since this film is written as a

---

[14] The term refers in particular to members of the British Women's Social and Political Union (WSPU), a women-only movement founded in 1903 by Emmeline Pankhurst, which engaged in direct action and civil disobedience.

modern-day fairy tale, in a place which is 'the land of dreams' (Hollywood), she has to end up marrying Edward. Consequently, a great deal of the independence that she experiences at the start of the film, as a prostitute running her life without a pimp, is forsaken for the wealth and glamour (and also affection) that she has with Edward. There is a predominance for romance to prevail above all else, and arguably, even in the latter part of the twentieth century, some women would prefer to be swept off their feet.

Nikita, also a woman of the 1990s, is independent at the start of the film in a rebellious fashion, as a violent, nihilistic teenage drug addict. Once transformed by Bob and Amande she is no longer free, but has a sinister duty to perform. If Luc Besson had kept to the original ending of his film, the female lead would have departed the film in a 'Rambo' style, all guns blazing. However, in the version distributed to cinemas, she just disappears rather than be constantly subservient to the French Secret Service. Hayward considers her to be a 'recycled woman', like the *femme fatale* of a *film noir*, 'weakened by love and who must pay the price for it by disappearing off the face of the earth' (2000, 299).

The objective of this chapter was to compare the story of *Cinderella* with the myth of *Pygmalion* and then examine some elements itemised earlier in this chapter against five films chosen for their metamorphic narrative. After analysis, to the original list can be added: (a) transformation through instruction, usually by a male, who at least initiates the alterations, and who is in a powerful position either due to education or wealth vis-à-vis the female; (b) transformation of the male due to the beneficial influence of the female; (c) display of the transformed woman in a public situation as an object of desire to men and women alike. (See appendix— in this table the different outcomes are linked to both the historical period in which the narratives appeared, and also the audience expectation of what constitutes a happy ending in various circumstances, for instance, fairy tale or a Hollywood romance film.) Eliza, Rita and Nikita's outcomes are arguably the result of their progressive or left-wing authors, Shaw, Russell and Besson. Only two elements apply to all the stories: the physical transformation and the change of status of the female protagonist. Although the metamorphoses in these narratives are led by and are under the control of characters other than the protagonist, the outcomes are largely positive for all. The notion of a positive transformation is what drives some people to make New Year's resolutions, go on diets, have their teeth fixed, learn Chinese, or travel to broaden their minds. This idea of the positive transformation is what makes these narratives popular; it is an enduring feature in film, television and literature alike.

Appendix

Summary of comparisons between stories and films

Feature	Pygmalion	Cinderella	Pygmalion My Fair Lady	Pretty Woman	Educating Rita	Nikita
Creator	Pygmalion	…	…	…	…	…
Transformer	Venus	Fairy Godmother	Higgins	Edward	Frank	Bob Amande
Transformed	Galatea	Cinderella	Eliza	Vivian	Rita	Nikita
Outcome	Marriage	Marriage	Education	Marriage	Education	Socialisation
Rags to Riches	No	Yes	Yes	Yes	No	No
Physical transformation	Yes	Yes	Yes	Yes	Yes	Yes
Status changed	Yes	Yes	Yes	Yes	Yes	Yes
Name changed	N/A	N/A	No	No	Yes	Yes
Magical/divine intervention	Yes	Yes	No	No	No	No
Absent mother	Yes	Yes	Yes	N/A	No	No
Instruction	No	No	Yes	Yes	Yes	Yes
Male transformed	No	No	Yes	Yes	Yes	No
Display	Yes	Yes	Yes	Yes	No	Yes

Works cited

Andrews, Eleanor. 'Whither Shall I Wander? Up and Down the Staircase in Film.' *Spaces of the Cinematic Home: Behind the Screen Door*, edited by Eleanor Andrews, Stella Hockenhull and Fran Pheasant-Kelly. Routledge, 2016, pp.137-151.

Asquith, Anthony and Leslie Howard, directors. *Pygmalion*. Pascal Film Productions, 1938.

Basso, Riccardo. 2016. 'The 20 Best Uses of Mirrors in Cinema History.' *Taste of Cinema*. 13 September. http://www.tasteofcinema.com/2016/the-20-best-uses-of-mirrors-in-cinema-history/ Accessed 9 February 2019.

Berst, Charles A. *Pygmalion: Shaw's Spin on Myth and Cinderella*. Twayne Publishers, 1995.

Besson, Luc, director. *Nikita*. Gaumont, Les Films du Loup, Cecchi Gori Group Tiger Cinematografica, 1990.

Bettelheim, Bruno. *The Uses of Enchantment: The Meanings and Importance of Fairy Tales*. Penguin Books, 1991.

Block, Geoffrey. '*My Fair Lady*: From *Pygmalion* to *Cinderella*.' *Enchanted Evenings: The Broadway Musical from 'Show Boat' to Sondheim*, edited by Geoffrey Block. Oxford University Press, 1997, pp. 225-244.

Booker, Christopher. *The Seven Basic Plots: Why We Tell Stories*. Continuum 2004.

Bottigheimer, Ruth B. *Fairy Tales and Society: Illusion, Allusion, and Paradigm.* University of Pennsylvania Press, 1986.

Boucicault, Dion. *Grimaldi or The Life of an Actress.* [1855] Colin Smythe Ltd, 2010.

Branagh, Kenneth, director. *Cinderella.* Performance by Kate Blanchett, Lily James: Allison Shearmur Productions, Beagle Pug Films, Genre Films, Disney, 2015.

Brontë, Charlotte. *Jane Eyre.* [1847] Penguin Classics, 2006.

Brown, Rita Mae. *Rubyfruit Jungle.* Vintage Classics, 2015.

Bruzzi, Stella. *Undressing Cinema: Clothing and Identity in the Movies.* Routledge, 1997.

Butler, Stephen Henry. 'The Pygmalion Motif and the Crisis of the Creative Process in Modern Fiction.' *Unpublished Doctoral thesis.* University of Brandeis, 1984.

Cash, Thomas. *Encyclopedia of Body Image and Human Appearance.* Academic Press, 2012.

Collodi, Carlo. *The Adventures of Pinocchio.* [1883] Oxford World's Classics, 2009.

Cooper, Bradley, director. *A Star is Born.* Warner Bros. Pictures, Live Nation Productions, Metro-Goldwyn-Mayer, Peters Entertainment, Gerber Pictures, Malpaso Productions, Thunder Road Pictures 2018.

Cukor, George, director. *A Star is Born.* Transcona Enterprises, 1954.

Cukor, George, director. *My Fair Lady.* Performance by Rex Harrison and Audrey Hepburn: Warner Bros., 1964.

Davies, Stevie. 'Introduction and Notes to Charlotte Brontë's Jane Eyre.' Charlotte Brontë. *Jane Eyre.* [1847] edited by Davies, Penguin Classics, 2006, pp. xi-xxxiv.

Dayton, Jonathan and Valerie Faris. *Ruby Sparks.* Fox Searchlight Pictures, Bona Fide Productions, DragonCore Studios, 2012.

Deluzain, H. Edward. 1996. 'Names and Personal Identity.' *Behind the Name.* https://www.behindthename.com/articles/3. Accessed 2 February 2019.

De Santis, Giuseppe. *Roma, Ore 11 / Rome, 11.00.* Titanus, Transcontinental Films, 1952.

Duffy, Carol Ann. *The World's Wife.* Picador, 1999.

Du Maurier, George. *Trilby.* [1894] Oxford World's Classics, 2009.

Dundes, Alan. '"To Love My Father All": A Psychoanalytic Study of the Folktale Source of King Lear.' *Cinderella: A Casebook,* edited by Alan Dundes. University of Wisconsin Press, 1988, pp. 229-244.

—. *Cinderella: A Casebook,* edited by Alan Dundes. University of Wisconsin Press, 1988.

Geronimi, Clyde, Wilfred Jackson and Hamilton Luske, directors. *Cinderella*. Walt Disney, 1950.

Gilbert, Lewis, director. *Educating Rita*. Performance by Michael Caine and Julie Walters: Acorn Pictures, 1983.

Gillespie, Craig, director. *Lars and the Real Girl*. MGM, Sidney Kimmel Entertainment, Lars Productions, 2007.

Gottlieb, Michael, director. *Mannequin*. Gladden Entertainment, 1987.

Gresseth, Gerald K. 'The Pygmalion Tale.' *The Journal of the Pacific Northwest Council of Foreign Languages*. 1981, pp.15-19.

Grimm, Jacob and Wilhelm Grimm. *Household Tales*. Translated by Margaret Hunt. George Bell, 1884.

Hayward, Susan and Ginette Vincendeau, editors. *French Film: Texts and Contexts*. 2nd ed. Routledge, 2000.

Hayward, Susan. 'Recycled Woman and the Postmodern Aesthetic: Luc Besson's "Nikita" (1990).' *French Film: Texts and Contexts*, edited by Susan Hayward and Ginette Vincendeau. 2nd ed. Routledge, 2000, pp. 297-309.

—. *Luc Besson*. Manchester University Press, 1998.

Hitchcock, Alfred. *Vertigo*. Alfred J. Hitchcock Productions, 1958.

Hughes, John. *Weird Science*. Universal Pictures, 1985.

Innes, Christopher, editor. *The Cambridge Companion to Bernard Shaw*. Cambridge University Press, 1998.

Iscove, Robert, director. *She's All That*. Miramax, Tapestry Films, FilmColony, All That Productions, 1999.

James, Paula. *Ovid's Myth of Pygmalion on Screen: In Pursuit of the Perfect Woman*. Bloomsbury Academic, 2013.

Jameson, Raymond De Loy. 'Cinderella in China.' *Cinderella: A Casebook*, edited by Alan Dundes. University of Wisconsin Press, 1988, pp. 71-97.

Joshua, Essaka. *Pygmalion and Galatea: The History of a Narrative in English Literature*. Ashgate Publishing Ltd., 2001.

Law, Helen H. 'The name Galatea in the Pygmalion myth.' *The Classical Journal*, vol. 27, 1932, pp. 337-42.

Marshall, Gail. *Actresses on the Victorian Stage: Feminine Performance and the Galatea Myth*. Cambridge, 1998.

Marshall, Garry, director. *Pretty Woman*. Performance by Richard Gere and Julia Roberts: Touchstone Pictures, Silver Screen Partners IV, 1990.

McDonald, Tamar Jeffers. *Hollywood Catwalk: Exploring Costume and Transformation in American Film*. I.B.Tauris, 2010.

Méliès, Georges, director. *Cendrillon*. Georges Méliès, Star Film, 1899.

Morikawa, Hisashi. 'Myths and Legends in Bernard Shaw's Pygmalion.'
www.geocities.jp/shawsociety/mythslegendsinPygmalion.pdf.
Accessed 28 November 2018.

Mulvey, Laura. 'Visual Pleasure and Narrative Cinema.' *Screen,* vol. 16, no. 3, 1975, pp. 6-18.

O'Dea, Jenny A. 'Body Image and Self-Esteem.' *Encyclopedia of Body Image and Human Appearance,* edited by Thomas Cash. Academic Press, 2012, pp.141-147.

Ovid. *The Metamorphoses.* Translated by Henry T. Riley. Digireads.com, 2017.

Perrault, Charles. [1697] *The Tales of Mother Goose: Bilingual Edition: English-French.* Sleeping Cat Press, 2014.

Peters, Sally. 'Shaw's Life: A Feminist in Spite of Himself.' *The Cambridge Companion to George Bernard Shaw*, edited by Christopher Innes. Cambridge University Press, 1998, pp. 3-24.

Pierson, Frank, director. *A Star is Born.* Barwood Films, First Artists, Winters Hollywood Entertainment Holdings Corporation 1976.

Pollack, Sidney, director. *Sabrina.* Constellation Entertainment, Mirage Enterprises, Mont Blanc Entertainment GmbH, Paramount Pictures, Sandollar Productions, Scott Rudin Productions, Worldwide, 1995.

Propp, Vladimir. *The Morphology of the Folktale,* edited by Louis A. Wagner. Translated by Laurence Scott. 2nd. University of Texas Press, 1998.

Reinhold, Meyer. 'The Naming of Pygmalion's Animated Statue.' *The Classical Journal,* vol. 66, no. 4, 1971, pp. 316-319.

Rosenthal, Robert and Lenore Jacobson. *Pygmalion in the Classroom: Teacher Expectation and Pupils' Intellectual Development.* Rinehart and Winston, 1968.

Russell, Willy. *Educating Rita.* Methuen Drama, 2009.

Shakespeare, William. *The Winter's Tale.* [1623] Wordsworth Classics, 1995.

Shaw, George Bernard. *Pygmalion: A Romance in Five Acts.* Prestwick House Inc., 2005.

Shedden-Ralston, William Ralston. 'Cinderella.' *Cinderella: A Casebook,* edited by Alan Dundes. University of Wisconsin Press, 1988, pp. 30-56.

Shelley, Mary. *Frankenstein.* [1818] Wordsworth Editions, 1992.

Singer, Irving. *Cinematic Mythmaking: Philosophy in Film.* The MIT Press, 2008.

Tashlin, Frank. *Cinderfella.* Jerry Lewis Productions, 1960.

Uther, Hans-Jörg. *The Types of International Folktales: A Classification and Bibliography Based on the System of Antti Aarne and Stith Thompson vols. 1, 2 and 3.* FF communications Suomalainen Tiedeakatemia, Academia Scientiarum Fennica, 2004.

Vesonder, Timothy. 'Eliza's Choice: Transformation Myth and the Ending of *Pygmalion.*' *Fabian Feminist: Bernard Shaw and Woman,* edited by Rodelle Weintraub. Pennsylvania State University, 1977, pp. 39-45.

Vincendeau, Ginette. 'Family plots: The Fathers and Daughters of French Cinema.' *Sight and Sound,* vol.1, no.11, 1992, pp. 14-17.

Vitti, Antonio. *Giuseppe De Santis and Postwar Italian Cinema.* University of Toronto Press, 1996.

Warner, Marina. *From the Beast to the Blonde: On Fairy Tales and their Tellers.* Chatto and Windus, 1994.

Wartenberg, Thomas E. *Unlikely Couples: Movie Romance as Social Criticism.* Westview Press, 1999.

Weintraub, Rodelle. 'Bernard Shaw's Henry Higgins: A Classic Aspergen.' *English Literature in Transition, 1880 – 1920,* vol. 49, no. 4, 2006, pp. 388-397.

Weintraub, Rodelle. *Fabian Feminist: Bernard Shaw and Woman.* Pennsylvania State University, 1977.

Wellman, William A. and Jack Conway, director. *A Star is Born.* Selznick International Pictures, 1937.

Wilder, Billy, director. *Sabrina.* Paramount Pictures, 1954.

Zelnik, Frederic, director. *Mr. Cinders.* British International Pictures, 1934.

Chapter Six

Tailoring Cinderella: Perrault, Grimm and their Beautiful Heritage

Sally King

Introducing *Cinderella* and the focus on fashion and footwear

Cinderella's transformation from rags into a ballgown and slippers is one of the most memorable and significant moments of the fairy tale. Her slippers later enable the Prince to track down and identify her, giving shoes a prominent role within the tale. Yet the form taken by the ballgown and slippers varies considerably across different versions of the tale, with footwear and fashion offering insight into the ideologies, customs and motivations of each writer. Sartorial features serve to self-consciously parade the writer's or translator's affiliations, aligning them with their individual contexts and philosophies while distancing them from others. The focus of the analysis in this chapter will be versions of *Cinderella* by Charles Perrault, and Jacob and Wilhelm Grimm, and the respective first English translations. There is no doubt that these renditions are some of the most influential versions of the tale and constitute landmark moments in its development (see, for example, Blamires, 'The Early Reception' 63, 69, 77; Dutheil de la Rochère et al. 4; Lathey, *The Role of Translators* 82-83, 93; Warner, *Beast to Blonde* 202-203, 294). While these writers are generally recognized, lesser known are the translators who produced the first English translations of Perrault's French and the Grimms' German *Cinderella* tales, namely Robert Samber and Edgar Taylor respectively. Yet these agents equally exerted a major influence on the tale's trajectory, as has been highlighted by various scholars (Blamires 'The Early Reception'; Dutheil de la Rochère, 'Cinderella's Metamorphoses' 255; Lathey, *Role of Translators* 43, 55, 92; Lathey, 'Translator as Agent' 82,

90; Sutton 48-49; Tatar, 2010; Warner *Beast to Blonde* 105; Zipes, *Victorian Fairy Tales* xvii). This chapter will therefore examine fashion and footwear in the tales and consider how changes made to sartorial features across the different versions are indicative of broader motivations, starting with the French tale and its English translation.

Contextualising Charles Perrault and Robert Samber

Perrault worked in an aristocratic setting as an adviser in the court of Louis XIV and he recorded tales that were circulating in oral form and shared as part of the seventeenth-century French practice of literary *salons*. It is likely that Perrault would have read and been influenced by Giambattista Basile's earlier written Neapolitan tales, while honing his renditions to his own cultural attitudes (Bottigheimer 34; Warner, *Beast to Blonde* 322). Perrault adopted a 'false naïve' tone, so that while his tales seem to be aimed at children, with their combination of entertainment and didacticism, they contain sophisticated layers and were ultimately written for adults (Dutheil de la Rochère, *Reading, Translating, Rewriting* 3, 14, 19; Zipes, *Art of Subversion* 14-16, 20-21, 52; Zipes, 'Author Biographies' 838-840). His moralistic tone fluctuates between the serious and the satirical, as he both promotes and mocks courtly practices, while avoiding overt confrontation, a style that endows his tales with a degree of contradiction and ambivalence (Zipes, 'Author Biographies' 838; Zipes, *Happily Ever After* 33).

Perrault's *Cendrillon ou la Petite Pentoufle de Verre* was first published in his collection *Histoires ou Contes du Temps Passé* in 1697 (Perrault, *Histoires* 117-148). The first English version, *Cinderilla: or, the Little Glass Slipper* (Perrault, *Histories* 73-91) in *Histories or Tales of Past Times*, translated by Samber, was published in 1729. While Perrault's tales were not explicitly for children, Samber did translate them specifically for a younger audience, even if children's books were not yet an established and accepted category of literature (Dutheil de la Rochère, *Reading, Translating, Rewriting* 22; Lathey, *Role of Translators* 2, 9, 48, 53-54). It was these distinctions in the ages and cultural tastes of the French and English audiences, alongside other factors, that played an important part in the different depictions of characters' appearance and their attire.

Technical sartorial details and descriptions

In Perrault's *Cendrillon*, references to appearance feature prominently, with the stepsisters' and Cinderella's clothes and hairstyles having a central role in the tale and being presented with flourish and meticulous detail. The stepsisters boast about their outfits for the royal ball, which for the eldest sister is 'mon habit de velours rouge & ma garniture d'Angleterre' (Perrault, *Histoires* 122), which Samber translates as 'my red velvet suit, with French trimming' (Perrault, *Histories* 76). Perrault's choice of 'red velvet' has regal connotations with the red colour being particularly significant; when Perrault was still a *courtier* some twenty years before the publication of the tales, Louis XIV decreed that only members of his court were permitted to wear shoes with red heels (Blanchard; McDowell; Semmelhack *Shoes* 168). Through his depiction of the red velvet suit, Perrault was arguably demonstrating a cynical awareness of this practice of social differentiation, as well as drawing on a colour with connotations of promiscuity. The licentious associations of women wearing red are long-standing, with one prominent example, perhaps known to Perrault's contemporary readers, being the red stockings of the eponymous character in Geoffrey Chaucer's *The Wife of Bath's Tale* (c. 1387-1400). Drawing on these intertextual references to red clothing, Perrault thus depicted the stepsisters in a negative light.

While Samber leaves the red velvet suit intact, his translation shifts the trimming's country of origin from England to France. In Perrault's text the trimming is English. Indeed, 'Dentelle au point d'Angleterre' (lace with English stitch) indicates a famous lace from Brussels that was referred to and sold as 'English' in the seventeenth century (Centre National de Ressources Textuelles et Lexicales [CNRTL]). This marketing strategy suggests that 'English' tailoring was considered chic and an attractive selling point for French customers of Perrault's period. In Samber's rendering of the tale, the English trimming for French readers becomes French trimming for English readers, and rather than submerging English readers into a French setting and presenting English material as foreign, the situation is inverted. The foreignness of the suit's decoration is preserved in a typical example of domestication, defined by Lawrence Venuti as the translation approach that aims for the illusion of being transparent and an 'original' English work (Venuti, *Scandals of Translation* 16-17, 57, 65, 74-76, 98, 145; Venuti, *Translation Studies Reader* 341). Samber's word choice seems in particular to be motivated by matters of fashion, echoing Perrault's attention to what was *à la mode*, as many commentators point out that French fashion was attractive to English readers of Samber's text, offering an explanation for the change that he made (Dorner 27; Johnston and Woolley 29; Severn 56; Victoria and Albert Museum).

The younger sister's outfit is presented in similar detail with her 'juppe ordinaire', that is, 'common petticoat' compensated for by her 'manteau à fleurs d'or, & ma barrière de diamans' (Perrault, *Histoires* 122-123). This sister is drawn to another colour that has connotations of nobility and ostentation, and Perrault's in-depth description reads like an extract from a fashion magazine or catalogue. Samber translates this extract as 'gold flowered manteau, and my diamond stomacher' (Perrault, *Histories* 76), again incorporating French terms to give fashion pre-eminence in the tale. The sisters' outfits are described using fairly technical vocabulary from the sartorial realm in French and English alike, with this technique being used again later in the passage when Perrault writes how Cinderella 'godronoit leurs manchettes' (Perrault, *Histoires* 122). Samber's rendering reads that Cinderella 'plaited their ruffles' (Perrault, *Histories* 76). According to the 1694 edition of *Le Dictionnaire de l'Académie Françoise,* 'godronner' forms a moderately specialised term in the domain of clothes and laundering, meaning to make pleats or folds along a cuff or ruff when it is starched (Académie Française 526). By incorporating such specific fashion terms, Perrault highlighted that an up-to-date knowledge of sartorial practices was essential to thriving in a court context, which is an allusion that Samber maintained in his translation, even if it is slightly simplified for younger readers.

Technical detail can also be seen in the stepsisters' arrangement of 'les cornettes à deux rangs' (Perrault, *Histoires* 123), in which Perrault employs 'cornettes' to refer to a type of hairstyle or headgear that was popular among seventeenth-century women (CNRTL). Perrault writes that 'On envoya querir la bonne coëffeuse, pour dresser les cornettes à deux rangs'. Samber's translation 'They sent for the best tire-woman they could get, to dress their heads, and adjust their double pinners [...]' (Perrault, *Histories* 76) takes some liberties with the French text to convey these elements to English readers.

Other technical language specific to the fashion and culture of Perrault's time includes 'mouches' ('beauty spots') in the line '[...]on fit acheter des mouches de la bonne faiseuse' (Perrault, *Histoires* 123). In his 2001 translation, Jack Zipes renders the term as 'patches' and defines it in a footnote as 'small pieces of black silk or court-plaster worn on the face in the seventeenth and eighteenth centuries either to cover a blemish or to show off the complexion by contrast' (Zipes, *Great Fairy Tale Tradition* 450). 'Patches' also feature in Zipes' translation of Marie-Catherine d'Aulnoy's contemporary *Cinderella* tale, *Finette Cendron* (d'Aulnoy 460), suggesting that they were widely used cosmetic items in the aristocratic circles to which Perrault and d'Aulnoy belonged. In Perrault's tale, these 'mouches' are bought from the 'bonne Faiseuse', that is, the talented 'craftsperson' or 'artisan' (Perrault, *Histoires* 123), with Samber presenting this incident as 'they had their red brushes and patches from Mrs. *De la Poche*' (Perrault, *Histories* 76). As with the English/French trimming, Samber moves away from Perrault's wording, adding several of his own embellishments to conjure up his own image of costumes and fashion. Samber's addition of 'red brushes' bolsters the theatricality of the tale, while the reference to 'Mrs. *De la Poche*' shows the influence exerted by French language, civility and especially fashion on English society in this period. By the sixth edition translation of 1764, 'mademoiselle *De la Poche*' is adopted (Perrault, *Tales* 84), showing a tendency on the translator's and editor's parts to emphasise the French inflections in the tale, particularly in its sartorial references.

This freer, more creative approach to translation appears to conform to Susan Bassnett's description of the 'metaphor of the translator/portrait painter'. This stance, frequently re-appearing in the eighteenth century, was adopted and advocated earlier by poet and translator John Dryden, who argued that translators must demonstrate creativity and latitude, adapting to their own culture's aesthetic canons, all the while respecting the 'duty of making [their] portrait resemble the original' (Bassnett 60; Dryden). Although the translator/portrait painter comparison was adopted in a range of ways, it highlights the dual expectations placed upon a translator in this period to convey the original through his/her rendering, while also showing artistic flair, by treating the text as a piece of art (Bassnett 63). It is notable that Samber's role as 'painter' is particularly evident in extracts about fashion, hinting at the prominence he assigned to this feature. Martine Hennard Dutheil de la Rochère and Gillian Lathey both indicate that Samber was a jobbing 'Grub Street' translator and author. He had translations and other works of a range of genres to his name, among them travel guides, medical texts and even pornography, and he worked under considerable time pressures. As such, he often adopted a more direct or literal linguistic solution in his translations and mostly adheres closely to Perrault's text with *Cinderilla* in that his general language choices do not stray far from the French (Dutheil de la Rochère, *Reading, Translating, Rewriting* 22; Lathey, 'Translator as Agent' 83-84, 88). Yet, with sartorial elements in *Cinderilla* he does deviate, and expresses himself in a more painterly manner, which is rendered all the more remarkable given his usually word-for-word, metaphrastic approach in other parts of the tale and in his translations more generally (Barchilon and Pettit 48; Dutheil de la Rochère, 'Cinderella's Metamorphoses' 250-254). In other words, in these instances, Samber's work is in line with the seventeenth-century French translation adage of 'belles infidèles', in which divergence from the source text allows for a beautiful target text (Wittman 439). Notably, he follows this technique precisely where the source text makes most reference to ideals of beauty. As such, while Perrault peppers his tale with intricate, esoteric vestimentary language, Samber mimics this attentiveness to fashion through his own uncharacteristically creative approaches.

Expressing personality through appearance, beauty and clothing

Throughout the tale, the idea that appearance is tied up with personality is suggested through the positive depiction of Cinderella's fashion-related actions, as she demonstrates her kindness and good nature by helping her sisters prepare for the ball and doing so with exquisite taste. Perrault writes that 'Cendrillon les conseilla le mieux du monde, & s'offrit mesme à les coëffer; ce qu'elles voulurent bien' (Perrault, *Histoires* 123), which Samber translates as '*Cinderilla* advised them the best in the world, and offered herself to dress their heads; which they were very willing she should do' (Perrault, *Histories* 76-77), returning to his more literal translation approach, which also maintains the sentiment of Perrault's phrasing. Similarly, 'Une autre que Cendrillon les auroit coëffées de travers : mais elle estoit bonne, & elle les coëffa parfaitement bien' (Perrault, *Histoires* 124) is translated as 'Any one but *Cinderilla* would have dressed their heads awry; but she was very good, and dress'd them perfectly well' (Perrault, *Histories* 77). In an exaggerated manner in which superlatives abound, Cinderella provides the best possible help and gives the stepsisters hairstyles that are flawless. There is the implication that her strong fashion sense and excellent skills as a hairdresser signal her as an exemplary person, just as her beauty is, as Daniel Aranda describes, a 'tangible manifestation of the heroine's moral mettle' (Aranda 132). Later, the women at the ball admire Cinderella's clothes and hairstyle, aspiring to imitate and replicate this trendsetter, provided they can access beautiful fabric and highly skilled artisans (Perrault, *Histoires* 133; Perrault, *Histories* 82), as Cinderella is positioned as a cut above the rest.

Meanwhile, the stepsisters are presented as vain, always looking in the mirror (Perrault, *Histoires* 125; Perrault, *Histories* 77), and are chastised by Perrault and the readers for their vanity through the alignment of this characteristic with the unsympathetic characters. Mirrors are traditional emblems of vanity, linking to the Greek mythic figure Narcissus though predominantly associated with women, and they have similar connotations in other fairy tales, such as *Snow White* and *Bluebeard* (Shefer 601–602). Patricia Hannon suggests that the stepsisters' interest in fashion and obsession with their appearance align with their desire for power (Dutheil de la Rochère, *Reading, Translating, Rewriting* 272; Hannon 948). Their behaviour is portrayed as unpleasant, whereas similar comportment from Cinderella is acceptable or even laudable, as exemplified when she demands fine clothes from her Godmother before she departs for the ball, asking 'est-ce que j'irai comme cela avec mes vilains habits [?]' (Perrault, *Histoires* 130). Samber translates this phrase as 'must I go thither as I am, with these ugly nasty clothes?' (Perrault, *Histories* 80), and the collocation of 'ugly' and 'nasty' coming from the mouth of the heroine legitimates the view that ugliness means nastiness. The 1764 edition of Samber's rendering strengthens this depiction to refer to 'poison nasty rags' (Perrault, *Tales* 90), vehemently emphasising this point, and indicating the reinforcement of Perrault's message through translation.

Cinderella's 'vilains habits' are later referred to as 'méchans habits' (Perrault, *Histoires* 140) or 'old ugly clothes' (Perrault, *Histoires* 86), when Cinderella is 'fort mal vestuë' (Perrault, *Histoires* 141), that is, 'very badly dressed' (Perrault, *Histoires* 86), all of which provide pejorative qualifications for the attire. In other cases, 'habits' (clothes) are presented favourably with, for instance, the lizard-cum-foot-men wearing 'habits chamarez' (Perrault, *Histoires* 129), which are translated as 'liveries all bedaubed with gold and silver' (Perrault, *Histoires* 80). Similarly, Cinderella's ballgown comprises 'habits de drap d'or & d'argent tout chamarez de pierreries' (Perrault, *Histoires* 130), as her clothes are made from 'cloth of gold and silver, all beset with jewels' (Perrault, *Histories* 80). As such, the tale's representation and repetition of the word 'habit' seem to contradict the traditional French proverb 'L'habit ne fait pas le moine', literally translated as 'The cowl does not make the monk'. The tale's message is that, in fact, clothes do make the person; beauty and vanity coupled with an unpleasant personality are deemed worthy of castigation but, for a kind-hearted person, these same qualities are important and applauded. Cinderella is described as 'une si belle & si aimable personne' and 'aussi bonne que belle' (Perrault, *Histoires* 133, 146), which Samber translates respectively as 'so beautiful and lovely a creature' and 'as good as handsome' (Perrault, *Histories* 82, 89). There is the intimation that attractiveness is a prerequisite for goodness, which is a reading that is discussed by Hannon (950).

Perrault's message is in line with what D. J. Adams describes as 'the prevailing fashion [in Perrault's time] for making a connection between physical appearance and inner character' and the long-held 'belief in the inherent correspondence of character and appearance' (Adams 14). These traits, which can also be detected in the tales of d'Aulnoy and other contemporaries of Perrault, are given greater nuance by these Modern writers in contrast to the more clear-cut approach of their Ancient counterparts.[1] D'Aulnoy and other Modern writers allow for some discrepancy between physical appearance and personality (Adams 15), yet Perrault ultimately requires good characters to have a pleasant appearance even if unpleasant characters can be attractive too. After the slipper fits, proving that Cinderella is the person sought by the Prince, the Fairy transforms Cinderella's attire before she addresses herself to the Prince, suggesting that she will otherwise not be worthy of or recognised by him, yet in her transformed state he finds her more beautiful than he did initially (Perrault, *Histoires* 144–146; Perrault, *Histories* 88–89).

In the moral message, Perrault returns to the idea that to be good as a person, one must also look good. With tinges of irony, Perrault proclaims the virtues of grace over and above having a finely dressed head, yet simultaneously limits his message to those who are already beautiful by referring the moral to 'Belles' or 'fair ladies' (Perrault, *Histoires* 147; Perrault, *Histories* 90). Samber's handling of the linguistic structure of the moral also indicates a concerted effort to maintain ideals of beauty within the language itself, as he uses domestication, straying from the rhyme, rhythm and content adopted by Perrault to render the verse pleasing to English ears. Jean Boase-Beier writes how translators of poetry tend to place emphasis on the 'importance of the aesthetic properties of the target text' (Boase-Beier 480–481), and this is especially so with Samber's handling of the verse moral of *Cinderilla*. Moreover, Riitta Oittinen and Cay Dollerup argue that read-aloud qualities are an important consideration when translating for young children (Dollerup; Oittinen 34), which could partially justify Samber's use of a regular meter for *Cinderilla*. Yet Samber's attention to these features seems particularly pronounced for *Cinderilla*, compared with his treatment of the morals of the other tales in Perrault's collection. This attentiveness suggests that other—possibly sartorial and aesthetic—motivations come into play.

The description of appearance is not limited to the women in the tale and the importance of beauty extends even to the non-human characters.

---

[1] Perrault was a prominent figure in the *Querelle des Anciens et des Modernes*, a conflict in which the Ancients were in favour of Greek and Latin literature, while the Moderns promoted contemporary, domestic material. The fairy-tale form epitomises the issues of this debate, as it was seen as dirty and inferior by the Ancients, yet authentic by the Moderns (Warner, *Beast to Blonde* 169, 322).

They are portrayed based on a value judgement of their appearance, particularly through the use of 'beau/bel/belle', meaning beautiful, handsome or fine. When Cinderella's godmother asks her to pick a pumpkin, Cinderella chooses 'la plus belle' (Perrault, *Histoires* 126), that is, 'the finest' (Perrault, *Histories* 78) that she can find. Meanwhile, a mouse is turned into 'un beau cheval; ce qui fit un bel attelage de six chevaux, d'un beau gris de souris pommelé' (Perrault, *Histoires* 127–128), which Samber translates as 'a fine horse, which all together made a very fine set of six horses, of a beautiful mouse-coloured dapple grey' (Perrault, *Histories* 79). The repetition of 'beau' and its derivatives is rendered by Samber using 'fine' twice and 'beautiful', while the sixth edition uses three distinct words 'fair', 'fine', and 'beautiful' (Perrault, *Tales* 88). The larger vocabulary of the English language is utilised to create nuance, as different linguistic aesthetics are foregrounded by Perrault and Samber. The use of synonyms by the English translator suggests that domestication has been performed here, aligning the text with English norms and what is considered linguistically elegant and aesthetically pleasing.

The rat-cum-coachman too is described as having 'une des plus belles moustaches qu'on ait jamais veuës' (Perrault, *Histoires* 128–129), which is rendered as 'the finest whiskers as were ever seen' (Perrault, *Histories* 79). The transformation endows the rat with a beautiful moustache, so as the rat is made more useful, he is also made more beautiful, or vice versa, thus reiterating the merging of goodness with attractiveness. Similar deductions apply to the pumpkin-coach, the mice-horses and the lizard-footmen. Indeed, the fairy selects this rat from a group of three, due to it having a 'maîtresse barbe' (Perrault, *Histoires* 128) or the 'largest beard' (Perrault, *Histories* 79). The whiskers/moustache and large beard work with 'gros rat' and 'gros Cocher' (Perrault, *Histoires* 128)—'huge rat' and 'fat jolly coachman' respectively (Perrault, *Histories* 79)—to conjure up an image of quintessential masculinity, combining hairiness and largeness. Samber adds the quality of merriment and cheerfulness, using the common collocation, as his eighteenth-century audience and Perrault's seventeenth-century audience alike would have been attuned to this combination of characteristics. There is a long history of jolly, fat male literary figures that precede these tales, including Sancho Panza in Miguel de Cervantes's *Don Quixote* and Falstaff in William Shakespeare's *Henry IV* (Eknoyan 423-424). In particular, given that Samber translated the tale for a child audience, the addition of 'jolly' may have served as a form of explicitation, which is common in translations for children and involves rendering more obvious what may have been conveyed via allusion in the source text (O'Sullivan 'Children's Literature' 456). 'Jolly' reiterates that being fat is a positive attribute for an adult male, whereas Perrault's framing is implicit and assumed to be understood by his adult readers and their knowledge of intertexts, literary tropes and social norms.

The little glass slipper

The rat's masculine attributes contrast with the typical qualities of youthful femininity embodied in the glass slipper, which is small and smooth. Even while Perrault's propensity for satire comes into play, personality and appearance are closely interlinked, and size is also presented as a marker of characters' personal qualities and gender. During the shoe-test ritual, Perrault presents how 'les deux sœurs [...] firent tout leur possible pour faire entrer leur pied dans la pentoufle' (Perrault, *Histoires* 143), which Samber translates as 'the two sisters [...] did all they possibly could to thrust their foot into the Slipper' (Perrault, *Histories* 87). Fashion historians Lucy Johnston and Linda Woolley discuss how, in the late seventeenth century, many means were adopted, including use of pointed toe and high heel on a shoe, in women's attempts to create the illusion of the ideal, tiny foot (Johnston and Woolley 32). Perrault's description of the sisters struggling to fit the glass shoe suggests an element of scorn towards the size of their feet and their attempts to falsify the feet's natural largeness. Samber intensifies 'faire entrer', literally meaning 'make enter', to 'thrust', which is more emphatic and vicious, as the sisters aggressively attempt to fit their feet in the vaunted tiny slipper. In so doing, he amplifies the sisters' unladylike qualities.

The importance granted to size is highlighted in the title of the tale and its reference to the slipper. In full, Perrault's tale is named *Cendrillon ou la Petite Pantoufle de Verre,* which Samber translates as *Cinderilla: or, The Little Glass Slipper.* The lexical choice 'little' is particularly telling, since while reflecting child-like language, it presents the slipper in an affectionate, albeit mildly patronising, manner. Although it appears to be an asset, the word in fact suggests that Cinderella is deprived and limited (Aranda 127–128; May–Ron 149, 158). The choice of term is significant, considering how it differs from another translation for 'petit', the more neutral 'small' (OED little *adj.* A. I. 8), and even though the sibilance of 'small slipper' would have reflected the alliteration of 'p' in 'petite pantoufle', Samber opts for 'little'. The English language of Samber's time, which had a greater number of words than the French of Perrault's time, offered Samber a broader array of vocabulary, and he drew on this richer stock of words to amplify the nuances of the French term. In this way, Cinderella's and the slipper's diminutive size presents her as good yet vulnerable in a similar way to a character from another tale in Perrault's collection named *Petit Chaperon Rouge* (Perrault, *Histoires* 47), which Samber translates as *The Little Red Riding-Hood* (Perrault, *Histories* 1). In this title, 'little' describes a human girl, whereas in the title of *Cinderella*, 'little' describes the slipper, in such a way that the slipper almost replaces Cinderella in two-way synecdoche, a notion supported by the title's use of 'ou' (or). Dutheil de la Rochère writes that the double title for *Cinderella* indicates dual themes of the girl and the shoe (Dutheil de la Rochère, *Reading, Translating, Rewriting* 271, 289), however I would argue that the dual naming conceals a conflation of the two items, as girl and shoe become indistinguishable and their identities merge. Laura Mullen refers to the slipper as signifier and Cinderella as signified, suggesting that there is a degree of slippage between the two entities that together work as a sign (Mullen 287). Yet like words standing in for what they describe, the slipper and Cinderella have come to be perceived as mutually exchangeable.

The little glass slipper's part in the tale reinforces this framing. The idea of the slipper suggests a slight style of footwear (Semmelhack *Shoes* 300–301), which reinforces the 'little' that qualifies it, aligning with conventional views of women and femininity, being softer and lighter as word and object than 'shoe'. The slipper's material heightens and hyperbolises these qualities in an oxymoronic manner. Fashion historian Elizabeth Semmelhack presents how in seventeenth-century Europe, the more impractical and uncomfortable the clothes and footwear, the higher the marker of class and status (Semmelhack *Heights of Fashion*). Cinderella's glass slipper is therefore an amusing indicator of ultimate prestige. Dutheil de la Rochère argues that 'Perrault resorts to the marvellous to mask his critique of the pettiness, intrigues, and vanities of the world of the court', often adopting superlatives to caricature and satirise courtly rituals (Dutheil de la Rochère, 'Cinderella's Metamorphoses' 259; Dutheil de la Rochère, *Reading, Translating, Rewriting* 274). The glass slipper seems to be part of this approach, as fashion is spectacularized for ultimate impact.

Zipes comments that the glass slipper is a characteristically ironic, humorous and paradoxical quirk inserted by Perrault, as a glass slipper would be at considerable risk of breaking if it fell off a foot, yet somehow remains intact when Cinderella drops it on the stairs (Zipes, *Great Fairy Tale Tradition* 444). Even so, Kathryn Hoffmann highlights how glass is a common feature of fairy tales, and in particular she positions the glass slipper among many other glass and crystal objects that abounded in the seventeenth-century aristocratic context, hence giving a certain logic to glass footwear (Hoffmann). The fact that glass can only be broken once endows the protagonist with a virginal aura (Delarue, 'From Perrault to Walt Disney' 111). As such, the shoe's material, while suggesting prestige and high status, also portrays Perrault's Cinderella as vulnerable, inexperienced and unblemished. In this way, she is aligned with Perrault's Little Red Riding Hood, whose fate is to be devoured by the wolf, compared with the more proactive character in earlier oral versions, who manages to escape from the wolf by tricking him (Delarue, 'The Grandmother's Tale'; Hayton).

The glass slipper's qualities of being rigid and not stretchable are what heighten its value, as well as emphasising its unique fit to Cinderella's foot, even while, like solid wax, it derives from a malleable form (Dutheil de la Rochère, *Reading, Translating, Rewriting* 293; Hoffmann 61). Indeed, wax is the very material used by Perrault in his metaphorical description of the slipper-fitting. The stepsisters struggle in the shoe-test ritual, yet when Cinderella tries, 'elle [the slipper] y entroit sanspeine, & ... elle y estoit juste comme de cire' (Perrault, *Histoires* 144). Samber translates this extract as 'it [the foot] went in very easily, and fitted her, as if it [the shoe] had been made of wax' (Perrault, *Histories* 88). Samber makes slightly ambiguous use of 'it' for both the foot and slipper, and Perrault's line translates more literally and explicitly as 'the slipper joined her foot effortlessly and fit it like wax', with Zipes' translation reading 'he [the Prince's gentleman] saw it [the slipper] go on very easily and fit like wax' (Perrault, 'Cinderella' 29). Hannon writes that the synecdochic description frames the slipper as 'an integral part of her body, a representation or possible substitute for that body', possibly prompted by her translation that reads 'was exactly like wax' (Hannon 951), altering the meaning slightly by missing out the pivotal 'y' in 'y estoit juste comme de cire'. Instead, I would argue that the simile in fact highlights the idea of coating the foot in a foreign agent that comes to control it rather than being integral to it. As such, besides its sexual connotations, wax evokes the idea of entrapment, as Cinderella's foot is encased in a snugly-fitting and uniquely shaped mould. While in other cases I agree with Hannon that the slipper's relationship to Cinderella verges on synecdoche, for example in the two-way synecdoche seen above in the tale's title, here the metaphorical language highlights the separate entities of foot and shoe that are fused together while remaining distinct.

In the context in which Perrault was working, arranged or forced marriages were commonplace, involving young women being compelled to marry much older aristocrats, which was the plight of several of Perrault's contemporary female fairy tale writers, such as Henriette-Julie de Murat (Warner, *Beast to Blonde* 169, 265–266; Zipes, 'Author Biographies' 839). With this context in mind, the wax simile seems to evoke the idea of entrapment and being shackled in wax. Despite problematic depictions prevailing in his tale, Perrault was relatively pioneering and progressive in terms of women's rights, suggesting that this wax simile symbolises the injustice of arranged marriages. Nevertheless, the inflexibility of glass and solid wax too emphasises the essentialist understanding that is embedded in the *Cinderella* tale, as the idea that the slipper fits onto only one foot suggests that the owner has innate qualities that are unmatched and irrefutable. The tale's essentialism is accentuated and parodied via the glass slipper in a similar way to Perrault's use of superlatives.

Through technical language, adjectival choice and metaphorical language, Perrault therefore emphasises the importance of beauty and fashion, while aligning largeness with masculinity and smallness with femininity. Samber retains these elements through his own linguistic techniques, particularly through greater use of creativity in rendering passages relating to appearance. These features are also prominent in the Brothers Grimm's tales and their English translations, which both too have their own distinctions.

Contextualising the Brothers Grimm and Edgar Taylor

Between 1812 and 1857, Jacob and Wilhelm Grimm produced seven editions of the *Kinder– und Hausmärchen* (*Children's and Household Tales*). In successive editions, the tales were altered, particularly by Wilhelm, to adhere to the Brothers' social, religious and pedagogical beliefs and conventions, and to moralise more explicitly about these aspects. The tale's reshaping was also affected by the new audience of children who had not been intended in earlier editions that were aimed at mostly adult readers, with the first edition specifically having an erudite agenda. In the editing process, there was also a desire to ensure internal coherency within each tale, with the most significant changes occurring between the first and second editions (Blamires, as 'The Early Reception' 66; Warner, *Beast to Blonde* 294; Zipes *Art of Subversion* 48, 58). Despite their insistence on the humble sources of their tales, the Brothers themselves were members of the bourgeoisie and most of their informants belonged to the rich, middle-class, educated and literate sectors of society. The Brothers thus carried out a conscious process of sorting, sifting and assimilating to streamline the tales to their own vision, while claiming that they were unearthing the natural, most authentic form of the tale (Blamires,

Telling Tales 148; Zipes, *Art of Subversion* 47, 55; Zipes, 'Cross-Cultural Connection' 866).

Another significant contextual factor was the threat of French domination and Napoleonic rule in the Grimms' hometown of Kassel. The Brothers Grimm were part of a larger early-nineteenth-century, German movement that aimed to assert German identity, stir national pride and unite the people—in a not yet unified Germany—against invading groups.[2] The Brothers used fairy tales of supposedly Germanic origins, collecting them and endeavouring to make them distinct from the French versions (Blamires, 'The Early Reception' 66; Zipes, *Breaking the Magic Spell* 70, 73, 90–91; Zipes, 'Cross–Cultural Connections' 867; Zipes, *Oxford Companion* 167). The idea of distancing the tales from French affiliations can be observed through the depiction of clothing and footwear in the Brothers' various editions of their *Cinderella* tale, *Aschenputtel* (Grimm and Grimm, *Kinder* 1st ed. 88–101; Grimm and Grimm, *Kinder* 2nd ed. 114–123; 7th ed. 119–126).

The first English translation of a selection of the Brothers Grimm's tales was published as *German Popular Stories* in 1823, followed by a second volume with other tales in 1826, in which the *Cinderella* translation, *Ashputtel,* appeared (Grimm and Grimm, *German Popular Stories* 33–46). We saw that while Perrault's tales were essentially for adults, Samber translated them specifically for children. Similarly, the Brothers' tales, initially for adults, were translated into English for a young audience (Blamires, *Telling Tales* 159). While the translations were a collaborative endeavour between Edgar Taylor and David Jardine, Taylor was responsible for translating the Brothers' *Aschenputtel* (Sutton 9–10, 75–76). The translations and the alterations wrought by Taylor in the translation influenced the Brothers in the changes they made in subsequent editions of their collection, such as rendering their tales more child-friendly (Blamires, 'The Early Reception' 69; Sutton 48–49, 56, 102). Through the Brothers' phases of editing and Taylor's translation, appearance, beauty, fashion and footwear remained prominent features of the tale, even if the techniques used to convey these ideals somewhat shifted. In each case, the philosophy and morality of the writer or translator was reinforced through these elements.

---

[2] German unification was orchestrated by Otto von Bismarck and the German Empire, or Second Reich, was proclaimed in 1871 following the Franco-Prussian War.

Wooden shoes

Cinderella is cast out and ridiculed by her stepfamily through the attire they force her to wear, which includes 'einen grauen alten Kittel' (Grimm and Grimm, *Kinder* 2nd ed. 115) or 'an old gray frock' (Grimm and Grimm, *German Popular Stories* 34). By the final edition the frock is accompanied by what are described as 'hölzerne Schuhe' (Grimm and Grimm, *Kinder* 7th ed. 119), with 'hölzerne' in this context being ambiguous, meaning 'wooden' in both senses of awkward and the material. Her exclusion is demonstrated by her ingenue stiffness alongside the drabness of her garments, not new nor coloured, and whose 'grayness' merges her with the surrounding dust and dirt. Later in the tale, to try on the slipper in the shoe-test ritual, Cinderella removes her shoe, which in early editions is the first reference to this shackling shoe, and it is described as 'schweren Schuh' (Grimm and Grimm, *Kinder* 2nd ed. 122), which Taylor translates as 'clumsy shoe' (Grimm and Grimm, *German Popular Stories* 45). The final edition, although it was ambiguous earlier in the tale, here presents the shoe that is removed as 'schweren Holzschuh' (Grimm and Grimm, *Kinder* 7th ed. 126), meaning a clog, sabot or wooden shoe that is difficult, awkward, heavy or clumsy, and suggests a hardwearing, loose-fitting peasant shoe for use in dirty conditions. As such, while the material of the shoe is not specified in early editions, by the final stages of the final edition it is presented as wood.

The symbolism of the wooden shoe or clog can be understood more clearly in light of Warner's article 'Those Brogues', in which she briefly discusses clogs, writing of the various senses in which 'clog', as noun and verb, is used (Warner, 'Those Brogues' 30). In particular, she highlights how clogs, like brogues, are often associated symbolically with land and country (Warner, 'Those Brogues' 30). Moreover, pattens and clogs were commonly worn over other shoes to protect them when going outdoors, and they have pastoral links to rural life, muddy paths and roads (Victoria and Albert Museum). As such, clogs may well have assisted the Brothers Grimm in aligning their tales and their character with the German *Volk*, so the incorporation of clogs in later editions seems to be an effort to increasingly Germanise the tales. In the Brothers' German translation of an Irish folktale, they render 'brogue' as 'Holzschuh', shifting a leather shoe to a wooden one in their domestication of the tale (Sutton 281, 283), indicating the symbolic nature of this footwear, the importance of its material and its distinctive connotations in the German context.

Warner comments that, besides constituting a form of footwear, 'clog' also means 'encumbrance' or 'impediment' (OED *clog* *n.* 3), so that

Cinderella's removal of the clog suggests liberation. As such, while the clogs are a burden to Cinderella, they also work to align the heroine with a peasant or inhabitant of the German countryside, framing her in a positive manner even if she is shackled. Hilary Davidson writes, in reference to the clogs in *Aschenputtel*, that 'Clogs [...] are poor, cheap, always unmagical footwear, signifying gross rustics who never rise beyond their earth-bound, labouring positions' (Davidson 28), pointing to the possible motivations for the Brothers' inclusion of clogs. Yet I would go further to highlight the specific significance of the wooden material, the fact that it is a supplement to later editions of the tale, and that its bucolic connotations seem to be presented somewhat positively. In view of the meaning of clog as encumbrance, Cinderella taking off this wooden shoe is an exceedingly symbolic act of liberation and it suggests that ordinary members of the German population can undergo similar transformative experiences. However, just as Perrault seems to deny the idea that marriage is liberating through his comparison of the glass slipper to wax encasement, the Brothers Grimm's unclogging and liberating of Cinderella from the burdensome wooden shoe comes at the cost of entrapment in the gold slippers in which her feet are later shod.

Diminishing sartorial details from first to second edition

Besides the inclusion of the clog, another passage that reveals the Brothers' editing hand deals with the stepsisters' preparation for the King's feast. As in Perrault's tale, the Brothers' first-edition Cinderella helps them when asked and resembles Perrault's character, with her involvement being willing and paramount. The Brothers have it that 'Aschenputtel gab sich alle Muhe und putzte sie so gut es konnte' (Grimm and Grimm, *Kinder* 1st ed. 90), as Cinderella puts in considerable effort to dress her stepsisters the best she can. The second edition Cinderella is also ordered to 'kämm uns die Haare, bürst uns die Schuhe und schnall uns die Schnallen' (Grimm and Grimm, *Kinder* 2nd ed. 116), as the stepsisters demand Cinderella to 'comb our hair, brush our shoes, and tie our sashes for us' (Grimm and Grimm, *German Popular Stories* 36). Cinderella follows the orders, but her enthusiasm and thoroughness are not expressed, rendering this second-edition Cinderella more reluctant than her first-edition counterpart when it comes to fashion. The Brothers Grimm view Cinderella's act of helping in contrast to the role of the (French) courtier.

Similarly, the description of the ball dresses and accessories in later editions are much less detailed than in the first edition. It should be noted that in the editing process, the tale is shortened, yet it is significant that many of the elements that are omitted relate to fashion and hence considered unnecessary or counter to the Brothers' ideological project. In the first edition, Cinderella's first outfit comprises 'ein prächtig silbern Kleid […], Perlen, seidene Strümpfe mit silbernen Zwickeln und silberne Pantoffel' (Grimm and Grimm, *Kinder* 1st ed. 93), as the Brothers offer an inventory of her magnificent, silver dress, pearls, silk stockings with silver gusset and silver slippers. Cinderella is described as being as beautiful as 'eine Rose, die der Thau gewaschen hat' (93), that is, a dew-washed rose. Her second outfit is 'ein Kleid […] noch viel herrlicher und prächtiger als das vorige, ganz von Gold und Edelgesteinen, dabei goldgezwickelte Strümpfe und goldene Pantoffel' (Grimm and Grimm, *Kinder* 1st ed. 96), and readers are again treated to a description of an even more wonderful and splendid dress than the former one, adorned with gold and diamonds, golden stockings with gold gusset and gold slippers. Referring to the dress, the Brothers Grimm describe the dress shining like the midday sun when they write, 'glänzte es recht, wie die Sonne am Mittag' (96). These rich costume descriptions and the complementary figurative language are considerably reduced in subsequent editions. Second-edition Cinderella wears 'golden und silbern Kleid', 'ein noch viel stolzeres Kleid' and 'ein Kleid […] das war so prächtig wie es noch keins gehabt hatte' (Grimm and Grimm, *Kinder* 2nd ed. 118, 119, 120), which Taylor translates respectively as 'gold and silver dress', 'a still finer dress' and 'a dress still finer than the former one' (Grimm and Grimm, *German Popular Stories* 39, 41, 43). As such, while the 1812 edition is much more akin to Perrault's tale with its inclusion of lush details about the outfits, by later editions the Brothers Grimm have very much made the tales their own, toning down the fashion descriptions. It seems likely that as they edited their tale, the Brothers removed many passages relating to fashion and costuming due to its French connotations, as they marked out their German tales as distinct from these foreign fashion-oriented versions. In the translation Taylor continued this tendency, offering more neutral descriptions of the outfits. The Brothers present the dress as 'so prächtig wie es noch keins gehabt hatte', that is, 'of unrivalled splendour', which is supplemented in the final edition with 'und glänzend' to refer to its brilliance (Grimm and Grimm, *Kinder* 124). The description is presented more modestly in the English translation as 'still finer', perhaps motivated by the desire to reduce elaborate linguistic constructions for child readers.

In line with her costumes, in the first edition, Cinderella's means of transport to the balls start with 'ein Wagen mit sechs federgeschmückten Rappen und Bediente dabei in Blau und Silber' (Grimm and Grimm, *Kinder* 93–94), which depicts a carriage with six black horses adorned with plumes and footmen in blue and silver. At the next ball, she is brought by 'ein Wagen mit sechs Schimmeln, die hatten hohe weiße Federbusche auf dem Kopf, und die Bedienten waren in Roth und Gold gekleidet' (Grimm and Grimm, *Kinder* 96), this time a carriage with six white horses, with tall, white plumes on their heads, and footmen wearing red and gold. Social progression is defined by what she wears and how she travels, with the array of colours and intricately listed decoration becoming increasingly regal at subsequent balls. The pageantry of these passages from the first edition, not present in subsequent editions of the tale, resemble the spectacular and performative aspect of Perrault's tale and the carriage brings to mind the grand carriage used for Louis XIV's wedding (Bettelheim 263). As such, the beautifully attired transportation with its specifically French connotations is omitted by the Brothers from later editions in their pursuit of German authenticity and purity.

Smallness in the tale

The editing process performed by the Brothers and Taylor's approach to the translation of the tales can also be observed through Cinderella's ball slippers and the changes made to them between different versions of the tale. In the second edition, Cinderella's shoes at the three balls are described as 'Seide und Silber ausgestickte Pantoffeln' and 'die Pantoffeln waren ganz golden', with the shoes at the second ball not even being mentioned (Grimm and Grimm, *Kinder* 2nd ed. 118, 120). In English, Taylor renders these extracts respectively as 'slippers of spangled silk' and 'slippers which were all of gold' (Grimm and Grimm, *German Popular Stories* 39, 43). The 'Silber' ('silver') and 'ausgestickte' ('embroidered') qualities of the first slipper become the 'spangled' features of the English translation, depicting different nuances of the shoe while preserving the level of detail. By the Brothers' final edition, these moderately descriptive references to footwear are embellished in that the third pair of shoes becomes 'klein und zierlich und ganz golden' (Grimm and Grimm, *Kinder* 3rd ed. 143; 7th ed. 124). While less detail is given about Cinderella's dresses in subsequent editions, we learn more about her shoes as the Brothers Grimm use this characteristic feature to express their patriarchal values. The slipper is depicted as little, dainty and graceful, which equate and conflate smallness with beauty for women, and this metonymic allusion naturalises a problematic depiction that was also witnessed in Perrault's tale.

The Brothers amplify the depiction of smallness, particularly small feet and shoes, as feminine, childlike, attractive, prestigious and lovable yet lacking. It was seen that Perrault's use of 'petit' presented size as a measure of gender, personality, social status, youthfulness and aspiration. Throughout the *Aschenputtel* tale, suffixes '-chen' and '-lein' are used to form diminutives of nouns, including girls/maids, doves, a saucepan, tree, smock, oil lamp, daughter and grain. While these endings could indicate a friendly, familiar quirk of dialect, it is noteworthy that most of the words qualified as little, small or cute relate to Cinderella, her mother, her bird companions and the domestic sphere. By way of comparison, diminutives that are used in the Grimm's tale *Sneewittchen* (*Snow White*) mostly describe the dwarfs and their possessions (Grimm and Grimm, *Kinder* 2nd ed. 185–193), while in *Das Todtenhemdchen* (*The Little Shroud*), they describe the seven-year-old male protagonist (Grimm and Grimm, *Kinder* 2nd ed. vol. 2, 391). In *Aschenputtel* the diminutives relate to Cinderella, a woman, not a dwarf nor a child, emphasising the daintiness of this female protagonist and of the ideal woman. Of particular note is the use of 'Mädchen' in *Aschenputtel*, which is translated variously by Taylor as 'little girl', 'little maiden', 'maid', 'maiden' and 'lady' (Grimm and Grimm, *German Popular Stories* 34, 37, 40, 42). On the one occasion that 'Mädchen' refers to the stepsister, Taylor adds the adjective 'silly' to alter the connotations (43). Although Zipes argues that 'Perrault endows his heroine with innate qualities while the Grimms' young girl must earn these qualities' (Zipes, *Enchanted Screen* 152), I would suggest that various features, including the use of diminutives, intimate that the Brothers' Cinderella, compared with her stepsisters, is innately small and has the tiny foot to prove it. The smallness of Cinderella's feet and shoes is made to seem natural and normal through the use of these linguistic techniques that infuse the tale on many levels.

Perrault, Grimm and their beautiful heritage?

Cinderella's wardrobe in its early French, German and English manifestations shows that in versions of the tale by Perrault, Samber, Grimm and Taylor, fashion and appearance are significant features and they are bound up with the ideological, philosophical and moral stance of the writers and translators. Different techniques are used to express beauty, goodness and worth, but in each case there is the message that appearance does matter, and that smallness is a feminine attribute. Many scholars have referred to the Brothers' handling of the tales in subsequent editions as a form of sanitising, purification or cleansing (Klingberg 12; O'Sullivan *Comparative Children's Literature* 82; Sutton; Zipes *Art of Subversion* 49–53). More specifically, we have seen that with *Cinderella* cleansing takes the form of beautification, which was a prime motivator in the changes wrought by the Brothers, but also by Perrault, Samber and Taylor in each of their iterations of the tale. Given their considerable legacy, a return to these works of Perrault and the Brothers Grimm and the first English translations helps to enrich our understanding of the *Cinderella* tale, and its adaptation according to the authors' and translators' social and cultural agendas. As the tale has evolved across time, place, language and media, fashion and beauty have remained central features. By analysing some of the key early moments of the tale's intercultural and interlingual exchange, we learn more about how and why the tale evolved and continues to evolve to this day, all the while problematic representations of women and femininity persist.

Works cited

Académie Française. *Le Dictionnaire de L'Académie Françoise, Dédié Au Roi. A–L.*, vol. 1, Jean-Baptise Coignard, 1694.

Adams, D. J. 'The 'Contes de Fées' of Madame d'Aulnoy: Reputation and Re-Evaluation.' *Bulletin of the John Rylands University*, vol. 76, no. 3, 1994, pp. 5–22.

Aranda, Daniel. 'Moral Adjustments to Perrault's Cinderella in French Children's Literature (1850 1900).' *Cinderella Across Cultures. New Directions and Interdisciplinary Perspectives*, edited by Martine-Hennard Dutheil de la Rochère, Gillian Lathey and Monika Woźniak, Wayne State University Press, 2016, pp. 124–40.

Barchilon, Jacques, and Henry Pettit. *The Authentic Mother Goose Fairy Tales and Nursery Rhymes*. Alan Swallow, 1960.

Bassnett, Susan. *Translation Studies*. Revised ed., Routledge, 1991.

Bettelheim, Bruno. *The Uses of Enchantment: The Meaning and Importance of Fairy Tales*. Thames and Hudson, 1976.

Blamires, David. *Telling Tales: The Impact of Germany on English Children's Books 1780–1918*. Open Book, 2009.

—. 'The Early Reception of the Grimms' *Kinder– Und Hausmärchen* in England.' *Bulletin of the John Rylands University Library of Manchester*, vol. 71, no. 3, 1989, pp. 63–77.

Blanchard, Tamsin. *The Shoe: Best Foot Forward*. Carlton Books, 2000.

Boase-Beier, Jean. 'Poetry Translation.' *The Routledge Handbook of Translation Studies*, edited by Carmen Millán and Francesca Bartrina, Routledge, 2013, pp. 475–487.

Bottigheimer, Ruth. 'Cinderella: The People's Princess.' *Cinderella Across Cultures: New Directions and Interdisciplinary Perspectives*, edited by Martine-Hennard Dutheil de la Rochère, Gillian Lathey and Monika Woźniak, Wayne State University Press, 2016, pp. 27–51.

Centre National de Ressources Textuelles et Lexicales (CNRTL) 2012. https://www.cnrtl.fr/ Accessed 26 March 2020.

Chaucer, Geoffrey. *The Canterbury Tales.* c. 1387–1400.

d'Aulnoy, Marie-Catherine. 'Finette Cendron.' *The Great Fairy Tale Tradition: From Straparola and Basile to the Brothers Grimm*, edited and translated by Jack Zipes, W.W. Norton, 2001, pp. 454–67.

Davidson, Hilary. 'Sex and Sin: The Magic of Red Shoes.' *Shoes: A History from Sandals to Sneakers*, edited by Giorgio Riello and Peter McNeil, Berg, 2011, pp. 272–289.

de Cervantes, Miguel. *Don Quixote.* Francisco de Robles, 1605.

Delarue, Paul. 'From Perrault to Walt Disney: The Slipper of Cinderella.' *Cinderella: A Folklore Casebook*, edited by Alan Dundes, Garland, 1982, p. 110–114.

—. 'The Grandmother's Tale: To Come of Age.' *Little Red Riding Hood Uncloaked: Sex, Morality and the Evolution of a Fairy Tale*, edited by Catherine Orenstein, Basic Books, 2002, pp. 63–84.

Dollerup, Cay. 'Translation for Reading Aloud.' *Meta*, vol. 48, no. 1–2, 2003, pp. 81–103.

Dorner, Jane. *Fashion in the Forties and Fifties.* Ian Allan, 1975.

Dryden, John. *The Preface.* 2nd ed., Jacob Tonson, 1681.

Dutheil de la Rochère, Martine Hennard. 'Cinderella's Metamorphoses: A Comparative Study of Two English Translations of Perrault's Tales.' *Przekładaniec: A Journal of Literary Translation*, vol. 22–23, 2009–10, pp. 249–66.

—. 'Introduction: Cinderella across Cultures.' *Cinderella Across Cultures: New Directions and Interdisciplinary Perspectives*, edited by Martine-Hennard Dutheil de la Rochère, Gillian Lathey and Monika Woźniak, Wayne State University Press, 2016, pp. 1–24.

—. *Reading, Translating, Rewriting: Angela Carter's Translational Poetics.* Wayne State University Press, 2013.

Eknoyan, Garabed. 'A History of Obesity, or How What Was Good Became Ugly and Then Bad.' *Obesity and Chronic Kidney Disease*, vol. 13, no. 4, 2006, pp. 421–427.

Grimm, Jacob, and Wilhelm Grimm. *German Popular Stories, Translated from the Kinder Und Haus-Märchen.* Translated by Edgar Taylor and David Jardine, vol. 2, James Robins, 1826.

—. *Kinder- Und Haus-Märchen Gesammelt Durch Die Brüder Grimm.* 1st ed., vol. 1, Realschulbuchhandlung, 1812.

—. *Kinder- Und Haus-Märchen Gesammelt Durch Die Brüder Grimm.* 2nd ed., vol. 1, G. Reimer, 1819.

—. *Kinder- Und Haus-Märchen: Gesammelt Durch Die Brüder Grimm.* 7th ed., vol. 1–2, Verlag der dieterichschen Buchhandlung, 1857.

Hannon, Patricia. '*Corps Cadavres*: Heroes and Heroines in the Tales of Perrault.' *The Great Fairy Tale Tradition: From Straparola and Basile to the Brothers Grimm*, edited by Jack Zipes, W. W. Norton, 2001, pp. 933–57.

Hayton, Natalie. '*Little Red Riding Hood* in the 21st Century: Adaptation, Archetypes, and the Appropriation of a Fairy Tale.' PhD Thesis. De Montfort University, 2013.

Hoffmann, Kathryn A. 'Perrault's *Cendrillon* among the Glass Tales: Crystal Fantasies and Glassworks in Seventeenth-Century France and Italy.' *Cinderella Across Cultures: New Directions and Interdisciplinary Perspectives*, edited by Martine Hennard Dutheil de la Rochère, Gillian Lathey and Monika Woźniak, Wayne State University Press, 2016, pp. 52–80.

Johnston, Lucy, and Linda Woolley. *Shoes: A Brief History.* 2nd ed., Victoria and Albert Publications, 2015.

Klingberg, Göte. *Children's Fiction in the Hands of the Translators.* Gleerup, 1986.

Lathey, Gillian. *The Role of Translators in Children's Literature: Invisible Storytellers.* Routledge, 2010.

—. 'The Translator as Agent of Change: Robert Samber, Translator of Pornography, Medical Texts, and the First English Version of Perrault's *Cendrillon* (1729).' *Cinderella Across Cultures: New Directions and Interdisciplinary Perspectives*, edited by Martine Hennard Dutheil de la Rochère, Gillian Lathey and Monika Woźniak, Wayne State University Press, 2016.

May-Ron, Rona. 'Rejecting the Glass Slipper: The Subversion of Cinderella in Margaret Atwood's *The Edible Woman.*' *Cinderella Across Cultures: New Directions and Interdisciplinary Perspectives*, edited by Martine Hennard Dutheil de la Rochère, Gillian Lathey and Monika Woźniak, Wayne State University Press, 2016, pp. 143–61.

McDowell, Colin. *Shoes: Fashion and Fantasy.* Thames and Hudson, 1989.

Mullen, Laura. 'Wearing it Out.' *Footnotes: On Shoes.* Edited by Shari Benstock and Suzanne Ferriss, Rutgers University Press, 2001, pp. 282–288.

Oittinen, Riitta. *Translating for Children.* Taylor and Francis, 2000.

O'Sullivan, Emer. 'Children's Literature and Translation.' *The Routledge Handbook of Translation Studies*, edited by Carmen Millán and Francesca Bartrina, Routledge, 2013, pp. 451–63.

—. *Comparative Children's Literature*. Routledge, 2005.

Perrault, Charles. 'Cinderella or the Glass Slipper.' *Beauties, Beasts, and Enchantment: Classic French Fairy Tales*. Translated and edited by Jack Zipes, Crescent Moon, 2009, pp. 25–30.

—. *Histoires, Ou Contes Du Temps Passé, Avec Des Moralitez*. C. Barbin, 1697.

—. *Histories or Tales of Past Times. With Morals*. Translated by Robert Samber, J. Pote and R. Montagu, 1729.

—. *Tales of Passed Times by Mother Goose. With Morals*. Translated by Robert Samber, 6th ed., J. Melvill, 1764.

Semmelhack, Elizabeth. *Heights of Fashion: A History of the Elevated Shoe*. Periscope, 2008.

—. *Shoes: The Meaning of Style*. Reaktion Books, 2017.

Severn, Bill. *If the Shoe Fits: The Lively Story of Shoes and Shoe Making, from Egyptian Sandals to Astronaut Boots*. David McKay, 1964.

Shakespeare, William. *Henry IV: Part I*. Edited by Jonathan Bate and Eric Rasmussen, Random House, 2009.

Shefer, Elaine. 'Mirror/Reflection.' *Encyclopedia of Comparative Iconography: Themes Depicted in Works of Art*, edited by Helene E. Roberts, vol. 2, Fitzroy Dearborn Publishers, 1998, pp. 597–608.

Sutton, Martin James. 'The Sin Complex: A Critical Study of English Versions of the Grimms' *Kinder- Und Hausmärchen* in the Nineteenth Century in Comparison with the German Originals.' PhD Thesis. University of Auckland, New Zealand. 1994.

Venuti, Lawrence. *The Scandals of Translation: Towards an Ethic of Difference*. Routledge, 1998.

—, editor. *The Translation Studies Reader*. Routledge, 2000.

Victoria and Albert Museum. 'A History of Shoes.' *Shoes: Pleasure and Pain,* 2018. https://www.vam.ac.uk/shoestimeline/ Accessed 15 March 2019.

Warner, Marina. *From the Beast to the Blonde: On Fairy Tales and Their Tellers*. Random House, 1994.

—. 'Those Brogues: Marina Warner on Her Parents and Other Travellers.' *London Review of Books*, edited by Mary-Kay Wilmers, vol. 38, no. 19, Oct. 2016, pp. 29–32.

Wittman, Emily. 'Literary Narrative Prose and Translation Studies.' *The Routledge Handbook of Translation Studies*, edited by Carmen Millán and Francesca Bartrina, Routledge, 2013, pp. 438–50.

Zipes, Jack. 'Author Biographies.' *The Great Fairy Tale Tradition: From Straparola and Basile to the Brothers Grimm*, edited by Jack Zipes, W. W. Norton, 2001, pp. 821–42.

—. *Breaking the Magic Spell: Radical Theories of Folk and Fairy Tales: Revised and Expanded Edition*. University Press of Kentucky, 2002.

—. 'Cross–Cultural Connections and the Contamination of the Classical Fairy Tale.' *The Great Fairy Tale Tradition: From Straparola and Basile to the Brothers Grimm*, edited by Jack Zipes, W. W. Norton, 2001, pp. 845–69.

—. *Fairy Tales and the Art of Subversion: The Classical Genre for Children and the Process of Civilization*. Routledge, 1983.

—. *Happily Ever after: Fairy Tales, Children, and the Culture Industry*. Routledge, 1997.

—. *The Enchanted Screen: The Unknown History of Fairy-Tale Films*. Routledge, 2011.

—, editor and translator. *The Great Fairy Tale Tradition: From Straparola and Basile to the Brothers Grimm*. W. W. Norton, 2001.

—, editor. *The Oxford Companion to Fairy Tales: The Western Fairy Tale Tradition from Medieval to Modern*. Oxford University Press, 2000.

—, editor. *Victorian Fairy Tales: The Revolt of the Fairies and Elves*. Routledge, 1987.

CHAPTER SEVEN

'A GRAND CHRISTMAS PANTOMIME': NANCY SPAIN'S *CINDERELLA GOES TO THE MORGUE: AN ENTERTAINMENT*

NICOLA DARWOOD

In the late 1940s a new version of *Cinderella* came to the Theatre Royal in Newchester on the Tame, a theatre in a small provisional town in the north of England. At that time, the Theatre Royal had a well-deserved reputation for producing professional plays by touring companies who used the theatre as part of their pre-London tour. The theatre's programme consisted of plays such as those by Ibsen and J. B. Priestley, and a number of well-known actors had performed at the theatre over the years including Sarah Bernhardt and Henry Irving but, once a year, the theatre was thrown into the world of the pantomime. This particular year's pantomime did not have a stellar cast, although the principal actors were reasonably well known—the part of Prince Charming was to be played by Vivienne Gresham, the young ingénue Betty Byng was excited to be in the role of Cinderella and the DeFreeze brothers were reprising their comedy double act as the Ugly Sisters. With rising anticipation the press and local dignitaries gathered together on Christmas Eve for the preview performance of the latest pantomime to come from the pen of the director (who was also playing the part of Buttons), the well-known Hampton Court whose productions were always lavish, and whose costumes were magnificent despite the ongoing rationing of clothes following the end of the war.

HAMPTON COURT

Presents

A GRAND CHRISTMAS PANTOMIME

THEATRE ROYAL, NEWCHESTER

CINDERELLA

Characters in the Pantomime:

PRINCE CHARMING	*Vivienne Gresham*
DANDINI (his valet)	*Marylyn Franklyn*
BAD BARON DE BROKE OF HARDUP HALL	*Fred Cunningham*
PHOBIA) His two elder	(*Banjo DeFreeze*
MANIA) daughters	(*Harry DeFreeze*
CINDERELLA (his youngest daughter)	*Betty Bynge*
THE FAIRY QUEEN OF STARRY NIGHTS	*Esmerelda Greenaway*
BROKER'S MEN	*Mic and Mac*
THE FAIRY OF THE POWDER PUFF	*HAMPTON COURT*
THE MOUNT CHARLES MALE VOICE CHOIR	*Valenka*
THE ROYALETTES	
THE TWENTY-FOUR TOTTENHAM TOTS	*By courtesy of Mme Cariocola*
SPECIALITY NUMBER	*Banjo and Harry DeFreeze*
Stage Manager, Press Representative	*Tony Gresham*
Wardrobe	*Estelle Furbinger*

Costumes and scenery designed by Tony Gresham and executed by Atkins and Marshall, Newchester, Ltd.

Fig.14-1. Programme for Hampton Court's production of *Cinderella* at the Theatre Royal, Newchester, from Spain, *Cinderella* 7.

It was to be a memorable occasion, sadly though for all the wrong reasons. In the middle of the performance a most unfortunate accident occurred: the centre stage trapdoor had not been closed properly and when Prince Charming (Vivienne Gresham) moved across the stage in the middle of her number 'Searching for love, searching for love', she stepped into the hole where the trap door should be, and fell to her death. Her son, the stage manager and press officer Tony Gresham, was obviously distraught, but Hampton Court's pragmatic business mind quickly turned to the ramifications of a pantomime without a Prince Charming and approached Miriam Birdseye, a revue artist and passionate fan of the pantomime genre who, by chance, was visiting Newchester on the Tame at the time. Miriam agreed to take the part, and played it in subsequent performances with great aplomb, but with little regard for the script, often relying on speeches from Shakespeare to get her through the show. Miriam and her friend, and fellow performer, Natasha DuVivien, one-time member of the Diaghilev Ballet Company and recently divorced, also played a significant role in the ensuing investigation following Vivienne Gresham's death, an investigation which was faithfully recorded by Nancy Spain, a journalist of great repute.

Newchester on the Tame, the Theatre Royal and Hampton Court's production of *Cinderella* are, of course, fictional 'characters' in Nancy Spain's 1950 detective novel *Cinderella goes to the Morgue: An Entertainment*[1] a tale of murders, divorce, a suicide, one potential marriage, questions of paternity and forged clothing coupons. The publisher's synopsis on the first page of the 1950 Thriller Book Club edition[2] of the novel gives an idea of its tone:

> From the start it appears that the pantomime has the 'kiss of death' upon it, what with a drunken ballerina, those amiable little monsters, the Twenty-four Tiny Tottenham Tots and a murdered principal boy. [...] Miss Spain's amalgam of subtle irony, pace and humour is unique among detective story writers. This delightful book puts her among the first practitioners of the art. (1)

This essay explores Nancy Spain's appropriation of the fairy tale of Cinderella and its pantomime form; it traces both the antecedents of pantomime and the growing popularity of *Cinderella* as a pantomime; it considers the comedy that has its roots in the *commedia dell'arte* and French 'night pieces' and discusses how Spain draws on this tradition to recreate the world of pantomime in *Cinderella Goes to the Morgue*.

Author, author!

Before the discussion of the historical foundations of the Cinderella story in its pantomime form, it would be appropriate to consider the role of the author in this story. It is a tradition of theatre that, at the end of a

---

[1] Hereafter referred to as *Cinderella goes to the Morgue* or *Cinderella* in parenthetical references.
[2] Coincidentally, Nancy Spain's novel, *Cinderella Goes to the Morgue: An Entertainment.* (London: Thriller Book Club, 1950) was published in the same year that Disney's version of *Cinderella* was released.

performance, the author can be called to the stage; in the spirit of the topsy-turvy nature of pantomime, however, it seems right to start with the remarkable story of the life of Nancy Spain, a story that would not be out of place on a theatrical stage.

In brief, Spain was a prominent journalist and television presenter in the 1950s and 1960s who died in an airplane accident, together with her partner, Joan Warner Laurie (the editor of *She*), the pilot and two other passengers, on their way from Luton to the Grand National at Aintree Racecourse in 1964.[3] While Cinderella may have gone from riches to rags back to riches, Spain's life was not one which fits the Cinderella motif; educated at Roedean,[4] she also played lacrosse for Northumberland and Durham and hockey for the North of England, and was commissioned as an officer during the Second World War before starting her writing and presenting career in the post-war period. She shocked many with both her dress—a 'trouser-wearing character' (Spain, *A Funny Thing* 61)—and with her sexuality, openly living with Joan Werner Laurie, and was friends with many in the world of literature and theatre, including Marlene Dietrich and Noel Coward.

Writing following Spain's death, Coward said '[i]t is cruel that all that gaiety, intelligence and vitality should be snuffed out when so many bores and horrors are left living' (Coward in Collis, back cover). Her enduring sense of humour is to be seen both in her novels and in her autobiographies, commenting on *Why I'm Not a Millionaire*, Spain's second volume of her autobiography (1957),[5] Noel Coward wrote, 'I found it gay, amusing, occasionally touching and always enjoyable', continuing: 'I may of course be prejudiced in this view because there are so many glowing references to me in it, as you know I am a pushover for glowing references. […] It should and will be an enormous success' (quoted in Spain, *Why I'm Not a Millionaire* 3).[6] Her third volume of her autobiography, *A Funny Thing Happened on the Way* (1964) is described on its inside cover as '[p]astoral-comical, autobiographical, nostalgic-topographical …' (Spain, *A Funny Thing* inside front cover).

---

[3] Aintree Racecourse is in Aintree, Liverpool UK and is home to the Grand National, one of the foremost steeplechases in the British horse racing calendar. A report of the adjourned inquest can be found in the *Birmingham Daily Post* of 24th March 1965 (3).
[4] An independent girls' day and boarding school on the outskirts of Brighton, UK.
[5] Her first volume *Thank You – Nelson* (London: Hutchinson & Co Ltd, 1945) detailed her experiences during the Second World War.
[6] The book is dedicated to Noel Coward.

In her biography of Spain published in 1997, Rose Collis provides a brief portrait of Spain who was, she says:

> a successful amateur sportswoman, cub reporter, radio actress, member of the armed forces, broadcaster, crime novelist, biographer, autobiographer, lecturer, television and radio panellist, book critic, gossip columnist, children's author and illustrator and cookery writer? [...] she was also one of the great communicators of her time, delivering whatever she had to say in an exceptional voice and manner which never sought to patronize or excuse. (xiv)

Spain's literary output was extensive and included: three volumes of autobiography; two biographies including one on Mrs Beeton, Spain's great aunt and referred to in *Why I'm Not a Millionaire* as 'Mrs. Cook Book Beeton' (12); eleven novels; seven children's books and one cookery book. She wrote for newspapers, most notably *The Daily Express* and *The News of the World*, appeared on radio and on television and was a regular panellist on *What's My Line* with Frank Muir. Her detective novels attracted a range of reviews, some more positive than others. For example, Elizabeth Bowen's review of *Poison for Teacher* (1949) in the *Tatler* on 30 November 1949 was full of praise:

> [the novel] is to be recommended, albeit recklessly, to girls'-school fiction addicts. That here, also, we have a detective story of high distinction, I need hardly state: the signature is enough. An either intense or sombre approach to crime is to Miss Spain foreign: in her world an inspired craziness rules. The investigation of the Radcliff School mysteries [...] is as good entertainment as any at which you or I may every hope to assist.[7]
> At the same time, the plot has no weak links : it is flawless enough to satisfy any don or bishop [...] Miss Spain has yet to write a better book than this last one—no doubt she *will*, but meanwhile she leaves one reader perfectly satisfied. Her wit, her zest, her outrageousness, and the colloquial stylishness of her writing are quite her own. (Bowen 448, 449)

---

[7] Spain's use of the name of Radcliff Hall for the location of *Poison for the Teacher* is a reference to Radcliffe Hall, author of *The Well of Loneliness* published in 1928 which was initially banned in the UK, the USA and Canada due to issues around perceived obscenity in relation to its homosexual content. An article in the *Western Morning News* on 10 November 1928 on the case heard in the Bow Street Police Court on 9 November 1928 following the seizure of copies of the novel, reports that 'Mr Fulton, for the prosecution, contended that it was an obscene theme and the book on that should not be published.'

The wit in Spain's fiction, so admired by Elizabeth Bowen, can also be seen in Spain's autobiographies which are both amusing but also often self-deprecating and can be seen particularly in her self-portrait of her younger years which is rather more prosaic than the one penned by Collis. *A Funny Thing Happened on the Way* includes the following, self-penned description of the author:

> 'N. Spain' left school, went to war, wrote a book about it called *Thank You—Nelson*,[8] wrote a detective story called *Poison in Play* and so set herself up as an author in one London bedsitting-room after another. There by mischance out of financial insecurity, a trouser-wearing character named 'Nancy Spain' was born: a character who had as little to do with the N. Spain I knew when young as the old cow has to do with the little heifer. (61)

It took Spain quite a long time to become the 'trouser-wearing character'. Returning to Jesmond in the north east of England following four years at Roedean, she got a job writing brief reports about sports activities for a local paper, quite often reporting on the games in which she was actually participating. This was not quite the life that she had dreamt of—instead she saw herself as an artist or an actress. Her mother was not happy about this and, in an act which might go some way to understanding the development of Spain's character, took her to some of the worst theatrical boarding houses in Newcastle-on-Tyne. In a draft of *A Funny Thing Happened on the Way*, Spain recalls that painful brief episode when her mother took her on:

> a swift and ruthless tour of the theatrical lodging houses in Newcastle-on-Tyne … 'That's what the theatre really means,' she told me, 'grind, grind, grind and terrible food. You'd have to be as strong as an ox. Anyway you look like an ox. You have to look better than you do, and move better than you to go on the stage. If it was your sister I'd understand it. (Spain cited in Collis 30)[9]

---

[8] Her first volume of her biography published in 1945.
[9] Collis has drawn on the draft version of Spain's autobiography, *A Funny Thing Happened on the Way*, which was published posthumously. Spain had completed a final manuscript of the autobiography, collected by her publisher just a few days before Spain's death ('Publisher's Foreword' in Spain, *A Funny Thing Happened on the Way*, 5). However, this anecdote does not appear in 1964 Hutchinson & Co edition.

While Spain may well have drawn on this experience when writing *Cinderella Goes to the Morgue*, her mother's intervention appears to have focused Spain's attention on sport and sports writing, a decision that led, via a posting as a communications officer in the WRENs[10] during the Second World War and writing detective novels, to a lifelong career as a journalist and then as a broadcaster becoming, along the way, the 'trouser-wearing character' known as Nancy Spain. It is difficult, perhaps, to understand why Spain's choice of clothing should have been considered so outrageous in the 1950s; it is possibly best exemplified by an article that appeared in the *Sussex Agricultural Express* on Friday 18 April 1958:

> Miss Nancy Spain came in for some lighthearted criticism from her three male companions on a brains trust panel [with] Gilbert Harding, Godfrey Winn and Alan Melville, at the Corn Exchange, Brighton, on Saturday.
> A full house saw Miss Spain stand on her chair on the platform to show the audience what she looked like in trousers, after hearing her companions describe women wearing trousers as 'appalling' and 'revolting.' [...] Mr. Melville said that in his experience he had found that women wearing trousers were often allied with a certain uncleanliness and scruffiness behind the back of the neck. 'It is a lazy, dirty, ungainly, horrid habit,' he declared. (Anon 'Nancy Spain Shows' 9)

Spain's ability to get invited to the 'right' parties, lunches and dinners gave her the fodder that she needed for her newspaper columns about the theatre, film stars and directors, actors and playwrights, and for her future career as a novelist. She had managed, as Collis puts it, to 'get under the wire' (Collis xiv), making many friends along the way, including Noel Coward, Hermione Gingold, the crime writer, Marjorie Allingham and her husband Philip Youngman Carter (who is believed to have been the father of Spain's son). Another new friend was Elizabeth Bowen, an Anglo-Irish writer and dedicatee of *Cinderella Goes to the Morgue*, whom she met in Ireland during one of Spain's visits to her sister, Liz. Before Spain met her long-term partner, Joan Werner Laurie, she fell in love with a number of women, and Bowen was, for a while, the object of Spain's admiration. While Spain refers to Elizabeth Bowen as 'Miss Bowen' in *Why I'm Not a Millionaire* (113), it is apparent that theirs was a deeper friendship, one based on mutual admiration. In a letter to the Canadian diplomat, Charles Ritchie, written on 7 January 1950, Bowen wrote about a party she had just attended:

---

[10] Women's Royal Naval Service

The party was my new girl-friend Nancy Spain's. I can't think how she
does it—the champagne, I mean. She writes very enjoyable crazy detective
stories. Someone called her Firbank of the detective world. I think I will
send you one or two of them. I know you don't care for that genre as a
rule, but there really is something very attractive about hers. I had a
vacancy for a girl friend, and she just fills it; 'tho she's a great deal
younger than me. She's nice and gay and rattling … (Bowen in Bowen
and Ritchie 152).[11]

However, their relationship floundered when Bowen began to feel that
Spain was developing too strong an attachment. Victoria Glendenning
suggests that Bowen felt that Spain was too intense; commenting that
neither Bowen's husband, Alan Cameron, nor his friend Eric Gillet,[12] liked
the fact that Spain appeared to be constantly at Bowen's house in Clarence
Terrace in London (189). Other friendships did survive, for example the
lasting relationship with the actress Hermione Gingold: a friendship which
led to Gingold's 'appearance' as Miriam Birdseye in *Cinderella Goes to
the Morgue.*

English pantomime, Cinderella and *Cinderella Goes to the Morgue*

Nancy Spain was not the first, or indeed last, to adapt or appropriate the
story of Cinderella which has been retold in books and on stage many
times since its appearance in Perrault's story, *Cendrillon.*[13] However, in
her appropriation and parodic retelling of the tale, Spain takes the notion
of a dramatised Cinderella one step further, drawing specifically on

---

[11] Glendenning's footnote to this letter describes Ronald Firbank as 'a camp
novelist and great stylist.' (Glendenning in Bowen and Ritchie 152)

[12] Eric Gillet and Alan Cameron were lifelong friends, having met at school
(Glendenning 58).

[13] Nor is Spain the only one to adopt the tale of Cinderella in a detective story. See,
for example: *Cinderella* by Ed McBain and Christopher Lee's *The Killing of
Cinderella: a Bath Detective Mystery.* Romance stories based on the Cinderella
plot include: Alex Stuart's Mills and Boon novel, *A Cruise for Cinderella*; a
second Mills and Boon story by Carole Mortimer, *Glass Slippers and Unicorns*;
The Slipper by Jennifer Wilde; *That Cinderella Feeling* by Anne Styles; Susan
Sallis' *The Pumpkin Coach* and Gemma Fox's *The Cinderella Moment.* Other
notable novels based on the Cinderella tale include *A Fugue of Cinderellas* by
Bryan Guinness and Claudia Carroll's *Personally I Blame my Fairy Godmother.*
Copies of the covers of these novels can be found in the Cinderella archive at the
University of Bedfordshire.

pantomime tropes as the background to her detective story.[14] The notion of pantomime, a peculiarly British phenomenon, has its roots in the practices of *commedia dell'arte*, a style of Italian theatre established in the sixteenth century and which, in turn, was descended from Augustan *pantomimus* (Poesio 250). It is a form which has developed over the last three centuries, particularly in the nineteenth century, since its beginnings on the stage of the Theatre Royal in Drury Lane, London (Sutherland 99-102), and, arguably, the theatre's production of *The Tavern Bilkers*[15] written by John Weaver. First performed in 1702, *The Tavern Bilkers* was a 'mimed comedy dance' (Lewis 89) whose central character Harlequin was drawn directly from Arlechhino, the original Harlequin figure so prominent in many nineteenth-century pantomimes (MacQueen Pope 457-458).

However, although Weaver makes a claim for having produced the first pantomime, a lack of records for Weaver's production of *The Tavern Bilkers* makes this difficult to substantiate (Scott 128).[16] Virginia Scott argues that the first performances of productions which could definitely be seen to be pantomimic in nature came some fourteen years later when the first Lun[17] pantomimes were produced by John Rich in Lincoln's Inn Field.[18] During the same season, John Weaver ran two productions which followed Roman notions of pantomime known as saturnalia (Scott 125). Scott further identifies the influences of French 'Night Pieces' and *forain*

---

[14] Such tropes include: cross-dressing principal actors (for example, in a performance of Cinderella, a young female actor would play the role of Prince Charming, and older male actors would play the roles of the step-mother and the Ugly Sisters); the casting of well-known actors in lead roles (in the twenty-first century pantomime roles are usually given to soap stars, reality TV stars and comedians); slapstick humour (including falling through trap doors and food fights); a number of song and dance routines; magic tricks and a chorus consisting of local drama school children.

[15] A cheat – in this instance someone who runs away without paying his bill.

[16] Virginia Scott's essay provides a detailed discussion of the influences of French theatre on English pantomime.

[17] There appears to be some doubt as to the identity of Lun; this may have been a pseudonym of John Rich or, alternatively a French actor, Francisque Moylin (Scott 131).

[18] Theatre owner and friend of Henry Fielding, Jonathan Swift and Alexander Pope. John Rich also produced John Gay's *The Beggar's Opera* (1728), the mock-opera which paved the way for operetta and musical theatre (including Bertolt Brecht's *The Threepenny Opera* in 1928). The friendship between Fielding and Rich did not, however, mean that Fielding approved of the form of pantomime as can be seen in his satirical comments in his play *Pasquin*, first performed in 1737 (Nicholls 1108).

performances in pantomime, such as those found in Evaristo Gheradi's six volumes of *Le Thèâtre Italien* (Paris, 1700) and the nine volumes of LeSage and D'Orneval, *Le Thèâtre de la foire*, published in Amsterdam and Paris between 1723 and 1737 (126). She provides a description of a 'Night Piece' performed around 1702 and originally published in Charles Gildon's book, *A Comparison Between the Two Stages* (also published in 1702) which describes comedic scenes repeated (with some adaptations) in twentieth and twenty-first century pantomimes:

> … what a rout there was with a Night Piece of Harlequin and Scaramouch. With the Guittar and the Bladder! What jumping over Tables and Joint-Stools! What ridiculous Postures and Grimaces! and what an exquisite Trick 'twas to straddle before the Audience, making a thousand damn'd French Faces and seeming in Labour with a Monstrous Birth, at last my counterfeit Male Lady is delivered of her two Puppies Harlequinn and Scaramouch. (Gildon quoted in Scott 129)[19]

By the end of the theatrical season in 1717, the form of pantomime had been established, becoming 'a vehicle for parody' which included dance, mime, comedy, song and dialogue (Scott 131), elements which are easily identifiable in the Spain's fictional production of *Cinderella* in Newchester on the Tame. The pantomime form continued to develop, particularly in the nineteenth century: from a performance centred around the Harlequinade in which Harlequin and Columbine were pursued by Clown and Pantaloon (direct descendants of the characters found in *commedia dell'arte*) to performances in which the centrality of these routines was diminished as writers turned, in the case of the story of Cinderella in particular, to the tales of Perrault (Davis 1-2). The change in focus can be seen in the 1893 production of *Cinderella* at the Lyceum Theatre which received rapturous reviews, including one by William Archer in *The World* on 3rd January 1894 in which he stated that this particular production was the beginning of 'a new epoch in pantomime—an epoch of beauty, refinement, and, if not precisely wit, at least of reason an coherence' (quoted in Richards 387-388).[20] Subsequently, *Cinderella* became the most performed pantomime between 1896 and 1899 and in the

---

[19] Scott quotes from the edition edited by Staring B Wells and published by Princeton in 1942.

[20] William Archer was a renowned theatre critic and is regarded as the person responsible for translating and introducing Ibsen's plays onto the British stage—see, for example, Woodbridge's article written in praise of Archer and published just ten years after Archer's death (207-221).

1900-1901 season. During the 1899-1900 season it shared this honour with *Dick Whittington* and in the 1901-1902 season, playing at fourteen theatres, came second only to *Babes in the Wood* which was performed in fifteen theatres (Richards 27). More recently, during the 2013-2014 'panto' season, *Cinderella* was the second most popular pantomime, with thirty-eight productions during this period; the most popular was *Jack and the Beanstalk* which had thirty-nine different productions. It was more popular than *Aladdin* (thirty), *Snow White* (twenty-four), *Sleeping Beauty* (twenty-two) and *Dick Wittington* (eighteen) (Abbott 43).

While the relative popularity of these pantomimes may have waxed and waned over the decades, they are all ones that were being performed in the three fictional theatres in Newchester on the Tame in the 1940s where:

> [f]or the five winter months of the year the Theatre Royal[21] (in common with the Universe and the Pallindrome [the other two theatres in Newchester]) devoted itself to Pantomime. But whereas at the Universe and the Pallindrome there were, habitually, white-tongued Scots comedians laying in travesties of pantomimes like *Mother Goose* or *Goody Two Shoes* or even, one year, *Little Cock Riding Boots*; at the Theatre Royal the pantomime was always a classic like *Cinderella* or *Dick Whittington* or *Jack and the Beanstalk*. (Spain, *Cinderella* 13)

Pantomime has, since the latter part of the nineteenth century, been part of the British Christmas tradition, with people from all walks of life attending the performances. While in Newchester on the Tame the most important local dignitaries to watch the show are the Lord Mayor, Thomas Atkins, and his wife, Kidder, other theatres have seen more distinguished audience members. Indeed, in the nineteenth century pantomime performances were attended by a number of well-known authors, including Charles Dickens, John Ruskin, Wilkie Collins and Lewis Carroll (Davis 2). Such audiences would suggest an inherent value of the pantomime, whether as a vehicle for satire, or just as a means of entertainment, a view held by W. MacQueen-Pope. In 1957, just seven years after the publication of *Cinderella Goes to the Morgue*, he gave the 'Dr. Mann Juvenile Lecture' (subsequently published in *Journal of the Royal Society of Arts*), in which he extolled the virtues of pantomime in post-war Britain:

---

[21] It is interesting to note that Newchester's theatre shares its name with the Drury Lane theatre, the theatre most associated with the form of pantomime in the nineteenth century.

Pantomime is a thing of great importance. Let nobody, youngster or adult, rate it lightly. It really is important. To begin with it is probably the oldest form of entertainment known. Pantomime is the mid-winter revel of the people—which is always played in mid-winter. It is more than possible that some old chief of pre-historic days, noticing that the spirits of his people were low when the nights were very long and the days very short—when there was little for them to hunt or go to war—decided to hold a great feast and tribal dance around the communal fire, and so pantomime was born. (456)

MacQueen-Pope highlights the connection between twentieth century pantomime and ancient traditions, particularly locating the roots of modern pantomime with the Roman mid-winter feast of Saturnalia, 'a crazy topsy-turvy affair when the world went upside down, when women dressed as men and men as women, when slaves became the masters and masters waited on their slaves' (456).

Cross-Dressing and 'Gag books'

The notion of casting a woman as the principal boy and a man as the dame became the pantomime 'norm' in the second half of the nineteenth century, but it was seen as early as 1731 in a performance of *Dick Whittington* when the Cook was played by a male actor. Nearly ninety years later, Eliza Povey became the first female actor to play the part of the principal boy when she played Jack in *Jack in the Beanstalk* at Drury Lane in 1819 (Richards 29-30), a tradition of cross-dressing that is still seen in pantomime in the twenty-first century. Jennifer Schacker states that '[t]he figure of the Victorian principal boy was eroticized and regarded as potentially scintillating, at least by a good proportion of the audience', continuing 'the principal boy's ambiguous relation to gender categories positions her as an apt embodiment of the ambitions, desires and anxieties' prevalent at the time of individual performance (53-54).[22]

Hampton Court, it could be argued, while possibly aware of the advantages of having an attractive principal boy, does not appear to be aware of the ambiguity of the role when making his (or, rather, Nancy Spain's) casting decisions for the Newchester on the Tame production of *Cinderella* in which the principal boy, Prince Charming, is initially played by Vivienne Gresham and, following Vivienne's murder, by Miriam Birdseye (Spain, *Cinderella* 7). The record of Miriam Birdseye's first

---

[22] The primary focus of Schacker's essay is the Drury Lane 1899 production of *Jack and the Beanstalk*.

performance of Prince Charming suggests that it was a *tour de force* for '[h]er rhyming couplets were so clever, her speeches from Shakespeare were so apt, her voice was beautiful, and her legs so symmetrical, that the audience could do nothing but adore her, and scream its adoration' (Spain, *Cinderella* 115-116). It is a description which can be seen to follow David Pickering's definition of the principal boy, rather than the sexual ambiguity of the late Victorian period:

> The ostensibly male hero of pantomime plots [...] is usually by convention played by an actress. Such actresses are most definitely not male impersonators and retain their femininity in the role, generally wearing flattering costumes showing off their legs—to which they draw enthusiastic attention by giving them an occasional hearty slap [...] (29-30).

However, although Miriam, 'showing off her legs', and Betty Bynge (playing the role of Cinderella) had the titular leads of the Newchester pantomime, the central characters of Hampton Court's production are the Ugly Sisters—Phobia and Mania—played by Harry DeFreeze and, until his untimely death in the middle of the performance, his brother Banjo DeFreeze respectively.[23] The comic duo, known collectively as 'the DeFreeze brothers', are:

> bill-toppers in every music-hall in Great Britain. They had a line of patter and an educated elegance that was unique in England. They closely resembled Fred Astaire. But the impact of their act was doubled because there were two of them. As Ugly Sisters, they merely did a modified version of their music-hall turn, with a lot of silly topical lines thrown in about the residential districts of the particular city they were 'playing'. (Spain *Cinderella* 32)

Their routines, although based on their music hall act, can be seen to have their antecedents in the comedy of the Harlequinade and the 'Night Pieces' of the eighteenth century; these have remained an integral part of twentieth-century pantomime with comedians drawing on stock routines which had been perfected over many years. Some pantomime comedians (such as Henry Marshall) developed their own 'gag books' which provide details of many of these comedy routines. Henry Marshall's 'gag book' from the early 1940s contains approximately 234 different routines and gags, including, for example, a 'magic powder routine', a 'duck pie routine' and the 'Wiffenpuff gag', 'a mythical creature represented by a piece of

---

[23] Spain may be making a parodic reference here to Freudian terminology.

fur on a string which appears and disappears on different parts of the set'
(Abbott 45-47). According to Abbott:

> The mechanism for this is easy to set up with traditional twelve foot
> canvas and wood flats but difficult to translate to the mainly cloth-based
> sets seen in the bigger shows today since pulleys need to be inserted into
> the set. Operation of this routine involves the installation of multiple
> Wiffenpuffs in the form of the creature on a continuous loop of rope on
> many different parts of the set, with several well-rehearsed stage-hands
> needed to pull the ropes in order for the apparent single Wiffenpuff to
> appear to rush from one part of the stage to another (47).

The traditional pantomime relies heavily on such comedy set pieces and
this is particularly so in the case of Hampton Court's production; although
Prince Charming may see herself as the 'star' of the show, Banjo DeFreeze
is in no doubt of the importance of the comedy routines such as those
performed by him and his brother, Harry, and which are devised for a dual
audience comprising of both children and adults. Prior to the murder of
Vivienne Gresham and, of course, before he is found in his own dressing
room 'quite dead' (Spain, *Cinderella* 116), Banjo extols the importance of
his part in the pantomime tradition to Miriam Birdseye. The main point
about pantomime, according to Banjo, is:

> '[…] that you have to keep the theatre full of [sic] fifteen weeks and if you
> don't have them coming back again and again, in a little place like
> Newchester you can't keep the theatre full. Follow me? Now, that's why'
> went on Banjo, gently sliding one large hand along the arm of the stall
> between them, '*that's* why we need funny men in this business. More than
> we do glamour pusses like you. Follow me?' (37)

'Mix[ing] mirth with murder': [24] genetics, reviews and the final curtain

Although Banjo DeFreeze's speech may appear to be rather threatening, it
acts as a counterpart to the ludicrous situations faced by Miriam and
Natasha as they seek to unmask the murder(s). With its satirical humour,
Cinderella Goes to the Morgue has a place within a certain genre of
detective fiction written in the immediate post-war period; comparisons

---

[24] This subtitle is taken from an anonymous article ('For the Armchair Traveller')
reviewing *Cinderella Goes to the Morgue* in the *Western Morning News* on 10
May 1950, 4.

can be made, for example, with the novels of Edmund Crispin, the author of a series of novels which featured Professor Gervase Fen, an unconventional Oxford professor of English Language and Literature whose eccentricities 'were not on the traditional donnish pattern [… which] were suffered more or less gladly by his colleagues, who knew that any treatment of Fen at his face value resulted generally in their own discomfiture' (Crispin 27).[25]

As with Spain's fiction, the humour in Crispin's novels is targeted not just at the police, but at the main protagonist and his affectations, while also highlighting the apparent mundanity of a post-war Britain as seen in the shops of Newchester on the Tame. For example, published just four years before *Cinderella Goes to the Morgue*, Crispin's *The Moving Toyshop* recounts a tale of murder committed in a toyshop which disappears overnight; Gervase Fen determines to solve the mystery and careers around Oxford in his car called 'Lily Christine III'. The dénouement comes in a chapter titled 'The Episode of the Prescient Satirist', and there are frequent asides to the reader together with the occasional footnote, a technique also used by Spain in *Cinderella Goes to the Morgue* where the details of previous murders in which Natasha has been involved are provided in a footnote. The footnote is also an act of self-advertisement as the cases listed are also the titles of Spain's novels (Spain, *Cinderella* 43). The tone of *The Moving Toyshop* is very similar to that found in Spain's novels and is foreshadowed in a note by the author at the beginning of the novel:

> None but the most blindly credulous will imagine the characters and events in this story to be anything but fictitious. It is true that the ancient and noble city of Oxford is, of all the towns of England, the likeliest progenitor of unlikely events and persona. But there are limits. (Crispin 6)

While *Cinderella Goes to the Morgue* can be read in relation to other fiction published around the same time, it can also be seen in the context of her own novels, specifically in terms of her characters. Spain's first detective novel *Poison in Play* (1945) introduced her character Johnny DuVivien, an Australian wrestler; her next novel, *Death Before Wicket* (1946) involved Johnny's wife, Natasha DuVivien, a Russian ex-ballet dancer based, in part, on Spain's sister Liz. Spain's third novel, *Murder,*

---

[25] Edmund Crispin was the pseudonym of Bruce Montgomery, organist and composer, who published nine novels and a number of short stories. *The Moving Toyshop* is dedicated to Philip Larkin.

Bless It (published in 1948), further builds the characters of her two investigators, Natasha and Johnny DuVivien, but there's also a brief mention of Miriam Birdseye, 'an actress' whose character takes shape in later novels, particularly in *Poison for the Teacher* (1949) and *Cinderella Goes to the Morgue*. Collis argues that Spain based Miriam Birdseye on her friend, the actress Hermione Gingold, the eccentric comedy actress who had starred in a string of very successful revue shows. Gingold's attraction for Spain is perhaps easy to understand. Her obituary in the *New York Times* on 25 May 1987 describes her as an:

> irrepressible English-born comedienne [...] a tall, vibrant woman with a mobile face, large, heavy-lidded blue eyes and tousled blond hair. She delighted in television, and one of her funniest moments came on a show when she was asked whether her most recent husband was dead. 'That's a matter of opinion,' she replied.

Theirs was an unlikely friendship as the actress Anne Clements recounts in an interview with Rose Collis for Spain's biography: '[b]eing so avariciously heterosexual herself, Hermione found Nancy's lesbianism hard to fathom, but Hermione's criteria for judging anyone was only by whether they were fun, intelligent and entertaining, and she certainly found Nancy all of these' (Clements quoted in Collis 87).

Entertainment and comedy are, of course, highly subjective. Some reviews of *Cinderella Goes to the Morgue* were very positive, for example the anonymous reviewer in the *Western Morning News* on 10 May 1950 who referred to Spain as 'of a genre all too rare—a thriller-writer who can mix mirth with murder in her books' (Anon 'For the Armchair Traveller' 4), and John Dickie, writing in the *Sheffield Daily Telegraph* stated that:

> 'Cinderella Goes to the Morgue' never has a dull moment, because the casualty rate outpaces the police investigations almost to the end. [...] Miss Spain is completely at ease in the atmosphere of the provincial theatre and her portrait of Hampton Court the vulgar producer, unnerved by any calamity, is a delightful study (4).

However, the novel did not attract universal approval. Sean Fielding, editor and reviewer of *The Tatler* writing on 19 April 1950, for example, referred to the novel as

> [a]n odd sort of thriller—if that truthfully is what Miss Spain intended to write—which suffers abominably from its locale (a provincial theatre) and its characters. Is it, are they, credible? I could not feel so in the very least. On the other hand, those many people to whom anything whiffing of

greasepaint comes as unalloyed joy, will probably be amused and grateful. (Fielding 44)

In this, the reviewer appears to be under a misapprehension: Spain was not attempting to provide a novel in which characters and setting should be considered 'credible'; instead she offers an appropriation of the topsy-turvy world of pantomime and of the Cinderella tale. However, while Spain's novel certainly has its pantomime villains (Hampton Court and Thomas Atkins, Lord Mayor of the City of Newchester, and mastermind behind the distribution of forged clothing coupons through his department store, Atkins and Marshall), very little attention is focused on the action on the stage or to the story of Cinderella. Instead the reader learns of the petty arguments, the jealous rages, and the despotic tendencies of a director. It is the drunken exploits of the DeFreeze brothers and Hampton Court which cause havoc while the minor characters (for example, and rather ironically, Cinderella herself) look on in horror or amazement.

Indeed, Spain has misled us from the very beginning of the novel, as, in fact, Cinderella never actually goes to the morgue. Spain's appropriation of the tale should however be read as part of the tradition of both the form of pantomime, and the pantomime of *Cinderella* in which comic gags— which can trace their roots back, arguably, to the *commedia dell'arte* and French 'Night Pieces', through the development of the pantomime in the nineteenth century, and Henry Marshall's 'gag book' of the 1940s—all culminate in a novel which, while maybe not credible, is definitely, as the full title would suggest, 'an entertainment'.

Works cited

Abbott, C. 'Henry Marshall's gag book: pantomime routines for actors in twentieth century repertory theatre.' *Theatre Notebook*, vol. 69, no. 1, 2015, pp. 40-62.

Anon. 'For the Armchair Traveller'. *Western Morning News*, 10 May 1950, p. 4.

—. 'Nancy Spain Shows What She Looks Like in Slacks.' *Sussex Agricultural Express*, 18 April 1958, p. 9.

Bowen, Elizabeth. 'Dry and Sparkling', *The Tatler and Bystander*, 30 November 1949, pp. 448-449.

Bowen, Elizabeth and Ritchie, Charles. *Love's Civil War: letters and diaries from the love affair of a lifetime,* edited by Victoria Glendenning, Simon & Schuster, 2008.

Carroll, Claudia. *Personally I Blame my Fairy Godmother ... The fairytale ending was just the beginning ...* Avon, 2010.

Collis, Rose. *A Trouser-wearing Character: The Life and Times of Nancy Spain.* Cassell, 1997.

Crispin, Edmund. *The Moving Toyshop.* Penguin Books Ltd, 1946:1960.

Davis, Jim. 'Introduction' in *Victorian Pantomime: A Collection of Critical Essays,* edited by Jim Davis. Palgrave, 2010, pp. 1-18.

Dickie, John. 'How the Muse Defied the Cat.' *Sheffield Daily Telegraph,* 6 April 1950, p. 4.

Fielding, Sean. 'Shorter Notices.' *The Tatler and Bystander,* 19 April 1950, p. 44.

Fox, Gemma. *The Cinderella Moment.* HarperCollins Publishers, 2006.

Glendenning, Victoria. *Elizabeth Bowen: Portrait of a Writer.* Phoenix, 1997.

Guinness, Bryan. *A Fugue of Cinderellas.* Heinemann, 1956.

Lee, Christopher. *The Killing of Cinderella: a Bath Detective Mystery.* Gollancz, 1998.

MacQueen-Pope, Walter. 'The Story of Pantomime.' *Journal of the Royal Society of Arts,* 105:5002 26 April 1957, pp. 456-458.

McBain, Ed. *Cinderella.* Henry Holt & Co, 1986.

Miller Lewis, Elizabeth. 'Hester Santlow's *Harlequine*: Dance, Dress, Status and Gender on the London Stage, 1706-1734.' *The Clothes that Wear Us: Essays on Dressing and Transgressing in Eighteenth Century Culture,* edited by Jessica Munns and Penny Richards. The University of Delaware Press, 1999, pp. 80-101.

Mortimer, Carole. *Glass Slippers and Unicorns.* Mills & Boon, 1986.

Nichols, Charles Washburn. 'Fielding's Satire on Pantomime.' *PMLA,* 46, 4, 1931, pp. 1107-1112, https://www.jstor.org/stable/41366062

Poesio, Giannandrea. 'Theatre practices and meta-narratives: a reading of the illustrated gestures in the Chludov Psalter.' Bizantinistica: Rivista di Studi Bizantini e Slavi. Serie Seconda, Anno XIX, 2018, pp. 250.

Richards, Jeffrey. *The Golden Age of Pantomime: Slapstick, Spectacle and Subversion in Victorian England.* I B Taurus & Co Ltd, 2015.

Sallis, Susan. *The Pumpkin Coach.* Corgi Books, 2004.

Saxon, Wolfgang. 'Hermione Gingold, English actress, dies at 89.' *New York Times.* 25 May 1987. http://www.nytimes.com/1987/05/25/obituaries/hermione-gingold-english-actress-dies-at-89.html Accessed 8 June 2017

Scott, Virginia. 'The Infancy of English Pantomime: 1716-1723.' *Educational Theatre Journal.* 24:2, May 1972, pp. 125-134.

Schacker, Jennifer. 'Slaying Blunderboer: Cross-Dressed Heroes, National Identities, and Wartime Pantomime'. *Marvels & Tales*, 27, 1, 2013, pp. 52-64.

Spain, Nancy. *Poison in Play*. Hutchinson & Co (Publishers) Ltd, 1945.

—. *Death Before Wicket*. Hutchinson & Co (Publishers) Ltd, 1946.

—. *Murder, Bless It*. Hutchinson & Co (Publishers) Ltd, 1948.

—. *Poison for the Teacher*. Hutchinson & Co (Publishers) Ltd, 1949.

—. *Cinderella Goes to the Morgue*. Thriller Book Club, 1950.

—. *Why I'm Not a Millionaire*. Hutchinson & Co (Publishers) Ltd, 1957.

—. *A Funny Thing Happened on the Way*. Hutchinson & Co (Publishers) Ltd, 1964.

Stuart, Alex. *A Cruise for Cinderella*. Mills & Boon, 1956.

Styles, Anne. *That Cinderella Feeling*. Scarlett, 1998.

Sutherland, Lucie. 'Jeffrey Richards, *The Golden Age of Pantomime* (London: I. B. Tauris, 2014), 438pp.' *Nineteenth Century Theatre and Film*, 42, 1, 2015, pp. 99-102.

Woodbridge, Homer. 'William Archer: Prophet of Modern Drama.' *The Sewanee Review*. 44, 2, 1936, pp. 207-221.

Wilde, Jennifer. *The Slipper*. McGraw-Hill, 1987.

CHAPTER EIGHT

REAL PRINCESSES
IN ANNE THACKERAY RITCHIE'S
FIVE OLD FRIENDS
AND FRANCES HODGSON BURNETT'S
A LITTLE PRINCESS

REBECCA MORRIS

As Marina Warner states in *From the Beast to the Blonde,* 'protest and fairy-tale have long associated' (411). This statement is applicable to many Victorian writers who incorporated fairy-tale elements into their narrative. The fairy-tale genre with rags-to-riches storylines, magic and mythical creatures, and good characters being rewarded in contrast to the villains who were punished for their cruel actions, was particularly appealing for writers. In addition to English translations of Charles Perrault and the Grimm Brothers, and original tales by writers including John Ruskin and William Makepeace Thackeray, novelists also utilised aspects of the fairy-tale genre in domestic settings to critique Victorian society. The Cinderella narrative with the long-suffering protagonist being rescued was particularly popular, and realist writers including Charles Dickens and Charlotte Brontë incorporated this plot into their novels featuring oppressed orphan children who discovered they had inherited large fortunes. In her essay *For Whom the Shoe Fits: Cinderella in the Hands of Victorian Writers and Illustrators*, Bonnie Cullen examines the popularity of Perrault's version of Cinderella in Victorian England, stating that it appealed as 'it was the best vehicle for Victorian notions of femininity […] Perrault's Cendrillon is the least active, and he shifts the spotlight to her fairy godmother' (74). Perrault's Cendrillon represented the feminine ideal because she was domesticated, beautiful, submissive, and patiently waited to be rescued by her fairy godmother and handsome prince, in contrast to her predecessors from folk tales, Basile's Zozella, and Madame d'Aulnoy's

Finette.[1] The Grimm Brothers' resourceful Aschenputtel was unable to emulate Perrault's Cendrillon in Victorian England.

Times were beginning to change, and women led several successful campaigns for legislation to protect their rights. Elizabeth Garrett Anderson became the first woman to qualify as a doctor in 1865, and in 1869 Emily Davies established Girton College in Cambridge, the first university college to admit female students. Barbara Bodichon's activism resulted in the creation of four Married Women's Property Acts between 1870 and 1894, and Josephine Butler's dedication to repealing the Contagious Diseases Acts was finally rewarded in 1894.[2] Ongoing campaigns for women's voting rights occurred during the nineteenth century. The first organisation for women's suffrage was formed in Sheffield in 1851 by Abiah Higginbotham and Anne Knight, and a number of other regional societies appeared before Millicent Garrett Fawcett founded the National Union of Women's Suffrage Societies (NUWSS) in 1897.[3] Whilst the Cinderella plot was popular, Victorian authors were influenced by social changes, and incorporated Perrault's tale into their works to critique it. Among these were Anne Isabella Thackeray Ritchie (1837-1919) and Frances Hodgson Burnett (1849-1924).

Anne Isabella Thackeray Ritchie

Anne Isabella Thackeray Ritchie (1837-1919) was the eldest daughter of novelist William Makepeace Thackeray. She had a remarkable literary career beginning with the publication of her first novel *The Story of Elizabeth* in 1863. During her lifetime, she produced a variety of fictional and factual works: other novels included *The Village of the Cliff* (1867) and *Old Kensington* (1873), and she also published biographies of notable female literary figures including Jane Austen and Maria Edgeworth. Her collection of short stories *Five Old Friends* (c.1875) contained retellings

---

[1] Over 30 nineteenth century editions of Perrault's Cinderella are held at the British Library in addition to fairy-tale collections containing the story. In contrast, only seven editions of d'Aulnoy's fairy tales remain and not all of these feature her protagonist Finette (Cullen 60).

[2] See Millicent Fawcett's *Women's Suffrage: A Short History of a Great Movement* (1912) for more examples of women's rights campaigners in the nineteenth century.

[3] See Diane Atkinson's introduction to *Rise Up Women: The Remarkable Lives of the Suffragettes* (2018) for more details about individual female suffrage campaigners and societies in Victorian England.

of five traditional fairy-tales that Ritchie adapted by placing them in a contemporary Victorian setting to comment on societal attitudes towards gender. In her introduction to Ritchie's collection, Heidi Anne Heiner states that 'most of the stories on the surface, represent and uphold prevalent Victorian attitudes' but 'Ritchie's subtle version of feminism can be found throughout' (287). Heiner praises Ritchie's characterisation of the narrator Miss Williamson who delights in happy endings, whilst enjoying her spinsterhood at the same time. In addition, Ritchie scrutinises gender roles through her portrayals of fairy-tale figures, especially the submissive princess who patiently waits to be rescued.

Frances Hodgson Burnett

Frances Hodgson Burnett (1849-1924) is best known for her children's novels *Little Lord Fauntleroy* (1888), *A Little Princess* (1905) and *The Secret Garden* (1911). The protagonists are placed in realistic settings, but the texts include elements of magic. In her biography of Burnett, Anne Thwaite notes that Burnett 'wanted life to be a fairy story. She wanted to make dreams come true' (12). Her sister Edith stated that Frances was 'just like her own Sara Crewe [...] in the end things would come out right for everybody in a fairy-tale sort of way' (38–9). Burnett's story of Sara Crewe started to develop in the 1880s; a novella *Sara Crewe: Or What Happened at Miss Minchin's* was published in 1887 and this was followed by a play entitled *An Un-Fairy Princess* in 1902. Like Ritchie in *Five Old Friends,* Burnett critiqued the role of the fairy-tale princess through her portrayal of Sara Crewe, the oppressed protagonist who loses and regains her fortune. Elisabeth Rose Gruner examines Burnett's allusions to the Cinderella narrative and the plight of French Queen Marie Antoinette in her essay *Roles and Role Models in A Little Princess.* She applauds Burnett's characterisation of Sara stating that she 'offers a model of female development that differs significantly from her predecessors' (178). She also states that Burnett's story 'is hardly a critique [of the original Cinderella tale] as, for example, Anne Isabella Thackeray Ritchie's', arguing that 'rather Burnett's versions function as commentaries and/or supplements to the familiar story' (168). Burnett's tale does not feature all of the characters associated with the Cinderella tale as Ritchie's does, but it can be argued that her Cinderella is more subversive than her predecessor's protagonist because Sara demonstrates more capability at showing initiative, and is partially responsible for engineering her happy ending.

Inspirational Princesses for Ritchie's and Burnett's protagonists

This chapter compares Ritchie's short story *Cinderella* (c.1875) and Burnett's novella *Sara Crewe: Or What Happened at Miss Minchin's* (1887), and considers how they critique societal attitudes to gender, paying attention to their representations of fairy-tale characters. It examines how Ritchie and Burnett question the Cinderella ideal, and contemplates whether they are reflecting upon current models of the role and personality of the princess by examining the texts in relation to contemporary royal figures. In addition, the essay analyses how Ritchie and Burnett challenge fairy-tale stereotypes through portrayals of their equivalents of the fairy-godmother, and wicked stepsisters and stepmothers. It argues that Ritchie and Burnett are calling for the role of the fairy-tale princess to be updated so that girls appreciate the importance of independence.

One princess who possibly inspired both Ritchie and Burnett was Queen Victoria's sixth child Princess Louise, Marchioness of Lorne and Duchess of Argyll. Louise was born in 1848 in a period of political upheaval: the French throne collapsed, and the rise of Chartism and demand for social reform in England caused concern over the Queen's safety. After Louise's birth, Queen Victoria admitted that she thought her daughter would turn out to be '[s]omething peculiar', connecting the birth of Louise and the revolution, and indicating her feelings that her daughter would triumph despite the uncertainty (Longford 7). This sentiment is expressed about Sara in Burnett's novella when she is caught daydreaming by the schoolmistress Miss Minchin. After she reveals her fantasy of becoming a princess, one of the girls remarks 'I shouldn't be at all surprised if she does turn out to be something' (Burnett 241). Like Princess Louise, Sara is expected to eventually triumph despite her vulnerability. Queen Victoria's daughter certainly did live a remarkable life and was very unconventional for a member of the Royal family. Her biographer Lucinda Hawksley states that she was 'a woman ahead of her time' who 'paved the way for the royal family of the twenty-first century' (348). Louise proved to be an accomplished artist and, in 1868, she became the first princess to attend the National Art Training School. She was a supporter of feminist campaigns and corresponded with activist Josephine Butler, and doctor Elizabeth Garrett Anderson. Louise was passionate about providing health and education for young people and opened several new schools and hospital wings. Moreover, she enjoyed engaging with ordinary people, sometimes opting to disguise her royal identity when travelling. Her marriage to the Marquis of Lorne proved to be unsatisfactory, but it was idealised in the newspapers because she was the first princess to marry a non-royal for over two-centuries.[4] For feminist writers of fairy-tales in the Victorian era, Louise represented an ideal princess and role model.

Like many royal children, Louise was named after relatives and was christened Louise Caroline Alberta: Louise being the name of her paternal grandmother and maternal great-aunt, Caroline, to honour Albert's step-grandmother, and Alberta, a feminine version of her father's name. Ritchie drew upon the fairy-tale tradition when naming her protagonist in her version of Cinderella. The name Ella Ashford, is a shortened version of 'Cinderella' and the 'ash' in her surname is an indication of how she is marginalised in the family, implying that she is treated as a servant. This instantly sets up the fairy-tale narrative and it is established to readers with whom they are supposed to empathise. Significantly, Ritchie's naming of her protagonist also alludes to the Grimm Brothers' *Aschenputtel,* which featured a heroine who is considerably more resourceful and proactive than Perrault's Cendrillon. This subtle feminism, recognised by Heiner, is evident as the reader progresses through the text, and they discover that the narrator displays limited sympathy for Ella when she passively waits for her situation to change, instead opting to praise her for her accomplishments. As with royal princesses, Ella is subject to expectation when being named after her famous predecessor, but it is emphasised later in the text that she needs to break from tradition and develop her own individuality.

It is possible that Burnett's protagonist was inspired by Sarah Forbes Bonetta, a West African princess. Originally christened Aina, the princess was captured as a slave at the age of five in Dahomey during the Okeandan war. She was rescued by Royal Navy Captain Frederick Forbes in 1850 who convinced the King of Ghezo to give her to Queen Victoria as a gift.[5] Burnett's Sara Crewe grows up in a foreign setting in India before she is sent to school in England. Her plight after losing her fortune includes similarities to that of Sarah Forbes Bonetta, although less

---

[4] An article in *The Observer* revealed MP Vernon Harcourt's opinion on Princess Louise's marriage—'I do not believe there is any man in England who will regret that the Crown should be guided by a wise policy, and thus have bought itself into a more close and immediate relation with the people of this country' (3).

[5] Sarah's parents were both killed in the war and she was enslaved for three years. Captain Forbes convinced King Ghezo to spare her life informing him that Sarah would be 'a present from the King of the Blacks to the Queen of the Whites'. See Camille Silvy's article 'The African Princess Sarah Forbes Bonetta'.

dangerous because she is not at risk of being killed. The princess and Burnett's protagonist possess similar physical appearances. In a *Morning Post* article entitled 'Presentation of the Dahoman Princess to the Queen', a journalist observes that Sarah's hair 'is short, black and curling, strongly indicative of her African birth' (5). In Burnett's novella, Sara is described as having an 'interesting little face' and 'short black hair' (42). Moreover, in addition to sharing the same Christian name and hair, the girls' surnames also contain naval imagery: Sarah Forbes Bonetta was named after Captain Forbes's ship and Burnett's surname 'Crewe' relates to passengers on a boat. The use of the plural term in Sara's surname is significant because it symbolises how she will continue to remember those more vulnerable than herself when she rediscovers her fortune, and thus become a princess for the people.

Adornment and self-expression as a means of female independence

Ritchie's and Burnett's protagonists contrast physically, but the two authors are similar in their attitudes towards girls wearing lavish clothes and possessing luxuries at a young age. In *Fairy-Tales, Natural History and Culture* (2014), Laurence Talairach-Vielmas argues that 'the role that clothes play in adaptation and rewriting of folktales into literary fairy-tales is revealing of the way in which bourgeois mores and norms redefined the feminine ideal' (99). Mr Ashford and Captain Crewe comply with these bourgeois ideals as they supply their daughters with luxuries. Ella's jewellery box contains several lavish items including pearls with a diamond clasp and a carbuncle brooch which are removed from her room when her father remarries, and his new wife convinces him that Ella has 'had too much put upon her, is a little too decided, too prononcée for one so young' (900). The narrator, Miss Williamson, sympathises with Ella but acknowledges that 'perhaps it was as well after all that early in life she had to learn to be content with very little share of its bounties; she might have been spoilt and over-indulged if things had gone on as they began' (930–2). Similarly, in Burnett's text, Sara's wardrobe is filled with 'clothes so grand and rich that only a very young and inexperienced man would have bought' (Burnett 15). Sara's wealth causes her to be 'indulged a great deal more than was good for her' (28). Ritchie's and Burnett's protagonists' problems begin with indulgent fathers who encourage them to dress like young ladies. In Perrault's tale, readers are encouraged to empathise with Cendrillon's father who is powerless when he remarries, but Ritchie and

Burnett imply that the attitudes of ineffective fathers can be as detrimental to their children as the actions of cruel stepmothers.

Accomplishments are valued more than physical appearance and luxuries in both Ritchie's *Cinderella* and Burnett's *Sara Crewe*, echoing their importance in the lives of both Princess Louise and Sarah Forbes Bonetta who were reported in the print media to be intelligent and talented, with Louise receiving praise for her artistic ability. A journalist in *The Manchester Guardian* commenting on her *Portrait of a Clandestine Lady* opined that it reflected upon 'the ability of Princess Louise, the face being lifelike and expressive' (5). Furthermore, an article in *The London Reader* applauded her talent for needlework and her knowledge of different types of lace—'At a glance she can tell Florentine lace from Venetian, Spanish from Belgian' and can 'name the country it was made from and the possible district from whence it comes' (190). In Ritchie's text, the reader learns that Ella 'could sing charmingly, with a clear, true piping voice like a bird's' and '[h]er dancing was remarkable: she had the most beautiful feet and hands' (Heiner 854). Despite privileged upbringings, Princess Louise and Ella Ashford had limitations placed upon them: Louise was unable to participate in as many causes as she chose to because of her royal status, and Ella is deprived of her luxuries and denied the chance to help her father with his work. For example, Louise expressed enthusiasm and support for the feminist movement in a letter to social reformer Josephine Butler—'I take great interest in the happiness and wellbeing of women, and long to do everything that I can to promote all efforts in that direction' (Longford 24). She promised to assist Butler in her campaign to repeal the Contagious Diseases Acts of the 1860s, but even the most liberally minded members of her family deemed this to be too controversial.[6] The Queen demanded that Louise return Butler's book *Women's Work and Women's Culture* and forbade her daughter from associating with her friend. In addition, Louise's wish to volunteer as a nurse during the Franco-Prussian war in 1870 was denied, but she was determined to help and organised several bazaars and contributed to art exhibitions; the proceeds from her *Portrait of a Clandestine Lady* at the Old Bond Street Gallery in the British Institute were donated to German war widows and children. Despite having to compromise and accept that

---

[6] Louise's youngest brother Leopold gave his opinion on Butler in a letter to her in 1874 stating 'she is by many people considered the most beautiful woman in the world, and she is very clever and a great speaker, but she does herself a great deal of harm by violently taking up a subject which had better be left alone by ladies of any role' (Longford 180).

she could not be involved in campaigns for social justice as much as she would have liked, Louise was still able to have an impact on improving prospects for vulnerable people through her artistic talent.

In Ritchie's *Cinderella,* Miss Williamson expresses the opinion that it is important for young girls to dance because they are unable to express themselves in the way that boys can. Young men 'have a hundred other ways and means of giving vent to their activity', and in contrast 'girls have no such chances; they are condemned to walk through life for the most part quietly' (Heiner 856-8). After her father remarries, Ella is forbidden from dancing in the fields; interestingly, her stepmother also forbids her from doing domestic duties, removing her housekeeping books from her room, insisting 'I think Ella will not be sorry to be relieved of her cares' (858). However, the reader is aware that Ella enjoys helping her father in the house, so her stepmother has not only deprived her of her luxuries but also her pleasures and independence, which are 'treasures far dearer to her than the pretty coral necklace and the gold clasp bracelet' (910). Unlike her contemporary Princess Louise, Ella is unable to compensate for her losses. She grows up 'taller, and prettier and sadder every year' (920). Ella's development into a pretty but unhappy young girl emphasises to readers that being conventionally attractive does not guarantee happiness. Instead, Ritchie stresses that pursuing interests and learning to be independent will result in girls feeling more fulfilled.

Burnett's protagonist not only physically resembles Sarah Forbes Bonetta, but also shares her intellectual ability. Writing in his journal, Captain Forbes described her as 'a perfect genius', revealing that she 'speaks English well and has a great talent for music' and is 'far in advance of any white child of her age in aptness of learning, and strength of mind and affection' (Silvy). Queen Victoria also admired Sarah's academic ability, commenting in her journal that she was 'really an intelligent little thing' (Victoria 14). In *Sara Crewe,* Miss Minchin informs Sara that she might be able to teach the younger pupils when she is older as a way of payment for her allowing her to stay at the school, grudgingly admitting 'you are a sharp child, and you pick up things almost without being taught. You speak French very well, and in a year or so you can begin to help with the younger pupils' (Burnett 61). Whilst working as a servant, Sara does not have the same educational opportunities as the other girls, but she displays determination when studying 'at all sorts of untimely hours from tattered and discarded books' (132). She is resentful towards her fellow pupils who are unenthusiastic about their work and envious of girls who own books they never read. Being deprived of books impacts on her wellbeing: 'If she had always had something to read, she would not have been so lonely. She liked romances and history and poetry; she would read anything' (134). The range of literature Sara is prepared to read reveals the depth of her character and is indicative of her ability to engage with people from different cultures and backgrounds. Like Ella in Ritchie's *Cinderella,* Sara expresses little concern for losing her luxuries, but is frustrated when she is thwarted in her attempts to pursue her interests. The two girls are in contrasting situations with Ella being in a middle-class family and Sara a pauper without a penny to her name, but Ritchie and Burnett demonstrate that girls could potentially feel empowered even in the most trying situations if they had something to stimulate them.

Sara does have an advantage over Ella because she is able to find a method of dealing with her suppression by using her imagination which 'helped her to make everything rather like a story' (165). One of Sara's favourite pretend games is to imagine that she is 'a princess in rags and tatters' and she is proud of her ability to maintain her role as a princess because '[i]t would be easy to be a princess if I were dressed in cloth-of-gold; It is a great deal more of a triumph to be one all the time when no one knows it' (221). She is inspired by French Queen Marie Antoinette who, whilst in prison, 'had only a black gown on, and her hair was white […] she was a great deal more like a queen then than when she was gay and had everything grand' (223–5). Marie Antoinette seems a strange choice of role model for Sara because her lavish spending caused her to be an unpopular queen and she was eventually executed during the French Revolution. However, despite her unpopularity, Marie Antoinette performed many charitable acts throughout her reign (the phrase 'let them eat cake' has inaccurately been attributed to her).[7] Marie Antoinette's biographer Antonia Fraser shows how the Queen expressed empathy towards the poor on many occasions. In a letter to her mother, she argued that it was her duty to help others: 'It is quite certain […] that in seeing the people who treat us so well despite our misfortune, we are more obliged than ever to work hard for their happiness' (160). In Burnett's novel, Sara imitates Marie Antoinette's desire to help the poor in times of difficulty and prosperity. While on an errand, she discovers a fourpence on the ground and is excited to discover a bakery nearby, but after seeing a beggar child,

---

[7] The phrase 'let them eat cake' was used a century before by the Spanish Princess Marie Thérèse and had been used by a number of princesses since but not Marie Antoinette. Fraser remarks that this Queen would 'have been far more likely to bestow her own cake (or *brioche*) impulsively upon the starving people before her' (xviii).

she keeps only one bun for herself despite being hungry, deciding '[i]f I'm a princess—! When they were poor and driven from their thrones—they always shared—with the Populace—if they met one poorer and hungrier' (278–80). Burnett's Cinderella figure is downtrodden but she is able to triumph; her rags empower her because they confirm that there is more to being a princess than wearing lavish clothes, and she imagines that she is performing her royal duties despite being in a vulnerable position. Sara's attitude is possibly inspired by that of Princess Louise. A journalist in *The Leeds Mercury* reported that 'there was no more sweet and intellectual a face than that of the young princess. Her duties were long and must have been fatiguing but they were done gracefully and well'. ('The Princess Louise') Sara resolves that '[a] princess must be polite' (Burnett 219). She refuses to respond to insults because:

> there is nothing so good for them as not to say a word—just look at them and think. Miss Minchin turns pale with rage when I do it. Miss Amelia looks frightened, so do the girls. They know you are stronger than they are because you are strong enough to hold in your rage and they are not. (106)

Here, Burnett is indicating that princesses need to have resilience as part of their responsibility towards their people; identifying with Perrault's passive Cendrillon would be unproductive for Sara and other girls who are in difficult situations. In her novella, Burnett implies that future Cinderellas should be modelled on real inspirational women instead of helpless victims who lack ambition and wait to be rescued by a prince or fairy godmother figure.

Stepmothers and ugly sisters: women who uphold oppression

Whilst championing independent women, the two authors also acknowledge that many Victorian women are responsible for upholding oppression. Despite social changes and campaigns for suffrage, prominent women in society were opposed to women's rights including Queen Victoria herself. In 1870, she wrote to Prince Albert's biographer Theodore Martin revealing that she was 'most anxious to enlist everyone who can speak or write to join in checking this mad wicked folly of 'Women's Rights' […] God created men and women different—then let them remain each in their own position' (Marlow 17). Female characters in Ritchie's and Burnett's texts reflect upon Queen Victoria's views regarding unconventional women. Cecilia Lulworth is manipulated by Mrs Ashford and convinced that Ella 'has a difficult temper' and is 'a great anxiety to Mrs Ashford' (Heiner 770–5). The maid Carter accuses Ella of being a spy when she offers to assist her in tidying up the clothes. Cecilia's and Carter's perceptions of Ella demonstrate that Cinderella figures are not necessarily considered to be victims. Here Ritchie exposes the hypocrisy of a Victorian society which appeared sympathetic towards the tormented Cinderella in Perrault's tale but constantly denied women the same opportunities as men. Thus, Ella serves as a metaphor for how actual Cinderellas are treated in reality.

Sara differs from Ella because she is considered favourably by Miss Minchin at the beginning of the novella. The Headmistress regards Captain Crewe's wealth as an opportunity to raise her reputation. When on school walks, she makes sure that Sara is 'always decked out in her grandest clothes' and 'when the parents of any of the pupils came, she was always dressed and called into the parlour with her doll' (Burnett 28–30). After the loss of her fortune, Sara's fellow pupils 'began to look upon her as a being of another world' because they are 'dull, matter-of-fact young people, accustomed to being rich and comfortable' (87). The pupils at Miss Minchin's Seminary associate loss of luxury with a change in personality, and are incapable of realising that Sara is still a little girl like them. Like Ritchie, Burnett outlines societal hypocrisy through Miss Minchin's sycophancy and the schoolgirls' prejudices against Sara. By commenting upon class, Burnett goes considerably further than her contemporary because her Cinderella figure is poor and destitute in contrast to the oppressed Ella who comes from a comfortable home. Sara's fellow pupils are complicit in her torment despite being confronted with a Cinderella figure. The attitudes of Burnett's characters stress to readers that sympathising with oppressed princesses in fairy-tales is meaningless if society fails to learn about the importance of protecting vulnerable people.

Through their portrayals of Ella and Sara, Ritchie and Burnett demonstrate that a Cinderella figure can have more aspects to her character. They criticise bourgeois ideals about femininity and value talent and personality over lavish clothes and physical appearance. The attitudes of other characters towards the oppressed girls expose how society in unsympathetic towards oppressed women, and Burnett emphasises the lack of empathy towards the poor. In addition to critiquing the princess figure, the two authors also comment upon gender issues through characterisation of other key female roles in the Cinderella narrative: the wicked stepmother, jealous sisters, and the fairy-godmother.

Heidi Anne Heiner argues that 'Ritchie's character development makes all of her characters, even the supposed villains, sympathetic on some level' (Heiner 285–7). When depicting Lydia Ashford and her daughters, Lisette and Julia, Ritchie does not imply that they are physically unattractive. The narrator Miss Williamson comments that Lydia 'really was a beautiful young woman, and would have looked quite charming if she had left herself alone for a single moment, but she was always posing' (788–9). Julia and Lisette become 'tall fashionable bouncing young ladies; they pierced their ears, turned up their pigtails, and dressed very elegantly', which suggests that they are conscious of their appearances (918). However, all three women are preoccupied with their looks because they are hoping to impress: Lydia's posing indicates that she is trying to mould herself into something she is not, and her two daughters adopting the same style suggests that they are lacking in individuality. Ritchie has defied the fairy-tale stereotype of the 'ugly' villains, instead demonstrating that women's preoccupations with being attractive and following the latest fashions causes them to become competitive and resentful towards each other. Like Ella's father, Lydia, Lisette and Julia conform to bourgeois mores regarding femininity, and are thus complicit in upholding patriarchal ideals in society.

In *Sara Crewe,* Burnett does not suggest that Miss Minchin is beautiful, but there is no suggestion that her behaviour is linked to insecurities about her physical appearance. She is described as having 'cold, fishy eyes, and large cold hands, which seemed fishy too, because they were damp and made chills run down Sara's back when they touched her' (Burnett 26). Miss Minchin's coldness foreshadows her cruel treatment of Sara after her father dies and she loses her fortune. Miss Minchin does not aim to make herself physically attractive like Mrs Ashford, but she is concerned about attracting more affluent pupils to her school, and hopes Sara's wealth will help her, eagerly informing other parents that 'her father was a distinguished Indian officer, and she would be heiress to a great fortune' (30–2). As discussed previously, she even has to acknowledge that Sara could prove useful to her even after she loses her fortune because of her academic ability and resists the temptation to dismiss her from the school, with the intention of employing her as an unpaid teacher when she is older. Thus, Miss Minchin is not motivated by jealousy towards Sara, but by her ambition to enhance her school's reputation which causes her to display ruthlessness and lack compassion.

Ritchie and Burnett both give the reader insight into explanations for their wicked stepmother figures' behaviour towards Ella and Sara, although they make it clear that their cruelty cannot be excused. After Ella is deprived of her luxuries and forbidden from helping her father, Miss Williamson states that '[t]he only excuse for Mrs Ashford was that she was very much in love with her husband, and so selfishly attached to him that she begrudged the very care and devotion which little Ella had spent upon her father all these years past' (Heiner 910–2). This relates to Heiner's argument because Ritchie is humanising Mrs Ashford by suggesting that she is capable of love, but it has become problematic because it has caused her to be jealous of Ella and deny her the same opportunities as Lisette and Julia, without appreciating that her husband has happily welcomed her two daughters into the family. In Burnett's text, it is even more difficult for the reader to sympathise with Miss Minchin's change in attitude towards Sara. Instead of displaying empathy towards Sara after learning of Captain Crewe's death, Miss Minchin is merely concerned with her own predicament: 'To be suddenly deprived of a large sum of money yearly, and to find herself with a little beggar on her hands, was more than she could bear with any degree of calmness' (Burnett 57–9). In contrast, Sara's grief is not caused by her loss of money but by the death of the father she loved. Ritchie's wicked stepmother figure does at least have some redeeming qualities in the sense that she genuinely loves her husband and daughters, but Burnett's Miss Minchin is reprehensible and hardened by her ambition. Both authors are condemnatory of their wicked stepmother figures, but they utilise them to question societal ideals about gender. Through Lydia Ashford, Ritchie stresses that female preoccupation with male approval has the potential to cause damage, and Burnett's portrayal of Miss Minchin shows that a woman's obsession with retaining a good reputation results in her lacking empathy. Thus, Ritchie and Burnett defy fairy-tale stereotypes through representation of their villains because they show that their motives for their behaviour are more complicated than being jealous of the Cinderella character's beauty.

When scrutinising letters of the British royal family, it could be argued that Princess Louise probably felt like a Cinderella in her own home. Queen Victoria described her as 'very naughty and backward' in a letter to her eldest daughter Victoria, Crown Princess of Prussia (Hibbert 94). After her sister Helena's marriage in 1866, Louise became her mother's secretary. Queen Victoria proved to be a demanding employer, and Louise regularly had to miss her art lessons because she was needed at home. In addition, she was constantly prevented from attending social engagements. In a letter in February 1868, her brother Alfred remarked upon '[h]ow much Lenchen [Princess Helena] seems to have been visiting about' and stated that he wished Louise 'could have some amusement of that sort' (Longford 102). After Albert's death, the Queen appeared to favour her youngest daughter Beatrice, who was able to misbehave without being punished, and was even allowed to have a dance to celebrate her eleventh birthday, despite the other siblings having to abstain from birthday celebrations during the Queen's mourning (Hawksley 55, 99). It would be inappropriate to categorise the royal family into fairy-tale roles as Louise was able to maintain strong relationships with her mother and sisters despite Queen Victoria's fastidiousness. However, it is apparent that Ella Ashford and Sara Crewe can relate to some of Louise's youthful experiences: Ella in the sense that she has a difficult relationship with her stepmother and is denied opportunities to attend balls, and Sara because Miss Minchin's demands prevent her from studying as much as she would like.

Suffrage and the role of the fairy godmother

Ritchie became acquainted with Princess Louise when they were both holidaying in France in the 1880s. Louise chose her to be her companion and informed Ritchie that she regularly opted to travel incognito. Ritchie remembered one occasion when they went to visit an old lady at a farmhouse, and Louise offered to stir the potato soup so the lady could continue with other tasks. Ritchie's biographer Henrietta Garnett describes the incident as 'a scene so much like a fictitious episode that Anny might have written herself'. Ritchie stated in a letter that she was reminded of 'a fairy-tale, a real cottage, and a real Princess stirring potatoes and *me* looking on' (Garnett 252). In addition to assisting people with domestic chores, Louise was also unafraid to nurse the sick, being devoted to her younger brother Leopold, who suffered from haemophilia. When residing in Canada with her husband, an outbreak of scarlet fever occurred at Rideau Hall and Louise nursed the patients back to health. Throughout her life, Louise worked to improve school and hospital facilities for children. In 1882, she opened a new wing at the Victoria Hospital for Children, and she paid regular visits to Ragged Schools. Writers in *The Ragged School Union Quarterly* applauded Louise for her attitude. One claimed '[m]any of the children were assembled in the gymnasium, Her Royal Highness having expressed a wish to see them' (91). Another stated that Louise was 'most kind and gracious in her demeanour, shaking hands with those who had been foremost in providing and arranging the exhibits' (113). All these instances show that Princess Louise regularly took on the role of a fairy godmother and was possibly an inspirational figure for writers who created independent Cinderella figures.

In Ritchie's tale, Ella struggles to find coping mechanisms to compensate for her stepmother's oppression, her only hope seems to be to repress her desires to attend social events to encourage Mrs Ashford to change her mind: 'she smiled through her tears, and thought to herself, that since her temper was so bad, she had better begin to rule it that very instant' (Heiner 959). This tactic is only successful to a certain extent though: Ella is permitted to accompany her sisters to their rich cousin Lady Jane Peppercorne's house, but she is still forbidden from attending any balls, and like Perrault's Cendrillon, is driven to tears when Lisette and Julia leave for the Crystal Palace. A fairy godmother figure arrives in the form of Lady Jane Peppercorne. The reader learns that she 'was very rich, had never married and was consequently far more sentimental than ladies of her standing usually are', which suggests that she will take pity on Ella (936–8). However, her reaction to Ella's tears contrasts significantly to that of the fairy godmother in Perrault's tale. She exclaims 'don't you know it is very naughty to cry no matter how bad things are?' (1007). Here, Ritchie undermines the fairy-tale narrative, and also subtly comments upon societal attitudes towards unmarried women because it is evident that Lady Jane does not display much sentimentality towards Ella. After assuring her that she will make arrangements for her to go to the ball and provide appropriate clothing, Lady Jane requests that Ella helps her unpack the hamper. She is impressed with Ella's ability to arrange the flowers: 'Why, you would be a first-rate girl, if you didn't cry' (1034). Interestingly, Lady Jane reluctantly provides a pumpkin after Mrs Ashford's insistence: 'I had it forced, my dear. Your stepmother tells me she is passionately fond of pumpkins' (1037). The unseasonal pumpkin highlights to readers they cannot necessarily rely upon fairy-tale endings. Ritchie's resourceful fairy godmother figure Lady Jane encourages girls to use initiative and help themselves and resist imitating Perrault's Cendrillon.

In *Sara Crewe,* there is no clearly defined fairy godmother figure. Sara confides in her doll Emily, who she believes is 'a kind of good witch and could protect her' (Burnett 100). However, she eventually has to concede that Emily is an inanimate object who 'can't help being a doll […] any more than those girls downstairs can help not having any sense' (128-30). Sara's equivalent of being able to go to a ball is being able to have access to books, and she despises the girls at the Seminary who take their education for granted. In his work *Disciplining Girls: Understanding the Origins of the Classic Orphan Girl Story,* Joe Sutcliff Sanders states that '[t]hrough stories, Sara exercises a great deal of control over most of the characters' (82). It is certainly true that other pupils are fascinated by her storytelling ability. When teaching Ermengarde St John about French history, Sara is able to make 'the travellers and historical people seem real', and the narrator suggests that Ermengarde has learned more than she would have done if she had been taught in class (Burnett 167). This reflects Sanders's point that Burnett's protagonist has demonstrated an equivalent of magical ability because she starts to transform Ermengarde into a more knowledgeable student, as the fairy godmother transforms Cinderella for the ball. However, Ermengarde also arrives in the form of a fairy godmother herself because she enables Sara to have access to books, so the stories do considerably more than teach because they bring the girls together. Sara also initiates the arrival of another fairy godmother figure who appears in the form of Mrs Brown, the lady at the bakery. After witnessing Sara donate her buns to the beggar child Anne, Mrs Brown takes an interest in both children. When Sara returns to the bakery after rediscovering her fortune, she discovers Anne working there. Mrs Brown explains that she 'told her to come here when she was hungry, and when she'd come, I'd give her odd jobs to do, an' I found she was willing, an' somehow I got to like her, an' the end of it was I've given her a place an' a home' (635–7). Burnett has once again gone further than Ritchie because she shows that women and girls can make a difference even if they lack affluence. She was possibly inspired by female suffrage movements in the nineteenth century, particularly the work of Millicent Garrett Fawcett. In 1866, Fawcett produced and collected the signatures for the first petition for women's suffrage when she was just 19 years old and too young to sign, and spoke at the first pro-suffrage meeting in London in 1869. She co-founded Newnham College in 1871, which was the second college to admit women at Cambridge University. Restricted in influencing political decisions, but dedicated to improving prospects for women, Fawcett was an inspirational figure. Her objective for women to obtain equal suffrage rights was not achieved until 1928, but she was able to have a remarkable impact on women's lives. Burnett's characters are more influential locally rather than nationally, but it can be argued that they create a culture of sisterhood like Fawcett because they are able to benefit from helping one another, despite being restricted in what they can do.

The idea of a handsome prince rescuing a princess is played down in both Ritchie's *Cinderella* and Burnett's *Sara Crewe*. In contrast to Perrault's prince who meets Cendrillon at the ball, Ritchie's Charles Richardson encounters Ella twice beforehand. Firstly, he witnesses her dancing in the field. He informs her that her 'dancing puts me in the mind of a fairy I once saw in a field at Cliffe long ago [...] She was very like you. I do believe it was you' (Heiner 1280–2). However, he also sees her at Lady Jane's house before she is dressed for the ball, but Ella never reveals this to him because she has to leave with her chaperone. Like Perrault's Cendrillon, Ella is transformed when she leaves the ball. She tears her tunic and her dress unravels: 'nobody would have recognised the beautiful triumphal princess of half an hour ago' (1315). Instead of going home without her shoe though, Ella loses only the diamond buckle, and there is no mystery about the owner because Mr Richardson knows she is staying with Lady Jane Peppercorne. By removing the shoe-fitting test, Ritchie stresses that women cannot be expected to conform to unrealistic expectations about femininity. Moreover, through Mr Richardson's memory of seeing Ella dancing alone and not remembering her as a sorrowful Cinderella figure, Ritchie demonstrates the superiority of independence to submissiveness.

In Burnett's novella, it is Sara's ability to play pretend games and take an interest in other cultures that helps her to rediscover her fortune. Sara is fascinated when she discovers the gentleman next door has an Indian servant who is impressed when she addresses him in Hindustani.[8] After sacrificing her buns to feed Anne, Sara returns to the Seminary to discover that her attic has been transformed: the room is full of luxuries and she has a banquet of food to feast on. It is the Indian servant who initiates the union between Sara and her guardian. When Sara returns the servant's monkey, the master in the house requests to see her when he hears them conversing in Hindustani. After questioning her, the gentleman has no doubt that Sara is his friend Captain Crewe's daughter. Upon rediscovering her fortune, Sara is determined to continue to help the poor: 'I know what it is to be hungry, and it is very hard when one can't even pretend it away' (Burnett 612). She promises to share her money with Mrs Brown to help her to feed hungry children. In addition, she gives the once homeless child Anne an opportunity to act as a fairy godmother by requesting that she distributes the bread. Once again, Burnett's Cinderella has proved to be an influential figure in her community by displaying compassion, emphasising the importance of open-mindedness, and encouraging others to help those who are less fortunate.

It is evident from analysing these texts that Ritchie and Burnett have drawn upon a variety of contemporary influential women to scrutinise the Cinderella ideal. Ritchie's narrative is more conventional as it follows the Cinderella plot in a domestic setting, and Ella is often portrayed as being submissive and helpless. However, she is also talented and has a key role model and ally in Lady Jane Peppercorne. Sara Crewe is more assertive in that she focusses on what she can do to improve her wellbeing and help others. In addition, Burnett's text is more radical because she gives

---

[8] The Indian servant Ram Dass and Sara's guardian Mr Carrisford from the 1905 novel were unnamed in the 1887 novella.

outsiders influential roles including the working-classes and people from other cultures. Ritchie's *Cinderella* and Burnett's *Sara Crewe* both emphasise that the submissive Cinderella figure is an unrealistic aspiration for women and girls.

Works cited

Anon. 'An Industrial Show and Royalty.' *The Ragged School Union Quarterly,* July 1885, p. 113. *ProQuest,* https://search.proquest.com/docview/3886077 Accessed 12 June 2018.

—. 'Mr Vernon Harcourt on the Marriage of the Princess Louise.' *The Observer.* 16 Oct. 1870, p. 3. *ProQuest Historical Newspapers: The Guardian and the Observer,* https://search.proquest.com/docview/475192373 Accessed 16 Oct. 2018.

—. 'Presentation of the Dahoman Princess to the Queen.' *Morning Post,* 16 Nov. 1850, p. 5. *British Library Newspapers,* https://search.proquest.com/docview/3886077. Accessed 4 June 2018.

—. 'The Princess Louise.' *The Leeds Mercury,* 29 Dec. 1870, p. 1. *British Library Newspapers Part 1 1800-1900.* Gale Document Number: BB3201654055. Accessed 12 June 2018.

—. 'The Princess Louise as a Needlewoman.' *The London Reader of Literature, Science, Art and General Information,* 25 Dec. 1875, p. 190. *ProQuest,* https://search.proquest.com/docview/8226090. Accessed 12 June 2018.

—. 'The Princess Louise at Deptford.' *The Ragged School Union Quarterly,* April 1886, p. 91. *ProQuest,* https://search.proquest.com/docview/4051513. Accessed 12 June 2018.

Atkinson, Diane. *Rise Up Women! The Remarkable Lives of the Suffragettes.* Bloomsbury, 2018.

Burnett, Frances Hodgson. *Sara Crewe: or, What Happened in Miss Minchin's Boarding School.* 1887. Kindle Edition, Amazon Media, 2012.

Captivating History. *Marie Antoinette: A Captivating Guide to the Last Queen of France Before and During the French Revolution Including Her Relationship with King Louis XVI.* Kindle Edition, Amazon Media, 2018.

Cullen, Bonnie. 'For Whom the Shoe Fits: Cinderella in the Hands of Victorian Writers and Illustrators.' *The Lion and the Unicorn,* vol. 27, no.1, 2003, pp. 57-82. *Project Muse,* https://muse.jhu.edu/article/39421. Accessed 31 May 2018.

Fawcett, Millicent Garrett. *Women's Suffrage: A Short History of A Great Movement.* 1912. Kindle Edition, Endeavour Media, 2018.

Fraser, Antonia. *Marie Antoinette: The Journey.* Weidenfeld and Nicolson, 2001.

Garnett, Henrietta. *Anny: A Life of Anne Thackeray Ritchie.* Chatto and Windus, 2004.

Gruner, Elisabeth Rose. 'Cinderella, Marie Antoinette and Sara: Roles and Role Models in *A Little Princess.*' *The Lion and the Unicorn,* vol. 22, no. 2, 1998, pp. 163-80. *Project Muse,* https://muse.jhu.edu/article/35395. Accessed 1 June 2018.

Hawksley, Lucinda. *The Mystery of Princess Louise: Queen Victoria's Rebellious Daughter.* Vintage, 2013.

Heiner, Heidi Anne, editor. *The Fairy Tale Fiction of Anne Isabella Thackeray Ritchie.* Kindle Edition, SurLaLune Press, 2010.

Hibbert, Christopher, editor. *Queen Victoria in Her Letters and Journals.* Sutton Publishing, 1984.

Longford, Elizabeth, editor. *Darling Loosy: Letters to Princess Louise 1856-1939.* Weidenfeld and Nicholson, 1991.

Marlow, Joyce, editor. *Votes For Women: The Virago Book of Suffragettes.* Virago, 2008.

Sanders, Joe Sutcliff. *Disciplining Girls: Understanding the Origins of the Classic Orphan Girl Story.* Johns Hopkins University Press, 2011.

Silvy, Camille. 'The African Princess: Sarah Forbes Bonetta.' *Black History Month UK,* 25 Aug. 2015. http://www.blackhistorymonth.org.uk/article/section/real-stories/the-african-princess-sarah-forbes-bonetta/. Accessed 7 June 2018.

Talairach-Vielmas, Laurence. *Fairy Tales, Natural History and Victorian Culture.* Palgrave Macmillan, 2014.

Thwaite, Ann. *Frances Hodgson Burnett: Beyond the Secret Garden.* The History Press, 2007.

Victoria, Queen. '11 January 1851.' *Queen Victoria's Journals,* Vol 31 http://www.queenvictoriasjournals.org/home.do Accessed 7 June 2018.

Warner, Marina. *From the Beast to the Blonde: On Fairy Tales and Their Tellers.* Vintage, 1995.

CHAPTER NINE

REPRESENTATIONS OF CINDERELLA AS MYTH AND FOLKLORE IN SPANISH VERSIONS OF THE TALE

MAIA FERNÁNDEZ-LAMARQUE

This chapter analyses the versions, adaptations and parodies of Cinderella and how they reflect the changing roles and experiences of women in Spain. I explore how the various retellings of womanhood in the tale reflect societal and political changes in the country, and analyse how the character of Cinderella, or *Cenicienta*, as she is called in Spanish, is mimetic of historical and social transformations as the tale has been nurtured by the cultural Zeitgeist. For example, the Spanish *La Movida* counter-cultural movement challenged the taboos imposed by Francisco Franco's regime following the dictator's death in 1975. The movement coincided with economic growth in the country and the formation of a new identity for women. As a consequence, the retellings of Cinderella moved from a conservative representation of femininity in the fifties to an alternative representation of Cinderella as a lesbian, feminist and counter-culture agent in the twentieth-first century.

There have been few studies of fairy tales in Spain and their origin has not been clearly defined. Jack Zipes' review of international fairy tales concludes that fairy tales in Spain in the eleventh and seventeenth centuries were a heterogeneous collection of texts composed of translations of Arabic texts, chivalric novels that make some allusions to the fairy tale genre, Sephardi Jewish writings and some of Lope de Vega's work (578). No version of Cinderella was recorded in all these works mentioned, and gender studies and Feminist scholars have pointed out this lack. In 2004, for instance, Patricia Anne Ober de Baubeta states in 'The Fairy-Tale Intertext' that, at that time, there were only a very few studies that intersect the topic of fairy tale intertextuality and feminism in 'Latin American or Iberian women's writing' (129). A few scholars, such as

Carolina Fernández-Rodríguez, have also studied global Cinderella versions from a feminist approach (1997); most recently in 2017, I discussed elsewhere the intertextuality with Pedro Almodóvar's *Hable con ella* (2003) and *Sleeping Beauty* in the context of comparative cultural studies and cinema from a feminist perspective. There is much to be gained from exploring this overlooked area of research and of the cultural history of Cinderella in Spain in particular.

The first adaptation encountered in Spain is in A. R. Almodóvar's compilation of stories, *Cuentos al amor de la lumbre* (1983) entitled 'Estrellita de oro'. The story, by an anonymous author, probably dates from the Middle Ages where the Jewish, Muslim and Christian cultures were in constant contact in Spain. In the story María receives a star branded on her forehead from the fairy godmother. A Muslim version also has a brand on the forehead (Mills 1982) reminiscent of several middle eastern and Asian religious traditions where women wear a dot in their forehead as a symbol of positive union and a high state of consciousness.

As I have discussed elsewhere María, the protagonist of 'Estrellita de oro', emblematises an enemy in the process of renaming, displacing and erasing (Lamarque 30). The medieval zeitgeist of cruelty and harsh treatment is made evident in the brutality of María's ill fate in the hands of her stepmother and sister. In this version, María's punishment consists of mutilation of her eyes and tongue. There is a pattern of institutionalised misogynistic depiction of women as lustful, untrustworthy, devalued and as a commodity of men (see Mirrer 1989). Louis Mirrer affirms that 'the portrayal of women in medieval Spanish literature […] has not been dealt with from a feminist perspective' (1989 4). Although male authors' representation of women abounded in this period, no female authors are recorded until the fifteenth century. In *Recovering Spain's Feminist Traditions* (2001), Lisa Volledorf argues that to study feminism in medieval Spain is an important act of 'feminist consciousness' raising. Harriet Goldberg goes beyond this and discusses the representation of antifeminism and antisemitism in medieval Spain as a tandem of two rejected groups. This first version of the tale highlights three reoccurring themes in Cinderella: the invisibility or erasure of the woman in a patriarchal society; the displacement of subordinate cultures; and the renaming or transformation of women's identity. These representations will mark the various axes of the forty-four versions of Cinderella encountered in Spain (Lamarque 9).

Invisible Cinderella[1]

Cinderella's invisibility in modern versions of the tale from the early twentieth century echoes women's status in Spain. Between 1920 and 1930, the institutionalised discrimination of women in many areas, and in education in particular, produced an average of approximately 58% illiterate women in Spain, making them invisible as political agents (Scanton 50).[2] *La Cenicienta*, a drama in three acts by Nobel Prize Literature winner Jacinto Benavente (1920), is representative of this conservatism and has only a few innovations to the story: Cinderella's father marries a rich woman, for financial reasons, allowing her to mistreat his daughter; Cinderella reacts to the ill treatment by protesting and questioning the abuse. There are three magical characters: Fantasía, the Poet, and the Old lady of the Forest. Cinderella is encouraged by these creatures to face her problems and confront them. However, her protests are easily dismissed and silenced for the rest of the story.

This story criticises individuals in power, suggesting that they do not work for the people but for their own economic benefit; it talks about political corruption and the unjust state of poverty in which the populace is kept. The nobility depicted comprise an egoistic King and a chronically depressed prince. The political context of this story surrounds Alfonso XIII, King of Spain (1902–1931), who was raised by his mother María Cristina in a strictly religious Christian environment. Criticised during his reign for his leadership, Alfonso XIII was pivotal in the failed Moroccan war (1921). He endured multiple assassination attempts as he was blamed for the Spanish defeat in Arwal, but was saved from an investigation by a *coup d'état* led by Antonio Primo de Rivera. After the victory of Socialist parties in the general election, Alfonso XIII went into exile and never returned to Spain; however, he never abdicated and, subsequently, Franco reinstated him as a Spanish citizen and returned his properties. Alfonso XIII's son, Juan de Borbón, was later selected by Franco to succeed the throne in 1970. The political undertones in Benavente's version are strong,

---

[1] No versions of Cinderella in Spain were recorded until the twentieth century. In Jack Zipes' recount of fairy tales in Spain, he states that the eighteenth century constitutes a 'tremendous gap; the almost total absence of fantasy short narrative in that period' (583).

[2] Emilia Pardo Bazán, despite the votes against her and political battles with administrators (all men) from the university, became the first woman graduated from a higher education institution and the first to become a professor in 1916.

and the absence of Cinderella as the central figure of the tale is clear in this version, underpinning the invisibility of women in this political struggle.

A second version of Cinderella from the 1920s gives a different perspective on education for girls: 'Cenicienta' was published under the pseudonym Elena Fortún (María de la Encarnación Aragonés). Her version of Cinderella appears as a short story in her book *Celia lo que dice* (1928). Solita plays the Cinderella character and is friends with the protagonist of the series, Celia. The seven-year-old Celia is able to ask questions which would have been forbidden to older girls. In her naïvety, Celia questions the lack of opportunities for her friend, Solita, who is an orphan girl and works as a maid in Celia's home. When Solita tells Celia about the dress she would wear to the ball, Celia doubts her since she knows the girl's financial situation. The story ends with Celia's inquiry of the maid, Juana: '*¿Solita, tiene madrina?*' [Solita, does she have a fairy godmother?] (69) Celia's question reveals the social differences and unjust hierarchy oppressing Solita (Cinderella). Fortún was known for questioning the repressive Spanish education system where a girl's education was focused solely on roles in the home. 'Las virtudes domésticas' [domestic virtues] were seen as the only and most important trait for women and which were promoted in popular publications as *La ciencia de la mujer al alcance de las niñas* (1865) by Mariano Carderera. Former Minister of Education, Pidal y Mon's argument highlights the ultra-reactionary agenda that Fortún was opposing:

> Sustraerla [a la mujer] a la educación maternal para entregarla al brazo laico y secular del Estado que la sumerja en una de esas escuelas en que la promiscuidad de sexos y la ausencia de todo pudor [que se marchó con el crucifijo de la escuela] les ha merecido el nombre gráfico de porquerizas. (Scanlon 17)

> [Taking her away [women] from the maternal education and placing her under the secular protection of the state would be a disaster. The state would submerge her into those schools in which the sexual promiscuity and the absence of all modesty [that left with the crucifix] have gained them the graphic name of pigsties.]

The first school for boys and girls was not created until 1857 through the *Ley de Instrucción Pública*. Women were prohibited from studying sciences or classical studies at university level according to Geraldine M. Scanlon (*La Polémica* 18), and in the *Escuelas Normales* women were educated only and exclusively to be teachers. The first decades of the twentieth century were characterised by the battle for better education for women by feminist groups and, as a result, Elena Fortún's children's stories became very popular and sold well.

Dissident Cinderella

In 1931, women were given the right to vote and the equality of rights was established. In this era, new possibilities arose for women in the areas of politics, the arts, sciences, and knowledge in general. The climate of the Republican period nurtured these social changes for women and, in addition, encouraged their involvement as political subjects. During this era, names of Republican intellectuals like Margarita Nelken, La Pasionaria and Victoria Kent stood out for their intellectual efforts concerning rights and equality for Spanish women. Margarita Nelken, as a representative of the Popular Front during the war, dealt with social themes concerning the position of women. She championed the working woman and, in fact, led the first women workers' strike in Madrid. For Nelken, women had been raised assuming attributes falsely considered 'feminine', which for her, served as a tool of submission. The parameters and models assigned and labelled by *La Sección Femenina* as part of 'being a woman' constituted a delay in progress, which she aimed to shed. All these advances disappeared when Franco rose in power after the defeat of the Republicans in 1939.

Antonio Robles' 'Cenicienta' (1936) captures this ideological spirit of the Second Republic. Cinderella refuses to be a princess and wears a Pierrot dress to the ball. This version is in opposition to that which was proposed by the Falange through *La Sección Femenina* during the Franco regime (1939–1975) when women were conditioned to the private sphere and confined to a mould of restricted behaviour. Women formed part of the ideological tenets as a support to men, with pre-established parameters and limits. 'La mujer muy mujer' [The woman, the real woman] that Pilar Primo de Rivera describes, who would later become the founder of Obligatory Social Service, synthesises the assigned place for the woman according to Franco's ideology in an official diary of the era as: 'enamorarse. Que es una de las tres únicas cosas serias que puede hacer una mujer. Las otras dos, ya sabéis, son coser la ropa de su marido y darle todos los hijos que se ofrezcan' (Martín Gaite, *Los usos* 71). [falling in love. Which is one of the only three important things that a woman can do. The other two, as you know, are sewing your husband's clothes and giving him all the children you can] (67). With the diffusion and promotion of the ideology of the Social Service, the advances achieved by women during the Second Republic disappeared.

In Robles' version of Cinderella, the 'essential' characteristics of women promoted by Francoism are completely discredited (see Lamarque *IRCHL* 2014). This is symbolised by the dress of the protagonist. In Franco's Spain, all Spanish women should attempt to show 'decency' and 'femininity' in dress: '[L]a decencia en el vestir se interpretaba como síntoma de españolidad' [modesty in clothing was interpreted as an indication of Spanishness] (Martín Gaite, *Los usos* 20). Any hint of a sense of 'liberality' in dress was overseen and immediately penalised and/or stigmatised by society. Clothing marked a line of behaviour and signalled the values of the woman in Francoist society. In this sense, the clothing in Franco's Spain served to define women and determined their 'moral' values and behaviour. However, in this version of 'Cinderella', the clothing that the young girl wears to the ball (the Pierrot costume) forms part of a discourse that not only fails to reinforce, but rather rejects completely, on a textual level, the 'feminine' attributes and values of the Francoist ideology.

Cinderella moves from the Angel of the Home to the workplace

Franco's ultraconservative and retrogressive agenda is reflected in the versions of Cinderella written during the 1940s and 1950s. In the romantic novel *El despertar de Cenicienta* by José Mallorquí (1943), the heroine is a shy girl named Renna Barney affianced to Fred Paine. Although the story reflects the economic struggle of the post-civil war poverty in Spain, it is set in New York and the couple are poorly paid employees. Fred inherits thirty million dollars as a consequence of a good deed he did in the past and they are able to live happily ever after. A more overt homage to Franco is seen in the original script found in the National Library in Madrid of Luis Escobar's *La Cenicienta del Palace* a musical first performed in *Teatro Eslava* in Madrid on March 1st, 1950 starring the famous Spanish actress Celia Gámez. This version opens the adaptation with a political salute to the dictator of Spain: '¡Saludo a Franco y Arriba España!' [A Salute to Franco and Viva Spain!].

The paradigmatic *fin de siècle* image of the *Ángel del hogar* (Home's Angel) is depicted in the Cinderellas of the 1940s and 1950s which portray protagonists who are naïve, simpleminded and innocent, who are over-shadowed by their male partners. In these adaptations, the feminine ideal of the eighteenth century is reflected in women whose aim in life and 'professional career' was marriage. All these women leave their jobs to marry and start a family following the ideological scheme of the time.

Home was glorified and the public sphere or work was described as a world full of defeat and deception for women (Scanton 60). Women in the 1950s faced a societal and legal system embedded within a patriarchal order, which placed extreme restrictions upon them. For example, according to the Spanish law of the time, the legal age for a woman to be a responsible adult was twenty-five. Before this age, a woman was under the strict rule of her father and then, when married, under the supervision of her husband. There were a number of restrictions under the Spanish penal code and punitive laws were created, supported and promoted against women's rights. Women were not allowed to inherit property and the rules on social conduct were even more rigid. Adultery by women was penalised as a crime but laws were much more relaxed for men who committed adultery (Caballé 236).

In the 1960s there was a shift in the depiction of *Cinderella* triggered by the decade's political and economic changes in Spain. In the 1940s and 1950s, women's work was seen as a shameful activity for her and for her husband (Scanton 62). The Socialist Party militant Margarita Nelken attempted to convince women that labour activity was an economic factor that was of relevance to all individuals, and not a space only dedicated to men. In *La nueva Cenicienta* a musical version directed by George Sherman (1964) Marisol's (Cinderella) most precious desire is not to marry the prince but to find a job. As a woman, Marisol traverses the angelical *picara* who is the supporter and mother figure in the family, to the determined woman who searches for employment as a flamenco dancer fulfilling her dream. *La nueva Cenicienta* revisits the spirit of the pre-Francoist era, where the Second Republic staged women as part of the economic force in Spain. Marisol's status becomes balanced as she, in the last scene, dances with both the prince of reality (her work supervisor) and the prince of pleasure, the American actor Bob Conrad (Lamarque 51).

Porn Cinderella

After Franco's death in 1975, Spain experienced a massive cultural explosion, with Madrid at the epicentre. Freedom from almost forty years of social constraint imposed by an oppressive regime created a hedonistic sociocultural phenomenon that erupted in many areas of artistic expression. These years produced the well-known countercultural movement called *La Movida*. The protagonists in *El Calentito* (2005), the name of a Madrid night club, are women in a punk music group, whose open sexualities and gender identities represent the spirit of the moment (Lamarque 93). The threat of a *coup d'etat* from the last remaining Franco supporters energises the members of the club and the film portrays the political and cultural moment very effectively through the story of a teenage girl coming of age in these transitional years. Released in 2005, this is a depiction of a previous era.

However, the diametrical change in women's roles in Spain experienced during the *La Movida* artistic movement was vividly portrayed at the time by Nazario Luque-Vera's subversive and anti-establishment version of Cinderella. *La princesa que perdió el pie de su zapatilla* [The princess who lost the foot of her shoe] (1979) is a pornographic remake of the tale. This version is an underground comic which appeared in *El Víbora*, an adult magazine published from 1979 to 2005. In the fairy tale, Cinderella's sexual desire or sexual attributes are not made explicit, it is an innocently romantic story. Luque-Vera subverts this and with it the mythical premise that women are not interested in sex or pleasure, and depicts Cinderella as an avidly sexual being out to find fulfilment and satisfaction. In *La princesa que perdió el pie de su zapatilla* the shoe symbol is replaced by a penis, which Cinderella looks for by trying different ones in the search for the right penis that would give her the most pleasure. There are explicit illustrations of sexual acts, incest and zoophilia in this version (Lamarque 163).

In the 1980s, *La Movida* disrupted many of the traditional and heteronormative conditions spread and reinforced by Franco's regime, particularly his ideology on gender roles. This countercultural initiative culminated in the approval of gay marriage in March 2005 in Spain. In *Cenicienta en Chueca: mujeres que aman a mujeres* by María Felicitas Jaime (2003) Cinderella has no name and is a lesbian. It is important to observe that the portrayal of women's queer sexual identities, homosexual desire, homoeroticism and/or queer' subjectivity does not abound in Spanish-speaking fiction and is only recently emerging in its English counterpart (Lamarque chap. 5). This lack is evident in Spain as versions of a gay Cinderella have not proliferated over the years, despite the many progressive political and social changes attained in the country. It is not a surprise, as this thematic void resonates with the 1971 Social Dangers Law which proposed methods and measures for the 'rehabilitation' of homosexuals, both men and women.

Proactive Cinderella

After Franco's death, in the mid-seventies a number of women's movements appeared clandestinely in the political arena, particularly *Las Jornadas por la Liberación de la Mujer* in Madrid in December 1975 and *Las Jornadas*

Catalanas de la Dona in May 1976. Additionally, in 1975 The United Nations proclaimed an annual International Women's Day to raise awareness of women's issues (Moreno Sardá 152). This change is reflected in the shift in women's traditional roles in Spain in the 1980s. New ideas put an emphasis in women's autonomy and freedom to choose, which is reflected in the musical *La Cenicienta del Palace* directed by Fernando García (1985). The story unfolds at a hotel (Hotel Palace) when twin sisters, Delia and Celia, visit the city. One of the characters, the Baroness, divulges the information that one of the sisters is a millionaire and the other one is poor. Schemes, plans and intrigues are plotted by many at the hotel where the sisters are staying to trick the millionaire girl into marrying one of two desperate suitors. Starring singer Paloma San Basilio, this musical version ends with the marriage of Delia/Celia with the man who is honest and kind to her. At the end, it is discovered that there are no twin sisters and there is only one millionaire who, tired of all the ambitious, greedy and false suitors, fools all into thinking that one sister was poor and the other rich. It ends with Celia and Carlos' wedding and the last musical number, 'Cenicienta, Cenicienta porque el sueño fue una verdad' [Cinderella, Cinderella, because the dream was true]. In this musical version Cenicienta has the power of choosing the right man, the prince, for herself. She is witty and smart and, through various stratagems, finds her prince who is sincere and is not interested only in her fortune. Cinderella has at last the agency to choose her own partner.

In a more recent comic version *Idiotizadas* (2017) by Moderna de Pueblo, Zorricienta (Cinderella) is a host in a radio show advising men and women about relationships. Zorricienta is the quintessential representation of a liberated and progressive woman, who has confronted the discriminatory and biased social rules regarding men and women. In this version, Cenicienta appropriates the nickname she is given at the ball, because she engages in a romantic encounter with the 'prince'. While he is praised and admired for 'scoring' with Cinderella, she is repudiated, ostracised and insulted with the name: *zorra* [whore]. Through the use of harsh moral codes not applied to men, the adjective *zorra* paralyses women and positions them as valueless and unworthy. Zorricienta in turn, reconstructs her identity using this insulting epithet and becomes a 'princess' who is independent and does not submit to the unfair, irrational and one-sided morale of name-calling that has restrained women through fear throughout history and time. This rewriting mimics transfeminism theory, leaving the category of 'women' open while rejecting immobile and determined positions. Zorricienta's transformation of her subjectivity and her rejection of fixed parameters echoes the challenge of transfeminism to 'transform and revisit the category women for the feminist political stance as well as destabilising of gender difference and the gender identities that go along with it' (Puente 78).

Displacement and Cinderella's not so happy ending

Cinderella and Civil War Reflections

A number of portrayals of Cinderella from the 1980s onwards use the tale to comment on violence in Spanish society and, more widely, the abuse of women, and the effect of these issues on women's self-esteem. These representations highlight the current move to denounce and unveil women's pervasive ill-treatment in the domestic sphere.

Sara Suárez Solís's 'Cenicienta 39' published in 1989 is set at the end of the Spanish Civil War. The story tells of penury, food shortage and angst in time of war. Cinderella is Pili, a girl who loses a leg when her home town is bombed. Instead of the crystal shoe, Pili has a prosthetic leg and a shoe on it. Pili's father is a soldier who fights for the Nationalists group and is lost; she does not know if he is still alive. There is celebration when the end of the war is announced and Pili's stepmother and stepsisters join the populace on the streets forgetting that Pili is alone in the house. She falls down the stairs and is injured, with no one to help and, in this version, Cinderella is not rescued by a charming prince (Zipes 603). Many women during the Spanish Civil war, injured by repression, prison and exile were, like Pili, not heard or accounted for in the official story. As Shirley Mangini states in her book *Memories of Resistance: Women's Voices in Spanish Civil War* (1995), this version is one of what she calls, 'Memory Texts'. Mangini mentions novelists like Dolores Medio, who use memory texts to recount the state of metaphorical mutilation that they experienced during the war. The author highlights writers such as Ibárruri and De la Mora, who also give voice to women's presence in the Civil War from an autobiographical point of view. Pili, the amputated Cinderella, resembles the mutilated Spain after the war and the devastating contrast between the victor's joy and the disaster and pain left as a consequence of the war.

Cinderella and Gender Violence

Since the late 1990s, gender violence and femicides have received increasing attention in Spain (Monleón 17). Femicides are defined as 'the misogynist killing of women by men' (Radford and Russell 3) and have been theorised by Aleida Luján Pinelo in her dissertation 'A Theoretical Approach to the Concept of Femicide/Feminicide' (2015) as she highlights the redefinition of the term by Russell as 'the killing of females by males because they are females' (Russell, video). Almost a thousand women were murdered in Spain from 2010 to 2019 (Feminicidios.net). While this recurrent lethal violence against women existed before 2010, it only started to be documented in the early nineties. According to the Feminicidios.net 52% of women were murdered by their male partners and 26% of these women were twenty-nine years old or younger. Núria Vergés Bosch and Jaume Nualart Vilaplana report that, in Spain:

> an average of 63 women per year were murdered by their partners and in absolute terms it has increased since 2000. [...] The report shows that the age group between 25 and 34 encountered the majority of cases and the great majority of women murdered were Spanish nationals. The most common entailment between the woman and her murderer was marriage. The murder took place in close proximity and was very cruel. Almost half of the cases were murdered with knives, but also by being beaten, by strangulation, shooting or other methods. (5)

Lourdes Ortiz's retelling of the classical Cinderella story in *Los motivos de Circe* (1988), 'Cenicienta: Parábola en dos actos' can be seen as an early commentary on the grave global issue of *feminicidios* (femicides) as the story was written some years before the denouncing of women murders by men was made public. It is only recently that societal changes have highlighted this hidden historical societal illness. The story takes place years after the wedding between the prince and Cinderella and she is now the queen. The king and his advisors conclude that the use of magic in the past surrounding the couples' encounter and marriage was the product of witchcraft. In other words, Cinderella is believed to be a witch and should be punished for using her supernatural powers to seduce the prince. The Catholic church and the King conspire and make a plan to kill her without any proof or evidence of her 'crime'. All the details of her assassination are plotted in the privacy of the palace by both men close to Cinderella. Femicides are perpetrated usually by family members and/or relatives of the victim. The queen, Cinderella, in Ortiz' version is murdered by male members of the Catholic Church and the King, a retelling which highlights the increasing social disease of feminicides in Spain and all over the world.

Vives, Álvarez-Dardet and Caballero's study demonstrates that there was a notable rise in police reports of domestic violence in Spain between 1998–2001. The study showed that:

between the first and the last year of the study, formal complaints
increased by 27% and murders increased by 49%. In Spain, during the
period analyzed, one out of every 100,000 women was murdered by an
intimate partner and one out of every 200 women reported IPV. Women
aged 22–41 years and those aged 82–86 years presented the highest rates
of mortality from IPV (268).

They conclude that the number of battered and abused women is a serious
problem that has been increasing in the past decades. This grave social
issue is tackled in *Cenicienta tiene un mal sueño* (2002) by Julia Massip
and Chus Martínez two psychologists, who were part of a municipal
programme in Barcelona to educate women about domestic violence.
Nunila López Salamero, the author of *La Cenicienta que no quería comer
perdices* (2009), a feminist picture book version, was also a collaborator.
The prologue, written by three municipal authorities, states:

> El cuento que tenéis en vuestras manos, queremos que sirva de ayuda a las
> personas que sufren estas situaciones de violencia. Es también un vehículo
> de información […] la violencia es siempre un acto de cobardía y no tiene
> ninguna justificación. Cerrar los ojos ante esta lacra social también lo es.
> (2)

> [We wish that the short story that you have in your hands will help women
> who suffer domestic violence. It is also an informative vehicle […]
> violence is always an act of cowardice and it is never justifiable. Closing
> your eyes before this social illness replicates it and is also an act of
> cowardice]

Cenicienta tiene un mal sueño erodes the familiar version of Perrault and
discusses the abuse of women as a social issue. The story starts at the end.
The prince turns into a violent man calling Cinderella ugly and abusing her
on several levels. Cinderella asks rhetorically, ¿Sería culpa de ella el
maltrato sexual? [Was the sexual mistreatment that she endures her fault?]
(20). She is naïve about her own sexuality and suffers from her husband's
abuse. Finally, she finds help, gets a divorce and establishes a vegetarian
restaurant employing many of the fairy tale female characters escaping
their 'fairytale ending'. The end of the story consists of final remarks and
awareness on the issue of women's domestic abuse:

> 'Y la Cenicienta lo consiguió. Dejó los tacones y las perdices y se hizo
> cocinera vegetariana. Y ahora está trabajando con otras mujeres como ella:
> Blancanieves y la Bella Durmiente que ya habían despertado, Caperucita,
> que había dejado al cazador por violento […] Y entre todas decidieron

cambiar sus papeles en los cuentos y empezar uno nuevo. ... Érase una vez unas mujeres que no estaban solas ... (Massip and Martínez n.p.)

[And Cinderella finally escaped the prince, leaving the high heels, the partridges and becoming a vegetarian cook. She is now working with other women like her, that have woken up: Snow White and Sleeping Beauty and Little Red Riding Hood, who has left the violent hunter [...] They decided to change their assigned roles in the tales and start new ones ... Once upon a time there were women who were not alone...]

A further violent social issue addressed through the tale is that of suicide as a consequence of rape. In Spain, rape was legally classed as a violation of human rights and the fundamental freedom of a human being in Assembly Resolution 48/104 at the 85th plenary session in 1993, a resolution which establishes the definition of women's violence. According to the study on suicide by Alvaro Meca et al, 'suicides in Spain exhibit a clear geographic pattern and occur at different rates between the genders. The results suggest an increasing number of suicides among women aged 35–49 years over the study period [1981–2008]' (381). Suicide in women as a mental health issue has increased as a consequence of rape in Spain and this can be seen in *Cenicienta en Pennsylvania* (2010) by Cristina Cerrada, where Mary has been the victim of sexual abuse as a child. This Cinderella has been exposed to physical violence against her, and becomes a very depressed, melancholic and unstable woman in adulthood.

The theme of mental health is also seen in *Cenicienta en sangre* (2010) [*Cinderella in Blood*] by Begoña Callejón, a collection of poems and short stories talking about Cinderella's feelings of abandonment, anger and deception. In the first one-page story 'Cenicienta expulsada en el país de las calabazas' [Cinderella expelled from the pumpkin country], Cinderella is the narrator and monologist. She is at the entrance of Ildaboth, which is the name of the demiurge or 'false god'. Her monologue is directed toward those who tricked her into believing that her mother was dead. She is in a state of limbo between the world that was given, a false world of fantasy and lies, and the world that she is about to enter. A voice says from inside Ildeboth: 'pasa, aquí solo verás lo que quieras ver. Calabaza o zapatito de cristal' [Come in, here you will only see what you want to see. Pumpkin or crystal shoe] (22). This literary version reflects and questions the cultural myth of the fairy tale character and how it has been a vehicle of deception for women. Cenicienta's eyes are finally opened and she is able to see the reality of the world; with her monologue, she appears to be the voice of women seeking self-understanding before the culturally encrypted concept of a Cinderella's identity. According to Helen Luu 'the genre (monologue) is defined not by its revelation of the speaker's self, but by its revelations about the speaking self' (19). In other words, in this version, Cinderella's use of monologue expresses her discontent and disappointment defined by the genre itself and by the context in which this sentiment is produced: society as the maker of Cinderella as a distorted, poor paradigm and identity for women. This adaptation also marks the consolidation period of the transfeminism movement in Spain between 2006 and 2010 (Puente 81). It is a moment of questioning the institutionalisation of feminism and a broader openness to various minorities within the production of discourse.

Lastly, a modern and extremely poetic version of the tale, in which Cinderella traverses epochs, lands, climates and social situations is *Te cuento ... La Cenicienta* (2015) by Juan Carlos Mestre and Juan Carlos Monedero. Cinderella is any woman anywhere in the world who is abused, diminished, raped and discriminated against for the fact of being so, and is a reflection on our convoluted and unjust times. This story offers narrative and historic images by photographer Clemente Bernad and Carolina Martínez, who were recently surrounded by controversy when a Spanish fascist group sued them for their documentary 'A sus muertos' (2018) (El diario Arístegui). The two formats of narrative and image work together to enhance the effect of the crude reality of real Cinderella stories around the globe.

As a cultural icon and metonymic object representing 'womanhood', Cinderella is without parallel around the world. In Spain, the fairy tale character has acquired multiple and varied faces, voices and postures as the witness, subject and agent to the country's political and social shifts and women's status within those structures. In particular, Cinderella has embodied women's experiences in Spanish culture as her role has changed from the muted, invisible, male-companion propagated in the early 1920s through Franco's almost forty-year retrogressive agenda for women, to the progressive gay and pornographic depiction of Cinderella following *La Movida* movement after Franco's death. Inscribed in the many Cinderellas that inhabit Spanish society and fiction are a sample of feminist constructs (Lamarque 6). These changing ideologies flow within three reoccurring themes: the invisibility or erasure of the woman in a patriarchal society, the displacement of subordinate cultures, and the renaming or transformation of women's identity. These adaptations of the paradigmatic character add a continuum to the fairy tale web (Bacchilega 18) as an ethno-fairy tale web illustrating the shifts in women's experience, women's achievements, women's identities and women's battles over inequalities not just in Spain but around the world.

Works cited

Almodóvar, A. R. *Cuentos al amor de la lumbre.* Alianza Editorial, 1983.

Almodóvar, Pedro, director. *Hable con ella.* El Deseo Producciones, 2003.

Aristegui, Miguel M. 'Dos cineastas se enfrentan a penas de cárcel por rodar un documental sobre un monumento franquista de Pamplona' Eldiario.es, 13 Nov. 2018, n.p. www.eldiario.es/navarra/cineastas-enfrentan-documental-Caidos-Pamplona_0_835367501.html Accessed 26 May 2020.

Bacchilega, Cristina. *Fairy Tales Transformed? 21st-Century Adaptations and the Politics of Wonder.* Wayne State University Press, 2013.

Benavente, Jacinto. *La Cenicienta, comedia de magia en un prólogo y tres actos dividida en quince cuadros.* Librería de los sucesores de Hernando, 1920.

Caballé, Ana. *El feminismo en España: la lenta conquista de un derecho.* Ediciones Cátedra, 2013.

Callejón, Begoña. *Cenicienta en sangre.* El Gaviero Ediciones, 2010.

Carderera. Mariano. *La ciencia de la mujer al alcance de las niñas.* Imprenta del Colegio de Sordo-Mudos y de Ciegos, 1865.

La Cenicienta del Palace. Director Fernando García de la Vega, performer, Paloma San Basilio, Luis Escobar. 2 Dec. 1985. Musical. Television.

La Cenicienta del Palace. Director and writer, Luis Escobar, writer and director, performer Celia Gámez and Alfonso Godá. Teatro Eslava de Madrid, Madrid. 1 March 1940. Performance.

Cerrada, Cristina. *Cenicienta en Pensilvania.* DVD Ediciones, 2010.

Clemente, Bernad and Carolina Martínez, directors, *A sus muertos.* Filmoteca de Navarra, 2018.

De Pueblo, Moderna. *Idiotizadas.* Editorial Planeta, 2017.

Dillard, Heath. *Daughters of the Reconquest. Women in Castilian Town Society,* 1100–1300. Cambridge University Press, 1984.

Escobar, Luis. *La Cenicienta del Palace.* Unpublished film script, 1940.

Estow, Clara. 'Women in the Historical Writings of Pedro Lopez de Ayala' *Revista de Estudios Hispánicos,* vol. 11, 1984, pp. 145–52.

Fernández-Lamarque, Maia. 'El bosque, el baile, príncipes y princesas: 'La Bella Durmiente' en *Hable con ella.*' *L' Érudit franco-espagnol,* vol. 11, 2017, pp. 52–66.

—. *Cinderella in Spain: Variations of the Story as Socio-Ethical Texts.* McFarland Publishers, 2019.

Fernández-Lamarque, María. 'Antonio Robles *La Cenicienta*: A 'Cinderella' Retelling Censored in Franco's Spain.' (IRCL) *International*

Research in Children's Literature, vol. 7 no. 1, 2014 pp. 78–94 with permission of *Hispania,* The American Association of Teachers of Spanish and Portuguese and Johns Hopkins University Press.

Fernández-Rodríguez, Carolina. *Las re-escrituras contemporáneas de Cenicienta.* Principado de Asturias. Consejería de Cultura. Universidad de Oviedo, 1997.

—. *La Bella Durmiente a través de la historia.* Universidad de Oviedo, 1998.

Folguera, Pilar. *El feminismo en España: dos siglos de historia.* Editorial Pablo Iglesias, 2007.

Fortún, Elena. 'Cenicienta' in *Celia lo que dice.* Alianza Editorial, 1928.

Grimm, Jacob and Wilhelm Grimm. *The Complete Fairy Tales of the Brothers Grimm.* Translated by Jack Zipes. 1812. University of Princeton Press, 2014.

Goldberg. Harriet. 'Two Parallel Medieval Commonplaces: Antifeminism and Antisemitism in the Medieval.' *Feminist Newsletter,* vol. 7, no. 5 1989.

Jaime, María Felicitas. *Cenicienta en Chueca: mujeres que aman mujeres.* Editorial S.L., 2003.

López Salamero, Nunila, and Sierra, Myriam Cameros. *La Cenicienta que no quería comer perdices.* Editorial Planeta, 2009.

Luján Pinelo, Aleida. A Theoretical Approach to the Concept of Feminicide/Feminicide. Diss, Director Dr. Peta Hinton, Universiteit Utrecht, The Netherlands Media and Cultural Studies Department, 2015.

Luque-Vera, Nazario. 'La princesa que perdió el pie de su zapatilla.' Comic. *El Víbora,* no. 168. Ediciones La Cúpula, 1993.

Mallorquí, José. *EL despertar de cenicienta.* Editorial Molino, 1943.

Mangini, Shirley. *Memories of Resistance. Women's Voices from the Spanish Civil War.* Yale University Press, 1995.

Martín Gaite, Carmen. *Los usos amorosos de la posguerra española.* Anagrama, 1986.

—. *Courtship Customs in Postwar Spain.* Translated by Margaret Jones. Bucknell University Press, 2004.

Massip, Julia, and Chus Martinez. *Cenicienta tiene un mal sueño.* Illustrated by Marisa Ordóñez. Ajuntament de Barcelona, 2002.

Meca, A.; Kneib, T; Gil-Prieto, R; Gil de Miguel, 'Epidemiology of suicide in Spain, 1981–2008: A Spatiotemporal Analysis.' *Public Health,* vol. 127, no. 4, 2013, pp. 380–5.

Mestre Juan Carlos, Monedero Juan Carlos. *Te cuento...Cenicienta.* Alkibla, 2015.

Mills, Margaret A. 'A Cinderella Variant in the Context of a Muslim Women's Ritual.' *Cinderella: A Casebook*, edited by Alan Dundes. University of Wisconsin Press, 1982.

Miller, Beth, editor, 'Sexual Humor in Misogynist Medieval Exempla'. *Women in Hispanic Literature: Icons and Fallen Idols*. University of California Press, 1983.

Mirrer, Louis. *Women, Jews and Muslims in the Texts of Reconquest Castile*. Ann Arbor University Press, 1996.

Monleón Pradas, Elena Edith. *In-Out House: Circuitos de género y violencia en la era tecnológica*. Editorial Universitat Politècnica de València, 2012.

Moreno Sardá, Amparo. 'La réplica de las mujeres al franquismo' *El feminismo en España: Dos siglos de historia*. Editorial Pablo Iglesia, 2007.

Ober de Baubeta, Patricia Anne. 'Fairy-Tale Intertext in Iberian and Latin American Women's Writing.' *Fairy Tale and Feminism: New Approaches*. Edited by Donald Hasse. Wayne University Press, 2004.

Ortiz, Lourdes. 'Cenicienta: Parábola en dos actos.' *Los motivos de Circe*. Ediciones El Dragón, 1988.

Perrault, Charles. *The Fairy Tales of Charles Perrault*. Illustrated by Harry Clarke, Introduction by Thomas Bodkin, Harrap, 1922.

Puente, Sonia Núñez. 'Activism Trouble: Transfeminism and Institutional Feminism in Spain.' *Feminist Formations*, vol. 28 no. 2, 2016, pp. 73–93. *ProQuest*, 19 July 2019.

Radford, Jill and Diana E. H. Russell, editors. *Femicide: The Politics of Woman Killing*, Open University Press, 1992.

Ramírez, Pedro Luis, director. *Cenicienta y Ernesto*. Prod. Cinematográfica S.A, 1957.

Ratcliffe, Marjorie. 'Adulteresses, Mistresses and Prostitutes: Extramarital Relationships in Medieval Castile.' *Hispania*, vol. 67, 1984, pp. 346–50

Robles, Antonio. *La Cenicienta*. Editorial Estrella, 1936.

Russell, Diana E. H., and Roberta A. Harmes. *Femicide in Global Perspective*. Teachers College Press, 2001.

Russell, Diana. *Feminicidio: una perspectiva global*. UNAM, Centro de Investigaciones Interdisciplinaria en Ciencias y Humanidades, 2006.

—. *The Origin & Importance of the Term Feminicide*. Video. 1993 www.dianarussell.com/videos_and_audio.html Accessed 21 March 2019.

Sherman, George, director. *La nueva Cenicienta*. Guión Producciones Cinematográficas, 1965. Film.

Scanlon, Geraldine. *La polémica feminista en la España contemporánea (1868–1974)* Trans. Rafael Mazarrasa. Ediciones Akal, 1986.

Suárez Solís, Sara. 'Cenicienta 39'. *Ábaco*, no 6. 1989 pp. 114-116. CICEES, http//www.jstor.org/stable/20795710 Accessed 11 Oct. 2017.

Vergés Nuria Bosh and Jaume Nualant. 'Feminicides in Area: Interactive Visualizations of Feminicides in the Spanish State.' CIMUAT: Congreso internacional de mujeres, arte y Tecnología, 2010.

Vives C., C. Álvarez-Dardet, and P. Caballero. *Violencia del compañero íntimo en España*, Departamento de Salud Pública. Universitat d'Alacant. España. Correspondencia: C. Vives Cases. Departamento de Salud Pública. Edificio de Ciencias Sociales. Campus Sant Vicent del Raspeig. Apdo. 99. 03080 Alicante. España.

Volledorf, Lisa. *Recovering Spain's Feminist Tradition*. Modern Language Association of America, 2001.

Zipes, Jack. *The Oxford Companion to Fairy Tales: The Western Fairy Tale Tradition from Medieval to Modern*. Oxford University Press, 2000.

CHAPTER TEN

HELPED BY A HONEYBIRD, CLOTHED IN CATSKINS, AND SWALLOWED BY A WHALE: EXPLORING THE IRISH VARIANTS OF THE CINDERELLA TALE

DONNA GILLIGAN

Ireland is renowned for its rich tradition of legend and folktales. With this in mind, it should be no surprise that the storytelling tradition also includes a number of variants of the Cinderella tale. While these tales may not be as well known within Ireland as some of the more popular native stories and folklore, they are significant examples of the ways in which the themes of the Cinderella tale travelled, spread, and combined with other national story motifs and subjects. This chapter does not intend to list all surviving versions of the Cinderella tale from Ireland; rather it seeks to provide a discussion which illustrates the breadth and variety of examples of this tale within a specific national context. Neither does this chapter intend to attempt to identify the sources of the tale variants—a subject long under investigation and contention by scholars of this subject. This work intends to provide an overview of the variants and aspects of the tale within an Irish setting, and to highlight the presence and prominence of the international folktale within an Irish context—a subject which may not be as publicly familiar as deserved.

In discussion of a number of representative examples of the Irish Cinderella tale, we can see the presence of a broad spectrum of the most prominent identified motifs of the international tale. From Irish Cinderella tale examples gathered from oral history, manuscripts, and early publications, there exists representation of the five most common tale motifs initially identified by the work of Marian Roalfe Cox in 1893—those of Cinderella (Type A), Catskin (Type B), Cap O'Rushes (Type C), Indeterminate (Type D), and Hero-Tales (Type E) (Cox). These motifs of the 'Cinderella Cycle' (Rooth) are often combined with tropes which are central to Irish legend and folklore, as well as international folktale themes and subjects. Exploration of the Irish Cinderella tale can be read as a case study of the ways in which a worldwide tale can be shaped, altered, and adapted by a specific country and its native traditions. The Cinderella narratives from an Irish context illustrate the combination of Irish folklore, legend, and contemporary societal influences with the customs of the broader international story, producing a distinctive and remarkable variant of the tale.

Scholarship and Sources for the Irish Cinderella

All research on variants of the international Cinderella tale builds from the work of Marian Roalfe Cox, whose pioneering publication on 345 variants of the story included two of the best-surviving accounts of the Irish version of the tale—'The Princess in the Cat-Skins' (Cox 272) and 'Fair, Brown and Trembling' (Cox 203). Anna Birgitta Rooth's 1951 work expanded on further surviving versions of the Irish variant, and Stith Thompson's revision of the tale type index of Antti Aarne further extended typologies of the story. Uther's additional work on the Aarne-Thompson catalogue is an extra useful application for examination of the surviving Irish versions. The work of Norwegian folklorist Reidar Christiansen has also contributed further to the collection and discussion of the Irish examples of the Cinderella tale.

With regard to primary rather than oral sources, Nutt (cited in Cox 535) has suggested that evidence from two early medieval Irish manuscripts may potentially record a variant of the Cinderella tale. A tale from a translation of the fourteenth century Book of Ballymote, also recorded in the twelfth century Book of Leinster (Cox 535; Joynt 91) discusses the sons of high king Eochaidh Mughmedón. In the story we are told that Eochaidh has four sons by his queen, Mongfhionn, and one by a captive princess named Caireann. Before the birth of her son, Niall, Caireann is maltreated by Mongfhionn and kept as a slave, but Niall overcomes the neglect he also faces to become a hero and chieftain. Nutt mentions a further tale from an annal of the fifteenth century (Nutt 138) telling the story of Raghallach, the seventh century king of Connacht. Raghallach is warned that he will be killed by one of his children, so orders his queen to kill any babies which may be born to her. The queen gives birth to a daughter, whom she gives to a swine-herd to kill. The swine-herd instead takes pity on the baby and leaves it to be reared by a hermit/holy woman. The king's daughter grows up to be the most beautiful woman in the land, and the king, ignorant as to her true identity, demands she be brought to him. He falls in love with her and becomes obsessed by her beauty, ignoring his wife and inviting the wrath of the saints for this rejection—which is hinted to ultimately lead to his untimely and shameful death (Ó hÓgáin 432).

Three popular nineteenth century published collections of Irish folktales preserved two of the best surviving Irish Cinderella stories. Patrick Kennedy's *The Fireside Stories of Ireland* recorded one of the few Irish versions of the 'Catskin' tale motif—'The Princess in the Cat-Skins' (81)—and the tale 'Fair, Brown, and Trembling' was recorded by Jeremiah Curtin in *Myths and Folk-Lore of Ireland* (8) and by Joseph Jacobs in *Celtic Fairy Tales* (169). Several more variants of the Cinderella tale can be found in the Irish oral history record. One of the richest sources of folktale collections in Ireland is that of the National Folklore Collection, housed at University College Dublin. This collection stores the vast collection of manuscripts recording the oral traditions of the country, collated by the Irish Folklore Commission in the early twentieth century. Of particular value for present-day researchers are the works of The Schools Collection of the Commission, the handwritten manuscripts of which have been recently digitised and made available to the public via the Dúchas website (Dúchas, The Schools' Collection).

The 'Schools Scheme', which ran from 1937 to 1938, was a programme which collected folklore through the assistance of senior level primary school children, who were tasked with recording traditions and stories from their locality and region (Briody 260). The recorded information includes topics such as local traditions, folk cures, games and pastimes, but of value to the Cinderella researcher is the 'Stories' section of the accounts, recording oral folklore and storytelling from the community. The stories recorded include several variants of the Cinderella tale, a number of which are presented in this chapter. The extensive, and as of yet largely non-digitised, wider collections of the National Folklore Collection, provide further possibilities for discovery and collation of additional examples of the Irish Cinderella story, with the examples discussed here being just a representative sample of the variant recorded from Irish oral history.

The Irish Cinderella

The tale of 'Fair, Brown, and Trembling' can be suggested to be the best known of the Irish examples of the Cinderella tale. Overall, the story fits into the traditional A Type Cinderella classification of Cox's groupings (xxv). In this story, Fair, Brown, and Trembling are three daughters of King Cúrucha of 'Tir Conal' (likely the Gaelic kingdom Tyrconnell, located in the area of modern-day County Donegal) (Curtin 78). Fair and Brown are the two favoured daughters of the King, and Trembling is the ill-treated heroine who is regarded as a servant. In order to visit the church her sisters are attending, Trembling is helped by an old henwife, who uses a 'cloak of darkness' and clippings from Trembling's old clothes to make extravagant robes and shoes for her to wear to go to the church. The henwife tells Trembling that she has 'a honey-bird here to sit on your right shoulder, and a honey-finger to put on your left. At the door stands a milk-white mare, with a golden saddle for you to sit on, and a golden bridle to hold in your hand' (Curtin 79). The heroine is warned that she must not go inside the door of the church, and must leave the minute that the Mass ends. The honey-bird and honey-finger accompany her on each of her further two horseback visits to the church, when each time she wears an outfit more elaborate than the last (fig 10-1).

"TREMBLING" AT THE CHURCH DOOR

Fig. 10-1. 'Trembling at the church door': an illustration of 'Fair, Brown, and Trembling' by John D. Batten for Joseph Jacob's *Celtic Fairy Tales*, 1892.

Trembling is admired by all at the church, including the prince of Emaina/Omanya. On her third visit as she tries to escape the crowd, her foot is grabbed by the prince, and she loses her shoe (Curtin 84), which is used by the prince to find the owner. He is accompanied in this quest by a number of the other Kings' sons, who are also in competition for Trembling's hand, and they traverse the country in their search. When the 'shoe marriage test' (Cox xxvi) is undertaken, the shoe fits Trembling and, with the help of the henwife, she reappears to the prince and her sisters in her previous gowns and with her magical steeds.

From this point onwards the tale starts to take a more unusual turn to that of the traditional Cinderella standard. The next stage of the story includes what is referred to in Cox as a 'second run' (Cox 189), where we learn more about Trembling's prince, and the heroine undergoes a second strange ordeal from which she must again be rescued. After Trembling's unveiling as the woman at the church, the prince of Emania is forced to fight the other competing princes in order to win her hand in marriage. He wins these duels and marries Trembling, who goes on to have a son. One day when the prince is out hunting, Trembling is pushed into the sea by her sister, and is swallowed by a great whale. Her sister Fair (who we are told resembles Trembling) takes on her identity. The next day, when the tide comes in, the whale throws Trembling onto the seashore where she is able to tell a young cow-boy of her plight, asking him to inform her husband about her situation (fig 10-2). She tells the cow-boy that the whale has her under its enchantment, and will swallow and cast her out three times—and unless she is saved by the fourth swallow, she will be lost. The cow-boy is hindered in his quest by a memory potion administered by Fair but, on the third day, Trembling's husband arrives, killing the whale and releasing her. As a result of her treachery, Fair is put out onto the sea in a barrel, with provisions to last her seven years.

Fig. 10-2. 'Trembling is cast out by the whale': an illustration of 'Fair, Brown, and Trembling' by John D. Batten for Joseph Jacob's *Celtic Fairy Tales*, 1892.

The corpus of Irish Cinderella tales features a number of commonalities as native variants. The more popularly known character of the 'fairy godmother' is generally represented in these tales by an elderly woman in the form of a henwife, a hag, or a witch. One of the aspects of a large number of the Cinderella tales which resonates with their contemporary recording in the nineteenth and twentieth centuries is the replacement of the well-known location of the party/ball with that of the church. Several of the Irish variants use the setting of a Mass as the 'meeting-place' for the performance of the 'heroine disguise' through the 'magic dresses' (Cox xxvi). During this long period of significant public adherence to the Catholic faith in Ireland, the use of Mass as a public meeting venue may have been particularly relevant to the audience for the stories, and may have been a more familiar and accessible connection than that of a ball. It is interesting to note that in an Irish context, the juxtaposition of the Cinderella tale of magic and enchantment alongside the prominent feature of a Catholic Mass service may potentially demonstrate the continuing presence of folk beliefs within an increasingly religious native population. The issues of enchantment and magical transformation do not necessarily lend themselves to traditional Catholic dogma and beliefs, but folklore collections such as the Dúchas archive show that public belief in folk magic, superstition, and fairy lore continued to survive alongside beliefs in organised religion up until the twentieth century.

It is interesting to examine the inclusion and prominence of the character of the 'prince of Emania' (Curtin 78) in the context of this Cinderella story. The name Emania is a derivation of the Irish place name of Emhain Mhacha or Navan Fort, located near Armagh city. Navan Fort is an ancient ceremonial pre-Christian monument which features prominently in Irish mythology, especially within the tales of The Ulster Cycle—a corpus of heroic tales in medieval Irish literature (Ó hÓgáin 487). The naming of the prince's kingdom as this area of mythological significance appears to ground the tale in Irish legend, as well as a specific geographical location. Emhain Mhacha/Emania was said to be the capital of the province of Ulster, and the base of the king (Ó hÓgáin 492), who held the legendary Red Branch knights in his service (Dix). The Ulster Cycle heroic tales are known for their common storytelling elements of epic battles, magical beasts, enchanted weapons, and tasks of worth to be completed by the hero in question. Such elements can also be seen to occur here in the tale of 'Fair, Brown and Trembling'.

The prince in this tale undergoes a series of challenges and tests before and after his marriage to Trembling, a common trope in Irish myth. This includes duels with 'all the princes and great men' who are also in competition for Trembling's hand (Curtin 88). The tale also uses the test of a sword to identify an imposter. When the prince becomes suspicious that Fair (masquerading as Trembling) may not be his wife, he puts his sword between them in bed, saying: 'If you are my wife, this sword will get warm; if not, it will stay cold' (Curtin 89). In the morning when he rises, the sword is cold, proving his suspicions. Themes of swords which 'spoke' without words can be found within Irish myth (Bernhardt-House 12) and are open to comparison with this plot device.

The prince defeats the whale who swallows his wife using a silver bullet shot from a gun, as instructed by Trembling (Curtin 90). The use of the silver bullet to kill is obviously a well-known premise of wider European werewolf folklore, but can also be seen in Irish folklore relating to the vanquishing of a king-otter, an animal who is only vulnerable to a silver bullet (Mac Coitir, *Ireland's Animal Myths* 204). Cox also cites Powell and Magnusson's discussion of Icelandic sea-monsters, which states that such beasts can only be defeated by the use of a 'silver shot' (Powell and Magnusson cited in Cox 488).

A similar variant of this story is recorded from a Scottish context in Cox's catalogue, titled 'The Snow-White Maiden, and the Fair Maid, and the Swarthy Maid, and Frizzle or Bald Pate their mother' (188). The heroine of this story follows a similar fate to Trembling, and is seized by the 'Great Beast Senseless' when her sister pushes her into a loch (Cox 188). Cox has suggested a potential Irish origin for 'The Snow-White Maiden', due to the use of the identifier of the 'King of Erinn's son' in reference to the prince in the tale (188). In both of these versions, we see the use of the unusual 'Jonah heroine'. Jacobs has suggested that these two tales are an amalgamation of the Cinderella tale with the Sea-Maiden tale (Jacobs, *Cinderella in Britain*, 276). He has further proposed that this combination is a 'specifically Celtic formula' of the Cinderella tale (Ibid.). It is interesting to note a specific plot device mentioned in 'Fair, Brown, and Trembling', which does not feature in 'The Snow Maiden'. The henwife in 'Fair, Brown, and Trembling' uses a 'cloak of darkness' as an aid to transform Trembling's rags into finery (Curtin 79). The element of the 'cloak of darkness' or 'cloak of invisibility' can be seen to occur in a number of Irish folktales. It could be suggested that such a supernatural element may be influenced by the mythological tale of the sea-god Manannan Mac Lir, who uses a cloak of invisibility (Spaan 176). This device is also recorded in use by the legendary hero Cúchulainn to help him defeat a foe (Spaan 180).

In the Group A Cinderella (Cox xxv) variant from County Leitrim entitled 'Cul-Fin, Cul–Din, Cul–Corrach' (Heiner 152), Cul-Fin (fair-haired) and Cul-Din (brown-haired) are two pretty daughters of a poor woman. Their youngest sister, Cul–Corrach (mangy or scabbyhead) is 'an ugly girl, and her sisters wouldn't let her be seen out'. All three sisters undergo a test of honesty set by an old woman from whom they fetch a light for their fire. The old woman leaves three heaps of money on the counter—'one of gold, the second of silver, and the third of copper', and watches the girls to see if they steal any. Both the elder sisters steal some of the gold and silver, but Cul-Corrach does not take any. The old woman bids Cul-Corrach to come to her when her sisters next leave for Mass, and transforms her by dressing her 'in the most beautifullest apparel that any lady could be seen in, and made her face beautiful too, so that she was to be admired, and she put her on a grey steed, and glass slippers on her feet.' (Heiner 153). She is given the usual warning of returning home immediately after Mass to change back into her old clothes.

Cul-Corrach returns to Mass in her finery another two times, with the lord's son stealing one of her slippers on the third occasion, later used to identify her during the 'shoe marriage test' (Cox xxvi). Cul-Fin and Cul-Din swear revenge on their sister 'that they would do their utmost to put her to death for getting such a noble lord'. This tale, like 'Fair, Brown, and Trembling' also features a 'second run' (Cox 189) which deals with Cul-Corrach's life as the lord's wife. When Cul-Corrach gives birth to her first child, her sister Cul-Fin takes the baby and throws him 'out on the heap behind the castle' (Heiner 154). The baby is found by a herdsman who takes him home to be raised by his wife. Cul-Fin puts a kitten in the infant's place, which is shown to the lord who responds 'Why, why, that's a shame; it's bad enough, but it might be worse!' (Heiner 155) This trick by Cul-Fin happens two more times, with the babies replaced by a pup and a pig, the herdsman raising the discarded babies, and the lord accepting the disappointment of the outcome. Cul-Fin and Cul-Din then attempt to drown Cul-Corrach by placing her and her bed in the sea, 'but it was a bed of phoenix feathers she had, and it could not sink' (Heiner 155). The herdsman saves her from the sea and tells the lord about the sisters' plot against Cul-Corrach, and presents their three sons whom he had raised. The old woman who had first helped Cul-Corrach comes to visit 'coming to do wrong right', and ordering the death of Cul-Fin, which is granted. The folklorist Leland Duncan, transcriber of this tale, noted that the plot device of fire-fetching could be seen in an Icelandic variant in Cox's collection, and that it could be proposed that the use of the copper, silver, and gold coins may be compared with the reference to copper, silver, and gold forests in some variants. He also matched the use of the 'changelings' in the child's cradle to a Grimm Cinderella variant from Mecklenburg (Heiner 156; Cox 492).

In 'The Princess in the Cat-Skins', (Cox's B-Type Catskins classification xxv) the heroine finds herself at the mercy of her stepfather, who wishes to marry his stepdaughter following the death of her mother. The heroine is helped by a magic filly who reveals herself to be a fairy who has watched over her since her mother's remarriage. The horse advises her to set three delay tactics for her stepfather, and to claim that she cannot accept his marriage proposal until she has three dresses:

> [...] say you must have first a dress of silk and silver thread that will fit into a walnut shell [...] another dress of silk and gold thread that would fit in a walnut shell [...] a dress of silk thread as thick as it can be with diamonds and pearls no larger than the head of a minnikin pin. Three is a lucky number you know (Kennedy 81-82).

On receiving the dresses, the heroine also finds a dress made of cat-skins on her bed, which she puts on. She takes the three dresses in the walnut shells, and alights on her enchanted horse. She obtains a position as a servant at the house of the prince where she becomes known as Cat-skin. She is guided by her horse to attend a ball that the prince is attending on three occasions, where each time she wears one of the three walnut shell dresses before escaping on the horse back to her servant quarters and catskin dress. She is finally recognised by the prince, not by a lost shoe, but by a small gold ring which he slips onto her finger at the ball. The 'helpful animal' (Cox xxvi) in this variant is the horse who reveals herself to be a guardian fairy for the heroine. Horses are the animals on which most emphasis is placed in Irish literature and folklore (Ó hÓgáin 284), where they are closely associated with the otherworld, and particularly with fairy belief.

A slightly different form of the Catskins motif can be seen in 'The Coat of Green Rushes', recorded in the oral history record from County Leitrim (Dúchas, The Coat of Green Rushes). In this tale, the heroine is again pursued for marriage by a father-figure, and runs away to escape the arrangement. She comes across the house of an old woman who feeds her, but who warns her that her three sons are giants, and that she must leave before she is eaten. Before she can leave, she is confronted by one of the giants who threatens her with death if she does not agree to marry him. He tells her that she will need to sleep with him that night to keep his back warm, and after undressing to her night-dress, she makes an excuse to go outside, and makes her escape.

The heroine hides overnight in a field of rushes, and makes herself a green coat of rushes in the morning to cover her night-dress. She finds work in spinning and knitting at a 'big house' (which we later learn is the residence of the king), and as she cries in despair at her tasks, a witch arrives to do the work for her. The witch meets the heroine again, appearing from under a rock at a spring, and asks why she does not attend Mass. When the girl tells the witch that she has no clothes fit to attend:

> the witch struck the rock with a hazel rod out stepped a lady dressed in white and dressed her like a queen and put glass slippers on her feet and pulled a small pony from under a fountain put her on the pony's back and said let you not take the wind, or the wind take you until you are back, and don't look or speak to any one and the poney (sic) will wait for you until you come out.

The girl returns afterwards and assumes her regular clothes and tasks. The next time the heroine attends Mass, dressed 'twice as nice' by the witch, the king's son pulls off one of her slippers. When the 'shoe marriage test' (Cox xxvi) is administered, the heroine is forced to hide behind the door by the queen. The witch arrives, announcing: 'boney heels and boney toes is put behind the door hiding', and the king's son finds her and discovers that the slipper fits her foot.

In a Longford variant of the tale titled 'Old Story Cinderella—A New Version' (Dúchas, Old Story Cinderella—A New Version), the heroine is aided by a magical hazel tree rather than a witch or enchanted animal. The heroine asks the tree for help to provide her with clothes to go to a dance that she had been forbidden to attend by her stepmother and stepsisters, chanting: 'Rustle and shake, dear hazel tree, Silver and gold shake down on me. And immediately a lovely pink dress and a pair of pink shoes came down.' This ritual is repeated on two further nights. On her attempts to escape the dance on the third night, Cinderella's foot gets 'caught in tar', and she leaves one of her shoes behind, which is found by the king. During the king's shoe test with the heroine's two sisters, their stepmother cuts off the toes of the first sister to allow the shoe to fit and to trick the king that she is the owner.

As the king takes away the sister on his horse, she is exposed by the magical hazel tree:

> When they went by the tree the tree said "There is blood upon the shoe that is not the true one for you["]. The king did not marry her. The shoe did not fit the second (sister) so they decided to cut of (sic) her toes also. When they went by the tree it said the same as before. But the shoe slipped on Cinderalla (sic). When they went by the tree it said: There is no blood upon the shoe. The king soon married her and lived happily ever after.

It is interesting to note that hazel trees hold particular significance in Irish folklore. Folk beliefs tell how hazel was believed to protect against evil, and could be used for magic. Irish legends and myth discuss the existence of a famed well of knowledge, surrounded by nine hazel trees of wisdom, and the otherworldly properties of the tree used for the shields of mythological characters, as well as for wisdom, truth, and magical ability (Mac Coitir, *Ireland's Trees*). In the earlier tale of 'The Coat of Green Rushes', we also see the use of a hazel rod by the witch to conjure dresses, shoes, and transport for the heroine (Dúchas, The Coat of Green Rushes).

In an untitled tale from Kilkenny (Dúchas, A Story), we see a possible Cinderella variant of Cox's Indeterminate Type D (xxv), with an unusual heroine titled 'Hairy Rockey'. In an origin story, we are told that the heroine's mother had been very ill, and under advice from the doctor, she held:

> her head under the eve (eave) of the house. Two sweet drops would fall into her mouth and not to hold her mouth for the third. The first two were so nice that she held her mouth for the third but it was very bitter. After a while there were three daughters born to her. Two nice girls to represent the sweet drops, and the other one was very ugly and her body covered with hair to represent the bitter drop.

The heroine is shunned and excluded by her sisters, but her neglect and underestimation works to her advantage to become the champion of the story. Hairy Rockey and her sisters are invited to stay overnight at the house of a giant and his family. Before going to bed, the giant gives red night caps to Hairy Rockey's sisters to wear, and green night caps to his own daughters. Ignored, Hairy Rockey 'slept at the fire where she used to sleep at home'. Aware that the giant plans to kill her sisters, she swaps the night caps of the giant's daughters with that of her sisters. The giant attacks in the night and beheads the girls in the red caps, mistakenly believing them to be Hairy Rockey's sisters, who flee with their sister from the house. Kennedy records a similar, expanded version of this tale in 'Hairy Rouchy', where the neglected and menial heroine outwits a giant in order to save her sisters and arranges marriages for them with the sons of the king of Spain (3). Hairy Rouchy is rewarded in the end of the tale for her loyalty and bravery when she marries the youngest son of the king. She is released from the spell which originally cast her unpleasant appearance, and her rightful physical beauty is restored to her (Kennedy 9).

Enchanted Animals, Cinderlads, and Magical Objects

Ó hÓgáin has noted that versions of over a third of the folktale variants with animal plot types from the international Aarne/Thomson catalogue have been collected from Irish oral lore, showing their popularity (14). As in the broader Cinderella tradition, helpful enchanted animals feature prominently within the plots of the Irish variants of the tale, guiding the heroine to better circumstances. Black sheep feature as the 'helpful animal' (Cox xxvi) within a number of the Irish Cinderella tales. An untitled tale from Donegal (Dúchas, no title) features a heroine who, abused by her stepmother, is forced to tend to the sheep on the hill without food to sustain her. Upon hearing that the girl has grown up to be 'very, very beautiful', the stepmother, who had hoped that the girl would starve without food on the hill, spies on her, only to find that 'there was an old black sheep in the flock that used to bring the poor girl food to eat and cloths (sic) to wear.' The stepmother demands that the butcher kill the sheep, and as the heroine cries over her loss, she meets a prince who falls in love with her and proposes marriage. She lives happily ever after, and as the tale ends, we are told of the fate of the stepmother—'she was choked when eating a piece of the old black sheep.'

The Ulster tale of 'Ashey Pelt' (Heiner 146) also features a black sheep as a prominent plot device. In this tale, we are told that 'it is a very lucky thing to have a black ewe', and Ashey Pelt, unhappy with her father's remarriage, is approached by one. The sheep bids her to find a rod behind a stone and strike it three times 'and whatever you want will come'. The heroine's wish to go to a party is granted, and 'Dress and horses and all came to her' with the midnight return proviso. When the prince searches for the owner of the silk slipper lost by Ashey, her jealous stepsisters force her outside to take care of the cows. As the prince leaves the house, sure that all have tried the slipper, the black ewe cries to him to stop, calling: 'Nippet foot, and clippet foot, Behind the king's son rides, But bonny foot, and pretty foot, Is with the cathering hides'. The prince finds Ashey amongst the cows, and they are married. Jackson has commented on the common occurrence of the black sheep in the Irish Cinderella tales, and that the black sheep is often presented as the mother of the heroine under enchantment (The International Folktale 273). Christiansen comments on a particularly unusual variant of the tale from County Kerry, where the Cinderella heroine has 'animal parentage' by a black sheep. An introductory episode provides information that the heroine is the daughter of a king and a woman under enchantment, who must live as a woman by night, and a black sheep by day (Christiansen 102).

The Irish Cinderella tales feature a number of variants of 'Cinderlad' stories, with a male protagonist. These forms of tales are recognised as Type E variants of the Cinderella tale by Cox, who identifies them typologically as 'Hero-Tales' (Cox xxv). One of the most common plot elements to the Irish hero tale is the inclusion of an enchanted bull, who guides the hero through his quest, and protects him even after the bull's death. This is a particularly common form of hero-tale recorded in the Cinderella tradition, identified as subtype AT511A (The Little Red Ox) in the Aarne-Thompson index, with examples known worldwide (Cox) (Rooth). In 'Jack and the Little Red Bull' from Kerry (Dúchas, Jack and the Little Red Bull), Jack escapes a neglectful stepmother and runs away, where he is followed by his own red bull, who carries him on his back. The bull encounters a number of other bulls who he must fight over the course of the journey. The bull informs Jack that 'when he was dead to cut his back, and he would find a magic strap and whenever he would be in danger to say, "Help. Help strap of leather".' The red bull defeats his first enemy, and a second two-headed bull, and is finally defeated by a three-headed bull. Jack cuts the strap from his back, and uses it to win success in three separate confrontations with a family of a witch and her three giant sons.

In 'The Little Red Bull' from Tipperary (Dúchas, The Little Red Bull), this story is expanded upon, with the bull providing Jack with food when he is starved by his stepmother—'"Strike my back" said the bull. Jack did as he was told. The bull's back opened and a fine dinner came out. This happened every evening and the step-mother noticed Jack getting fat.' The stepmother sends out her three daughters to spy on Jack, with one instructed to watch him each night. The first daughter is lulled to sleep during her watch by a musical instrument played by Jack, provided by the bull. The second sister, with 'three eyes two in her forehead and one in her poll' (possibly a derivation of the Irish word for nostril—poll sróine/polláire) meets the same fate. Each night after the spy falls asleep, Jack is free to eat as much as he likes.

However, with the third sister, with 'four eyes two in her forehead and two in her poll', Jack makes a mistake with his music, and is unaware that one of the four eyes does not close and fall asleep. The sister sees all, and reports back to her stepmother, who plans to kill the bull. Jack and the bull escape, and as in the former version of this tale (Dúchas, Jack and the Little Red Bull), the bull undergoes three fights on their journey—the first with a giant, and the next two with two bigger bulls. The bull tells Jack that he will die in the third fight, and gives him instructions for after his death. At the bull's death, Jack 'opened the bull and took out a coat of darkness, a steed of swiftness and a sword of light' (Dúchas, The Little Red Bull). Jack goes on to have encounters of the same manner of the other variants of this particular story. He has two confrontations with giants, who he beheads with the sword of light, and a third with a witch (likely mother of the giants as before), whom he also beheads.

The objects provided by the bull in this variant are reminiscent of a number of weapons and magical devices common to Irish myth and legend; most notably the 'sword of light'. The sword of light, known in Irish as An Claidheamh Soluis, features in Irish legend and folktales, where it is a magical weapon with powerful properties and mythological connections. It also features as a plot device in Scottish folk tales (Campbell). The inclusion of the sword of light in Irish folktales has been suggested to have been influenced by native stories of mythological weaponry such as the supernatural sword owned by the warrior Cúchulainn, which 'shone at night like a torch'. In folk tales, the sword of light is often 'possessed by a giant and won from him by a hero' (O'Rahilly 68), and it is wielded by the giant in the aforementioned variant tale of Hairy Rouchy (Kennedy 6). The idea of a sword of light has also been connected to the tale of the four treasures of the Tuatha Dé Danann, an Irish mythological race of supernatural beings. The four treasures of the Tuatha Dé Danann are suggested by some to have included the cauldron of plenty, the spear of victory, the stone of destiny, and the sword of light (Young 6). The sword of light of the Tuatha Dé Danann is linked to deities such as the sea-god Manannan Mac Lir (Young 67), and the hero god Lugh (Young 77). The bull in this Cinderella variant also provides the hero with a further object with potential mythological connections. While in 'Fair, Brown, and Trembling' the magic use of a 'cloak of darkness' helps the heroine (Curtin 79), here a 'coat of darkness' is provided to protect the hero and allow him to complete his quest.

In the Tipperary example of 'The Little Red Bull' (Dúchas, The Little Red Bull), the story has format similarities with 'Fair, Brown, and Trembling' in that it also has a 'second run' (Cox 189). In this case, Jack is told by his new master of 'a fiery draggon [sic] to come and try to kill the princess and whoever could save her could marry her'. Jack disguises himself in 'fine clothes' and heads off to fight the dragon—on his first confrontation injuring it, the second cutting out half of its tongue, and on the third 'he pierced the dragon in the heart and killed him'. As he rushes through the crowd to escape, the crowd take off one of his slippers. Jack's master tells him that whoever the slipper fits will be able to marry the princess. When those testing the slipper come to Jack's house 'Jack tried it and it ran in on his foot. He married the princess and lived happy ever after'. This is an interesting variant of the tale—combining the Cinderlad/Dragonslayer incidents with the most familiar trope of the 'shoe marriage test' (Cox xxvi). A similar format to this can also be seen in the recorded native tale 'Billy Beg and the Bull' (Sierra 44).

Fig. 10-3. Irish 5p postal stamp, 1922/1923, showing an illustration of 'An Claidheamh Soluis' (The Sword of Light)

A version of the same tale from Sligo (Dúchas, Jackeen and the Bull) specifically refers to the animal as a 'fairy bull', and the bull's gifts to Jack include 'a sword that would kill any fish in the sea', 'a suit that would shine in the darkness' and a crock of gold. In a change to the format, the tale involves a plot device seen previously in 'Fair, Brown and Trembling'. The story tells us of:

> a custom that every seven years a gentleman's daughter used to be swallowed by a whale. One day the lady was saying goodbye to all her friends. When the whale came up Jackeen killed it. The lady said he would have to marry her. Jackeen began to run away. She pulled off one of his shoes. She went round the village in a beautiful coach to see where was the boy who had saved her life .... The lady found him. They got married and had plenty of money and they lived together afterwards.

This section of the story combines the 'shoe marriage test' (Cox xxvi) more commonly seen in the traditional Cinderella variants, as well as a possible crossover element from 'Fair, Brown and Trembling' in the form of the whale and the swallowed female character. The crock of gold mentioned in this tale may be seen to link to common Irish fairy and leprechaun lore, and a further Limerick version of this variant also features specific help for Jack from a leprechaun to conquer the giants (Dúchas, Story—Poor Boy, Bull and Giants).

A final version of this hero-tale from Longford (Dúchas, The Little Bull) also uses the traditional Cinderella tale tropes of disguise through fine clothes and the use of the 'shoe marriage test' (Cox xxvi). Unusually in this example we are told that after defeating his foes of the giants, the hero wears 'the loveliest pair of glass slippers that were ever in the world', of which he loses one near to the king's castle. As with the traditional Cinderella format, the hero undergoes the 'shoe marriage test', where the shoe fits, and he marries the king's daughter.

Conclusions

Christiansen has commented that 'there is [...] no standard Irish Cinderella-story, neither can Irish variants have a common source' (Christiansen 101). The surviving Irish variants of the tale show a relatively wide variety and complexity of the Cinderella formats initially classified by Cox and Rooth. They combine story motifs and themes from both national and international influences, which make the Irish corpus of tales an interesting and valuable case study of the variation and popularity of the Cinderella tale. This examination of the Cinderella Cycle in a specifically Irish context provides an example of the breadth and diversity of the tale within particular regions, and the methods of tailoring the story for its regional audiences. The Irish Cinderella accounts can be seen to demonstrate the blending of Irish mythology and folklore with the conventions of the worldwide tale, producing a distinctive and fascinating native variant of the narrative. They demonstrate the native influence of the storytelling elements of the Irish mythological cycle, native legends and folktales. Aspects of Irish myth are married to the rudiments of the international Cinderella tale, with the use of Irish place-names, characters from Irish legend, and magical weaponry and objects which were well known to a contemporary Irish audience. The interesting juxtaposition of such features of Irish legend and folklore alongside the prominent feature of a Catholic Mass service potentially demonstrate the survival of folk beliefs alongside an increasingly religious native population.

Future research on the subject of the Irish Cinderella variants will hopefully uncover further enlightenment on both their adherences to the Cinderella tale tradition, as well as their native cultural influences and adaptation. Additional research in the Irish oral folklore archives will undoubtedly uncover a wider range of surviving examples of the tale which will impact significantly on a broader understanding of the Irish convention. This chapter hopes to contribute to the growth of this discussion, as well as an increased recognition and appreciation of the Irish Cinderella tale. The Irish variants of the Cinderella tale provide an entertaining and informative insight into the adoption and adaptation of an international folktale within a context of rich native folk traditions and mythology. Cinderella's Irish adventures—whether helped by a henwife, clothed in catskins, or swallowed by a whale—survive as unique and entertaining interpretations of one of the world's best loved fairy tales.

Works cited

Bernhardt-House, Phillip A. 'Warriors, Words, and Wood: Oral and Literary Wisdom in the Exploits of Irish Mythological Warriors.' *Studia Celtica Fennica VI* (2009), pp. 5–19.

Briody, Mícheál. *The Irish Folklore Commission 1935—1970: History, ideology, methodology*. Finnish Literature Society, 2016.

Campbell, J.F. *Popular Tales of the West Highlands: Volume I.* R. & R. Clark, 1890.

Christiansen, Reidar Th. 'Cinderella in Ireland.' *Béaloideas,* vol. 20, no. 1/2, 1950, pp. 96–107.

Cox, Marian Roalfe. *Three Hundred and Forty-five Variants of Cinderella, Catskin, and Cap O'Rushes. Abstracted and tabulated.* David Nutt for the Folklore Society, 1893.

Curtin, Jeremiah. *Myths and Folk Tales of Ireland*. Little, Brown and Company, 1890.

Dix, Rachel. 'The Hero of the Red Branch.' *The Irish Monthly*, vol. 44, no. 515, 1916, pp. 323-327.

Dúchas, *The Schools' Collection* https://www.duchas.ie/en/cbes Accessed 26 March 2020.

—. The Coat of Green Rushes, https://www.duchas.ie/en/cbes/4649698/4648234/4658781

—. Old Story Cinderella—A New Version https://www.duchas.ie/en/cbes/5009208/4997656

—. A Story https://www.duchas.ie/en/cbes/4758488/4748012

—. no title https://www.duchas.ie/en/cbes/4428331/4396401/4481517

—. Jack and the Little Red Bull https://www.duchas.ie/en/cbes/4706336/4703879

—. The Little Red Bull https://www.duchas.ie/en/cbes/4922139/4855998/5011519

—. A Folktale https://www.duchas.ie/en/cbes/5073887/4878170

—. Jackeen and the Bull https://www.duchas.ie/en/cbes/4701705/4694382/4760102

—. Story—Poor Boy, Bull and Giants https://www.duchas.ie/en/cbes/4922003/4917183

—. The Little Bull https://www.duchas.ie/en/cbes/5105151/4996395

Heiner, Heidi Anne. *Cinderella Tales From Around the World*. Sur La Lune Press, 2012.

Jackson, Kenneth. 'The International Folktale in Ireland.' *Folklore*, vol. 47, no. 3, 1936, pp. 263-293.

Jacobs, Joseph. *Celtic Fairy Tales*. David Nutt, 1892.

—. 'Cinderella in Britain.' *Folklore,* vol. 4, no. 3, 1893, pp. 269-284.

Joynt, Maud. 'Echtra Mac Echdach Mugmedóin'. *Ériu,* vol. 4, 1910, pp. 91-111

Kennedy, Patrick. *The Fireside Stories of Ireland*. McGlashin and Gill, 1870.

Mac Coitir, Niall. *Ireland's Trees—Myths, Legends and Folklore*. The Collins Press, 2015.

—. *Ireland's Animal Myths, Legends and Folklore*. The Collins Press, 2015.

Nutt, Alfred. 'Cinderella and Britain.' *Folklore,* vol. 4, no. 2, 1893, pp. 133-141.

Ó hÓgáin, Dáithí. *The Lore of Ireland: An Encyclopaedia of Myth, Legend and Romance*. The Boydell Press, 2006.

O'Rahilly, T. F., *Early Irish history and mythology*. Dublin Institute for Advanced Studies, 1957.

Rooth, Anna Birgitta. *The Cinderella Cycle*. Gleerup, 1951.

Sierra, Judy. *The Oryx Multicultural Folktale Series Cinderella*. Oryx Press, 1992.

Spaan, David B. 'The Place of Manannan Mac Lir in Irish Mythology.' *Folklore*, vol. 76, no. 3, 1965, pp. 176-195.

Thompson, Stith. *The Folktale*. Holt, Rinehart, and Winston, 1946.

—. *Motif Index of Folk Literature; A Classification of Narrative Elements in Folk Tales, Ballads, Myths, Fables, Mediaeval Romances, Exempla, Fabliaux, Jest-Books, and Local Legends*. Indiana University Press, 1966.

Uther, Hans-Jörg. *The Types of International Folktales: A Classification and Bibliography, Based on the System of Antti Aarne and Stith Thompson*. Suomalainen Tiedeakatemia, Academia Scientiarum Fennica, 2004.

Young, Ella. *Celtic Wonder Tales*. Dover Publications Inc., 2014.

CHAPTER ELEVEN

CREATIVE REFLECTION: CINDERELLA— THE ULTIMATE DOMESTIC NARRATIVE

VANESSA MARR

This paper examines the domestic origins and manifestations of the Cinderella tale, arguing that this story continues to inform and reflect the domestic expectations of women today. It is supported by a discussion of my artwork, which considers the Cinderella story within a domestic context, along with my ongoing research project that explores the relationship between women and domesticity.

My creative practice has established a yellow dusting cloth as a visual metaphor for domesticity, stitched by hand with red thread to represent traditional women's work and femininity. The duster is an object that I return to frequently; it continues as a running theme throughout my work. Traditional dusters were selected as a metaphor for domesticity because they are mundane, yet visually appealing in their brilliant bright yellow. The duster, the voices it manifests and the stories it tells, are a pivotal point for my investigations (see fig. 11-1).

It is acknowledged that there are many versions of the Cinderella tale, told the world over; however, for the purposes of this investigation, I will be positioning the Brothers Grimm, Charles Perrault and Disney versions as my main reference points, as these are most well-known. Unlike today when they are usually labelled as children's stories, in Perrault's time fairy tales 'captured the concerns of the Court and the social and sexual politics of the seventeenth century French upper class' (Orenstein 29). They were used to moderate behaviour and became a vehicle for 'sharp social criticism, frequently about marriage, love, education and the roles of men and women' (*ibid.*). In contrast, Disney was more interested in making money and showing off the abilities of his animated illustrators; what better way to do this than to borrow from the successful legacy of what are arguably the most famous tales of all? As Zipes writes: 'the purpose of early animated films was to make audiences awestruck […] in such a way that they would forget the earlier fairy tales' (Zipes 197). Disney's version of Cinderella is based on Perrault's (Lang 64–1) but borrows some of the wicked stepmother's worse traits from Grimm: a stew pot of drama, guaranteed to be successful!

In terms of the domestic roles discussed, my focus is on the role of the modern women in the home. I argue that the Cinderella tale is the ultimate domestic narrative, reflecting the imposed yet historically sustained view that domesticity is ultimately a woman's responsibility. In *Situating Everyday Life* Sarah Pink argues that 'researchers are in some ways always part of the lives and world they are researching' (Pink 31). My research is about the every day, and the stories surrounding the mundane domestic tasks that connect us all. The fairy tale of Cinderella explores exactly that.

Women's work, women's narratives

Fairy tales were originally told to women, by women, often while they worked: the original Old Wives Tale. These ever-evolving stories act an indicator of the moral and social compass of the time; through our often-unacknowledged recognition of them in speech, popular culture and contemporary narratives, they are responsible for shaping many of our expectations of love, sex, marriage and life in the home (Orenstein 11). In the days when stories were told orally and the Brothers Grimm and Charles Perrault had yet to adapt these tales towards a more patriarchal focus, women told each other these stories to help make sense of the world around them. Marina Warner states: 'the matter of fairy tale reflects […] lived experience, with a slant towards the tribulations of women [… These stories are] an historical source, or a fantasy of origin [that] gains credibility as a witness record of lives lived, of characters known' (Warner xix).

In *Women's Work: The First 20,000 Years of Women's Work* Elizabeth Barber argues that working with thread, spinning, weaving, sewing etc, historically became a woman's primary means of earning money out of practicality and necessity. 'The compatibility of this pursuit with the demands of child care' (Barber, 30) was crucial; it can be easily taken up and put down again, is by nature repetitive, portable and does not require absolute concentration to complete. It is also a task that can be shared, one which doubtless bound countless communities of women together. For the majority of women these tales would have been told while they worked:

cooking, cleaning, child rearing and, in many instances, running a business from home as well (see fig. 11-2).

Right to left: Fig. 11-1. Embroidering a duster. Fig 11-2. *What is Woman's Work.* Fig. 11-3. *Once Upon a Time.* Vanessa Marr, 2014.

Fig. 11-4. Seven hand-embroidered dusters, Vanessa Marr, 2014.

In today's society this feminine link with cloth has been lost on a practical level, although a predominantly female group will still select it as a craft. Until just fifty years ago women knitted and sewed their own clothes and even wove cloth for family use. These days, working women usually buy pre-made clothes and use childcare providers but the challenge of juggling home, work and child rearing remains a hot female topic (Hanauer xix). I am fascinated by this theme. As a working mother I can relate to this too; the creation of my artwork often mirrors this process. I make my art on the train on my way to work, whilst my daughter plays in the park and whilst the dinner cooks. My own concerns to protect and nurture, and the pain that life sometimes brings, are so accurately reflected in the tales of Cinderella and others that they cease to be tales of old but instead a reflection of life as I know it.

Personal creative practice: promises and expectations

From the legacy of women's work with cloth, I draw from skills passed down to me by both my mother and grandmother and work with thread to make my art. When seeking a visual and material embodiment of domesticity I selected a traditional yellow duster. Other commonplace cloth domestic objects such as aprons or tea towels were also considered but dismissed: because as they are usually adorned, they are already an object to be admired. The transformation of the dusters, which are unadorned, from tool to ornament, changes their purpose and meaning.

I first created a set of seven hand-embroidered dusters which, acting as a metaphor for domesticity, comment upon the expectations of women within both a domestic environment and a fairy tale context. They refer to popular fairy tale phrases, for example *Once Upon a Time* (see fig. 11-3) and *Happily Ever After* (fig 11-6) which are juxtaposed with definitions of brutality, protectiveness and femininity, taken from the dictionary. I selected a script font for the phrases to visually reference the ancient origins of these sayings, whilst the definitions are designed as concrete poetry and presented within forms that relate to cloth and domesticity: an apron, an iron, scissors and a thimble (see fig.11-5 a-d). Just as Annette Messenger embroidered proverbs that denigrate women into cloth to highlight the absurdity of these viewpoints (Iborra-Sanchez n.p.) so I invite viewers to question the definitions I've visuald: the implied fragility of femininity; why the dictionary definition of domestic refers specifically to housewives not husbands; and what 'happily ever after' really means. I chose an iron to hold the definition of brutality because I discovered it is one of the most common objects used in domestic violence. The thimble that embodies the definition of protectiveness would have saved another fairy tale heroine from a hundred years of slumber, its commonplace belonging in a sewing box reminds us to protect both ourselves and our families.

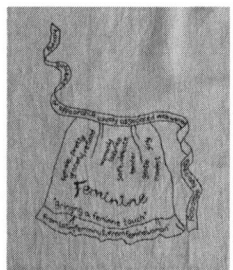 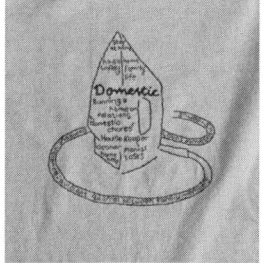 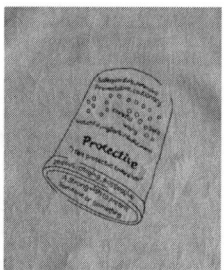

Fig. 11-5. A: Apron, b: Iron, c: Thimble, Vanessa Marr, 2014.

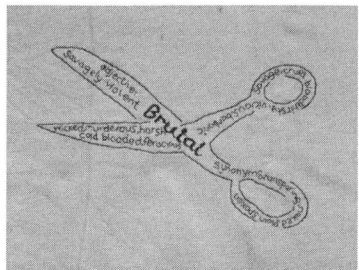 

Fig. 11-5. d: Scissors. Fig. 11-6. *Happily Ever After… This is not the End*, Vanessa Marr, 2014

Red thread is used to embellish the dusters with embroidery, which visually ties the project together both aesthetically to match the stitched edges of the duster and with meaning to represent femininity. Historically red is considered a symbol of womanhood representing fertility (Gordon 122). There are many examples of its use in textile form. Weavers often wore a red sash or string around their hips to praise Isis, the Egyptian goddess of fertility, and even today the colour is worn by women, from brides to exotic dancers 'hold[ing] the quality of sexual promise' (Gordon 38). Women seeking to become pregnant often wear red cords around their wrists, referencing a Jewish tradition still held in Bethlehem at Rachel's tomb. The DNA that identifies the duster artwork is a discussion of what it means to be a woman: red thread provides this visual link.

The choice of embroidery builds upon the feminine history of working with cloth as previously discussed but also reiterates a link to this practice that is particularly strong. In *The Subversive Stitch* Rozita Parker describes how embroidery 'has provided a source of pleasure and power for women, while being indissolubly linked to their powerlessness' (Parker 11). My claim of dusters and embroidery to make art that challenges patriarchal perspectives on a woman's domestic role undeniably references the craftivist movement, although I discovered this after I had begun. From education, to privileged pastime, from home making towards a claim of stitching by women for revolution, art and leisure, this skill still unmistakably visuals the feminine (see figs. 11-7, 11-8).

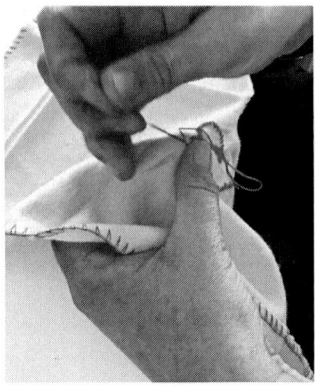 

Fig. 11-7 Left: Embroidering dusters in a workshop that accompanied an exhibition of the dusters in 2017. Fig. 11-8 Right: A selection of dusters on display at the University of Brighton, 2017.

Many other textile-based crafts are also still considered the pastime of women. As discussed in *The Culture of Knitting*, this task in particular conjures images of 'old women clicking needles […] hip young chicks knitting for peace […] or remembered clothes that mothers, aunties and grannies have made' (Turney 8). Textiles are often linked to domesticity and female fulfilment, a fact much referenced in contemporary art, for example through the textile sculptures of Louise Bourgeois (Celant). Notably even the Bauhaus directed its female staff and students towards the weaving room (Weltage 42) and, whilst we could consider the female Bauhaus artists restricted, the textiles they created suggest creativity, innovation and expression that more than equals the work of their less constricted male colleagues. If embraced, can working with textiles mean liberation rather than restriction? Can it cause a revolution?

Fairy tales are much maligned for their 'easy lies' and 'false hopes' (Warner 415) but fantasy also offers an escape and a collaboration of understanding. My selection of fairy tale phrases makes promises and sets expectations; the dusters imply a domestic context, and the objectified definitions challenge the reality of these promises. In sequence they tell a story of their own that is purposefully open to interpretation, inviting the viewer to reflect upon their own experiences and draw their own conclusions.

Women and domesticity—what's your perspective? A collaborative research project

Inspired by my original set of dusters and the theme of fairy tales and their domestic origins, I have been running a participatory arts-based research project since 2014 that explores the relationship between women and domesticity, asking anyone from the community, from all walks of life, artists and non-artists, to commit through thread their own views and experiences on this theme. Notably, predominantly women have responded. The result is a growing collection of over one-hundred hand-embroidered dusters featuring personal reflections and insights including poetic quotes, resentful statements, images and fond memories. Each duster is unique and hand-stitched, demonstrating skill, perseverance and time spent in creative investigation of the object, transforming it from a cloth kept under the sink into a voice for women today (see fig. 11-4, 11-8).

I'm particularly interested in the transformation that occurs to both object and participant when engaged with the cloth through stitching. Drawing upon the notions of collaboration, self-reflection and craft activism I am exploring how modern women see themselves in a domestic context whilst also taking inspiration from my own artistic practice. This project opens up opportunities for ongoing dialogue on the often-silent task of housework, discussing common social experiences and commenting upon the experiences and perspectives of women across the distinctions of age, social class and geographical context. The collection is the context for my academic research including both practical workshops and academic papers. It is also regularly exhibited, performing a collection of voices that call for acknowledgement.

Acts that build community

Cinderella worked alone, which was in itself a punishment. These days we also clean behind locked doors and live very separate lives from those of our female ancestors. Fairy tales were intended to be shared and to empower women but instead evolved to reflect the 'more general patriarchal view of women as domestics and breeders, born to serve the interests of men' (Zipes 80). This is most obvious when we look at the role of the persecuted heroine, of which Cinderella is a classic example. She is generally abused, seeks magic help, meets a prince, hides then reveals her identity and is ultimately married off. The duster *Happily Ever After... This is not the End*, (see fig. 11-6) references this narrative because I question her satisfaction with the happy ever after solution. Then what? A life of domesticity and breeding? Not enough has changed since these nineteenth century fairy tales, for women still predominantly hold these roles. We need a way of giving voice to this protest and importantly we need to share it. Our ancestors sewed together, and we can too, in the way that modern day life allows it. Workshops, discussions, presentations, Instagram, blogging—all have led me to personal friendships through the duster project. This act of sewing builds a community through the companionship of shared challenges and experiences. Sewing doesn't require a shout or a march, it takes time, thought and contemplation. As Sarah Corbett discusses in her book *How to be a Craftivist,* quiet protest is a valuable tool that often opens doors that would otherwise be closed. Cloth and stitch are crucial in this engagement, both as maker and receiver of the message. We have an intimate relationship with cloth. We wear it on our bodies, we wrap our new-borns and our dead in it. We clean with it, we adorn with it. The rise of craftivism in the past few years reflects a return to the values that the original fairy telling women held. They knew the value of a story accompanied by cloth.

The voices from the dusters are emancipatory; the process of saying it brings freedom and perhaps even permission to change things as the voices are subsequently acknowledged. Whilst experiences are reduced to a few choice words or images embroidered upon a duster, this is not a reductive process. Reflection and action build rather than reduce. The combined narrative of collective voices speaks a truth of experience that underpins the warnings woven into oral folktales. Based on my experience, I would argue that a modern-day Cinderella is no less likely to be enslaved by domesticity that her predecessor, but how will she deal with it in today's world? My personal Cinderella broke free from enslavement through a degree and a career. In a day and age when, in the West at least, women can in theory be and do anything, we need a story that shakes off the shackles of cleaning the toilet and empowers our daughters to bet on themselves over the Prince.

Disrupting domesticity

Warner cites fairy tales as 'words as weapons for women' (Warner 413) explaining women's arts within this arena as verbal: riddling, casting spells, conjuring and creating magic. This is the very practice of storytellers themselves; a voice that unites women's struggles: a 'social binding agent', which when mixed produces the 'colours of a painting' (Warner 414). The nature of these tales invites both the suggestion of the unrealistic and the recognition of the human condition, spun with colourful language and metaphor.

Fairy tales are fantastic and often unbelievable: brutal yet protective; alarming yet reassuring; but also, crucially, honest in their reflection of female characteristics both good and bad. The hidden, often unacknowledged, depths of these characters are buried within the stories. As these tales were passed down from one generation to the next, with evidence that the same stories even crossed continents, there was inevitable character development and manipulation of the plot (Warner xviii). However, the key plot points remained the same, as did the female characters that bound the tales together and who often provided the principle motif that defined the tale (Orenstein 72). These commonplace myths served to establish gender roles that haven't been challenged for centuries.

The collective voices that gather together through the duster project challenge the domestic myth of the ideal woman who is completely satisfied with making and maintaining her home. In his book *Mythologies* Roland Barthes establishes myth as a 'type of speech' defined 'by the way in which it utters [its] message' (Barthes 13). We receive these myths daily, often through advertisements that use images and messages to build complex narratives, which are then woven into our society. A happy woman (signifier) is shown completing a domestic task (the signified), then presented as the sign (or myth) that this where she belongs. It is possible to challenge this with the same process; the signifier (the embroidered duster) and the signified (domesticity and femininity) become the sign (meaning women and domesticity). The message embroidered upon the duster and the context of the question posed (Women and Domesticity: What's your Perspective?) are therefore framed within a visual context that supports the message that participants embellish upon the dusters. This gives the message the same importance and visual weight as an advertisement, thus presenting a new myth that disrupts the norm.

This new myth is much more diverse and much more realistic. Satisfaction is recognd in the collection of stitched proclamations but so are rage, frustration and above all else an imploring for acknowledgement (see fig. 11-9). The effort and time spent in creating these messages call out to be noticed, for it seems that the established myth of a happy housewife is also an invisible woman: rather like Cinderella, who meets the needs of others above her own. Politically, socially and domestically they are determined to no longer be ignored. Just as the Suffragettes needed to fight and agitate to get women the vote, the time has come to disrupt what is considered normal and for women to write their own domestic stories. If Cinderella is the ultimate domestic narrative, it should start with her.

Fig. 11-9. A selection of dusters completed by project participants on display at the De La Warr Pavilion, Bexhill-on-Sea, March 2016.

Fig. 11-10. *Rubber Glove – You shall go to the Ball!* Vanessa Marr, 2014.
Fig. 11-11. *There's No-one Like her,* Vanessa Marr, 2018.

Domesticity as punishment

Rubber gloves are worn for dirty domestic tasks. They protect you from germs and form a barrier between skin and task, skin and object. Stitched in red and in yellow to match the yellow duster theme, this work depicts domesticity as punishment (see fig. 11-10). To be made to wear them is to be made to complete an unsavoury task, a task which requires the wearer often to bend, to stoop, to get on one's knees to complete it. The punishment is ultimately servitude.

Cinderella's exclusion from the ball by her wicked stepmother is a well-known part of the tale and pivotal to the beginning of her transformation from skivvy to princess. The embroidered statement defies exclusion from the ball, promising something better. The underlying message is to 'take your punishment gracefully for you might be rescued'. Throughout the Grimm Brothers version there is reference to Cinderella's good and forgiving nature, which is directed towards her stepsisters on numerous occasions. The final line states:

> She was taken to the young prince, dressed as she was. He thought she was more charming than before, and, a few days after, married her. Cinderella, who was no less good than beautiful, gave her two sisters lodgings in the palace, and that very same day matched them with two great lords of the court. (Grimm n.p.)

There are contradictions in this message, a confusion of reward versus punishment. In her book *From the Beast to the Blonde,* Marina Warner writes of 'stories which centre on a heroine [...] suffering a prolonged ordeal before her vindication' (Warner 202). The implication is that it will somehow make her a better person. This is particularly supported by Disney's animated version of Cinderella (Disney 1950) where she completes the tasks with a weary yet happy smile and an implied sense of knowing that she is doing good.

Disney's animation also includes a scene that depicts Cinderella in tears beside the fire. Her body is slumped, and she looks defeated. She appears weak and unable to cope, surrounded by the tools of domestic drudgery: ripe for the rescue perhaps? The need for rescue is often suggested through stories we hear early in childhood. Bettelheim suggests that all children identify with the story of Cinderella because of their need to be rescued from 'degradation and [to] experience the most wonderful exaltation'. Further, they need the reassurance that their own efforts can achieve this. He also discusses that her 'dwelling in the ashes' presents her as 'dirty and uncouth' (Bettelheim 243). Within society's expected and projected morality for women this is about as low as it gets. So, we are confused; domesticity is presented as a punishment, but it holds the potential for a reward if completed virtuously. The Grimms also write that the Prince accepts her 'dressed as she was' (presumably in rags), which contradicts the aspiration for riches and status. Has all her virtuous domesticity transcended this?

Marie-Louise von Franz begins her book *The Interpretation of Fairy Tales* with the statement: '[f]airy tales are the purest and simplest expression of collective unconscious psychic processes' going on to say that 'they represent their simplest, barest and most concise form' (von Franz 1). When we see ourselves reflected in the archetypal characters playing out before us, there is an unconscious desire to play their role too. We unconsciously refer to them when interpreting a problem, going on to identify with them and subsequently decide upon a course of action. The unconscious is, metaphorically speaking, in the same position as the one who had the original vision or experience and wishes to share it. We become them and act out accordingly. This makes the fairy tale very hard to resist, it is the perfect persuasive messenger.

Domesticity as a goal

The myth of happy domesticity still persists; according to social standards presented by popular media culture, a woman's fairy tale dreams of happy ever after are no less relevant today. Let us all be like Cinderella, never complaining and ever happy with a broom in our hand! Yes, the tale saves her from the wicked stepmother and her kin, but why give up on all that domestic bliss?

As discussed earlier, happily ever after should in fact reference the beginning rather than the end (see fig. 11-6). The winning of the prize of life in the fairy tale castle marks the transference from one domestic context to another: from slave to wife. The Cinderella tale falls short of telling us how to live after the 'I do'. All we know if that it must be perfect, and happy, forever. Anne Sexton sums this up in the final stanza of her poem 'Cinderella' through reference to the girl and her prince living 'happily ever after, like two dolls in a museum case', apparently frozen in time and in contrast to the usual practical and boring realities of marriage such as 'diapers or dust' or 'telling the same stories twice'. Sexton points out that this fairy tale marriage does not reflect the real world, yet with 'their darling smiles pasted on for eternity' our fairy tale newlyweds appear to live out the unattainable dream (Sexton, 56–7).

Does Cinderella actually gain any power from this transference or is her role as server already too ingrained to change? 'Too often, Cinderella believes she belongs where she is' (Kolbenschlag 86) and she is so grateful for anything else, that the pattern of her role as server persists. Feminists have long since challenged the feminine role that fairy tales present, claiming 'that women had been imbued with a false consciousness, and thus needed to have their true consciousness raised' (Orenstein 140). 'One is not born, but rather becomes a woman' Simone de Beauvoir famously stated (Beauvoir 267). Unfortunately, fairy tale girls become women whilst dutifully waiting for the ultimate rescue of marriage, whilst the boys rush off for exciting adventures. Cinderella epitoms this through her ultimately passive approach to life. This need not be so, and fortunately these days it is much less the case, however when it comes to domesticity, certain motifs persist.

This passive Cinderella has not always existed. Early oral versions of the tale tell of a 'strong young woman' (Zipes 46) who actively uses her wits to regain her position in society; one that isn't defined by rescue from a prince but instead by a desire for personal recognition. Zipes discusses how in Perrault's version the Fairy Godmother and the Prince are introduced to keep Cinderella submissively in line. As a privileged man, Perrault selected a tale that amused him and adapted it to his own means, thus transforming it from a feminine tale of empowerment to one that positioned the woman as he perceived she should be: submissive, obedient and dedicated to the home. The Brothers Grimm undoubtedly contributed to this too but, Zipes argues, from the more noble standpoint of wanting 'the rich cultural tradition of the common people to be used and accepted by the rising middle classes' (Zipes, 61). However, contrary to popular belief, they were not sourcing their stories from oral tales as Perrault did, but gathering tales from the rising classes whilst developing new ones. Inevitably, popular social views of the time were highly influential on these new tales, resulting in a story that is essentially the same: that of a disempowered woman looking to a man to define her purpose.

The time has come for fairy tales to evolve from these male-manipulated versions that ultimately serve to keep a woman in her place. Disappointingly the recent Disney remake (Branagh 2015) did nothing to address this issue, positioning Cinderella once again with virtues of beauty and gentleness above all else. A modern version of Cinderella would do well to look back to the original oral tales for inspiration; the story should be empowering and radical, the tale of a forthright woman establishing and defining her position in society, not looking to the Prince for rescue. Instead, just one glance and she's hooked, perceiving the Prince as the solution to all her problems. What sort of a message is that to teach our daughters?

Pedalling the fairy tale dream

Advertisers often use the Cinderella tale to sell cleaning products, pedalling the dream of happily ever after and borrowing the idea from Perrault that they can used to influence societal behaviour. The 2012 Gif Actifizz commercial shows Cinderella magically wiping the dirt away, ultimately transforming from a caricature into a real-life satisfied housewife (Actifizz). By using Cinderella as the signifier for domesticity, the message is quickly communicated and understood. A quick *Google* search for 'Cinderella Cleaning Products' reveals that this is also evident in advertisements for dishwashers, cleaning services and even aprons to wear whilst you clean. They also often hark back to the popular modern understanding of the tale through visual references that are made to Disney. A cleaning advice article discovered on *Buzzfeed* concludes its long list of tips with an animated image of Disney's Cinderella admiring herself in a bubble, along with the line: 'Now enjoy your sparkling clean bathroom', thus presenting her likeness as a goal for time spent fussing over trivial domestic challenges *(buzzfeed.com/nataliebrown/ways-to-make-your-bathroom-cleaner-than-its-ever-been)*. It is apparent that reference to Cinderella prompts the immediate understanding of a domestic context whilst also projecting an aspirational domestic role for women within it.

As discussed in *The Routledge Companion to Media and Fairy-Tale Cultures,* 'advertisements function by employing a desire', which is also the very magic that drives a fairy tale. Both pedal dreams that sell 'magical transformations that are integral to […] these narratives'. The difference is that a fairy tale presents the possibility of a transformation, the advertisement tells you that the product it's selling 'is the transformation' (Greenhill et al. 155). Character arcs are trumped by the acquisition of a product: 'Constructing a positive transformation in a woman's life on the basis of her consumption and use of a washing machine renders her existence primarily in terms of a domestic role' (Greenhill et al. 156). Association with a fairy tale supports this. We know that Cinderella ultimately found domesticity transforming because her selfless servitude was rewarded by rescue from her plight and marriage to the Prince, along with the other dream that women are sold: their very own castle to keep all their amazing domestic appliances in. Who could fail to live happy ever after with all that on offer? In short, it leaves the 'world safe for gender hierarchy and capitalism' (Greenhill et al. 156) (see fig. 11-11).

Fig. 11-12. *When I'm feeling domestic I put my Pinny on,* Ana Valls, 2015.
Fig. 11-13. *Be a Good Girl,* Vanessa Marr, 2017.
Fig. 11-14. *Is this Domestic Bliss?* Vanessa Marr, 2016.

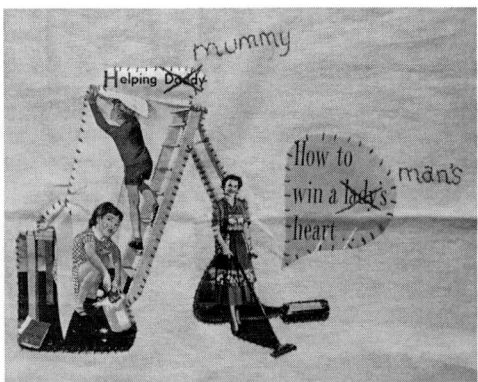

Fig. 11-15. *The Many-Handed Woman,* Vanessa Marr, 2016.
Fig. 11-16. *Be just like ~~Daddy~~ Mummy*, Jenny Embleton, 2016.

In the middle of the twentieth century post-war policies encouraged women back into the home, an idea that the advertising industry backed enthusiastically. Illustrations and advertisements from that era praise a woman's domestic ability and sell her products that are apparently guaranteed to make her happy and efficient (see fig. 11-14). Women are often used to sell to women in the same way as 'the misogyny of fairy tales engages women as participants, not just targets' recounting stories that suggest a 'world of female authority as well as experience' (Warner

208). This reassures her that this is a woman's way of doing things, i.e. behaving as Cinderella did and dutifully fulfilling her domestic tasks. It gives the role value, 'if a woman says such things [...] then the matter is settled' (Warner 209). Unfortunately, although messages are perhaps subtler these days, as evident in the Gif advertisement, this message persists today.

This social conditioning starts early; be just like Mummy and you too can become Cinderella. This idea has been subverted in Jenny's duster, which collages images from a post-war children's magazine of gendered parental and childhood stereotypes (see fig. 11-15 & 16). In contrast, an article describing a *Dream Photo Shoot* where little girls dress up like Cinderella with a mop in hand*,* featured in the *Daily Mail* in on 17 January 2015 (Mail Online Reporter), firmly positions domesticity as part of the little girl princess dream. Repeated images of women in popular media culture, happily completing domestic tasks, reinforce the idea that is a desirable goal, never mind the unrealistic expectations (see fig. 11-14).

In Emma Donoghue's retelling of Cinderella, the female protagonist cleans without the prompting of the wicked stepmother. The voices in her head have already established themselves, as have the voices of the media today.

> I scrubbed and swept because there was nothing else to do. I raked out the hearth with my fingernails and scoured the floor until my knees bled [...] Nobody made me do these things, nobody scolded me, nobody punished me but me. The shrill voices were inside. Do this, do that, you lazy heap of dirt [...] When everything that could possibly be done was done for the day, the voices faded. I knelt on the hearth and looked into the scarlet cinders until my eyes swam. (Donoghue 4)

Speaking and silencing the voice of the stepmother

The voices that Donoghue refers to also speak from the dusters, both my own work and those from the project, reflecting the domestic experiences of over a hundred modern women. This collective reflective practice holds, and when exhibited performs, the multitude of voices that exist inside our heads. The wicked stepmother is not far away from the modern female domestic experience, she whispers dissatisfaction into our ears; a list of 'should've' and 'have-to' through the inherited voices of our mothers, grandmothers and the women before them. Stitching upon a duster is a means of contesting and disrupting the voices that plagued Cinderella and continue to plague us today (see fig. 11-13).

Fairy tales recount experience disguised as tropes and archetypal characters that have an impact because we recognise them. We are able to see ourselves in Cinderella, scurrying around, completing a multitude of tasks with the expectation that we do so with a smile. We identify with her as a character and therefore will her to succeed. Many of the women participating in the duster project have already met and married their Prince Charming, which often only achieved their expected elevation to the media-spun fairy tale of the Domestic Goddess. More voices and more pressure! Embroidering upon a duster releases those voices and begins to challenge the expectations.

Frigga Haug's collective work on memories of female sexualisation uses a form of reflective story-writing within which sharing and collaboration form a pivotal force for change. She discusses the role of storytelling to 'expand our knowledge [...] sharpen social perception [... and] change our attitude to others' (Haug 71). Fairy tales are one of the oldest examples of storytelling. Cinderella's position within this collection establishes the tale as the root of domestic expectations. By drawing upon this legacy and telling our own stories we can borrow from the power of the fairy tale and, as Haug also writes, begin to 'live our lives more consciously'. June Crawford et al. built upon Haug's work some years later when dealing with emotion and gender: they too used storytelling to release experiences, notably 'uncovering the processes of the construction of self' (Crawford et al. 39). This presentation of self brings us back to our relationship with Cinderella. In her domestic plight we see our domestic selves. She, it seems, will have to change with us.

Researching the everyday

It's unfashionable to talk about domestic tasks, particularly in a professional context, yet the necessity of these tasks is something we all have in common, both men and women. If we didn't keep our homes clean, we would ultimately become sick. It doesn't get more important than that. Housework literally makes the world go around yet there is scant reference made to it in literature outside of the context of Cinderella and her contemporaries behaving like dutiful maidens or housewives, and until recently it was largely ignored in academia too. No great work of art is made about doing the washing up, yet undoubtedly artists are in some way involved in the preparation, consumption and clearing away of a meal as much as rest of us. A combination of society, industrialisation, maternity and practicality for hundreds if not thousands of years has left responsibility for the majority of everyday domestic tasks firmly in the lap of a woman. Whilst help might be offered and some households really do share it these days, in most cases the ownership of domestic tasks still sits with the women of the household, whether they work outside the home or not (see fig. 11-17).

Fig. 11-17. *All you need is a Magic Wand*, Angela Paine, 2015.
Fig. 11-18. *We all need to do our bit*, Joanna Kerr, 2015.
Fig. 11-19. *In the Land Faraway, Dreams Come True*, Vanessa Marr, 2014
Fig. 11-20. *Fairy Tale Castles in the Sky*, Vanessa Marr, 2017

In her book *The Second Shift* Arlie Hochschild attributes women with an extra month spent on housework each year in comparison to her male partner. This rises once children are born but is still significant when they are not a factor. The roots of my collaborative research project sit within this context. Hochschild's book was published in 1990, but I was intrigued to explore if, nearly thirty years on, anything had changed. My own experience and that of most my friends certainly had not. Hochschild also notes the enthusiasm of working women with busy lives to make time for research interviews and the 'feeling that the second shift was their issue' (Hochschild 6). This has been the case with my project too. The women who choose to stitch upon a duster are rarely those 'with time to do so' as someone once queried. They are usually stressed out, harassed and fed up with doing it all. They welcome the opportunity to have their voice heard and for importance to be placed on what others might perceive as petty moans. Whilst efforts are currently being made to expand the scope of the project, the demographic to date is largely female, professional and middle class; by world standards they are privileged. This has potential to take away from the importance of their voice, but I would argue that this doesn't diminish the extent to which they can feel taken for granted (see fig. 11-18).

The collection of different yet complimentary voices is one of the strongest elements of the project and something most frequently remarked on when the dusters are exhibited. Within this context women are neither applauded nor demonised for their concerns. Patterns have emerged but each voice is unique and as important as the next one. The juggle of everyday domestic life is a female topic, a common thread that binds us across social class, race and age. Love it or loath it, women have something to say about it, which brings me back to Cinderella. Crucially, she was not made to dig the garden or mend the roof. Hers was a female concern, that of the necessary domestic tasks that keep the world turning.

Conclusion

Cinderella models the ultimate domestic archetype. Whether the connotations are positive or negative, her link to domesticity is firmly established. The artwork entitled *Scrubber* epitomises this relationship (see fig.11.21). The derogatory reference implies the act of scrubbing but is also a name that is used to refer to a woman with loose morals. This brings us full circle, back to dirty tasks and negative connotations. Cinderella is a tale of contradictions, of tragedy and loss, of hard work and reward, of impossible dreams and domestic drudgery, much like the messages that the media still presents to women today.

Cinderella should empower us—she made a change, but one that contemporary women find restrictive and limiting. This contradicts the tricks played by advertisers who, like Perrault, use the fairy tale to keep women down with a multitude of domestic tasks that are never completed. She manifests our hopes and our dreams but also our enslavement. We have become the archetypal persecuted heroine of our own lives. Fairy tales are magical, but they are also everyday stories. Magic isn't a dishwasher, although it helps, it's a new Cinderella story. A story that I'd like to stitch upon a duster, so that it can take on a life of its own.

Fig. 11-21: *Scrubber*, Vanessa Marr, 2017.

Whether we take her as a heroine or a wench, it is impossible to separate her from the origins of her name, to sleep amongst the cinders is to integrate and define oneself with one's surroundings: the hearth, the home, the domestic. In *Little Red Riding Hood Uncloaked* Catherine Orenstein asks: 'have you read a fairy tale lately? Look around. Fairy tales are in the pages of People magazine, profiling Hollywood princesses […] in our movies […]' (Orenstein 10). Fairy tales are also used to sell us a lifestyle through the advertising we consume each day. 'We think we outgrow them. In fact, we internalize them' (Orenstein 11). If attitudes towards a woman's perceived domestic role are to change, then perhaps what we need is a new fairy tale (see fig 11-19. and fig. 11-20).

Works cited

Actifizz. Cif Advertisement. *How Cinderella got to the Ball – Fast!* 28 February 2012. http://www.youtube.com/watch?v=pC9-8sqULzs Accessed 1 June 2020.

Barber, Elizabeth. *Women's Work: The First 20,000 Years*. Norton. 1995.

Bettelheim, Bruno. *The Uses of Enchantment: The Meaning and Importance of Fairy tales*. Third edition. Penguin Books, 1991.

Branagh, Kenneth, director. *Cinderella*. Performance by Kate Blanchet, Disney. 2015.

Brown, Natalie. *Twenty-eight ways to make your bathroom cleaner than it's ever been!* https://www.buzzfeed.com/nataliebrown/ways-to-make-your-bathroom-cleaner-than-its-ever-been?utm_term=.aibKAPZO40#. os4Q5doORV Accessed 6 April 2016.

Beauvoir, Simone de Howard. *The Second Sex*, edited by Madison Pashley, Vintage Books, 1952: 1974.

Corbett, Sarah. *How to be a Craftivist*. Unbound, 2017.

Celant, Germano. *Louise Bourgeois: The Fabric Works*. Skira Editore, 2010.

Crawford, June and Susan Kippaz, Jenny Onyx, Una Gault, and Pam Benton. *Emotion and Gender: Constructing Meaning from Memory*. Sage Publishing Ltd. 1992.

Donoghue, Emma. *Kissing the Witch*. Hamish Hamilton. 1997.

Franz, Maria-Louise von. *The Interpretation of Fairy Tales*. Shambhala, 1996.

Geronimi, Clyde, director. *Cinderella*. Walt Disney Productions, 1950.

Gordon, Beverly. *Textiles: The Whole Story*. Thames & Hudson, 2011. 122.

Greenhill, Pauline and Jill Terry Rudy, Naomi Hamer, Lauren Bosc. *The Routledge Companion to Media and Fairy-Tale Cultures*. Routledge, 2018.

Grimm, Jacob and Wilhelm. 'Cinderella' in *Grimms Household Tales*. 2 Vols. Translated by Margaret Hunt, George Bell & Sons, 1884. http://germanstories.vcu.edu/grimm/cinder.html Accessed 20 March 2020.

Hanauer, Cathi. *The Bitch in the House*. Penguin. 2002.

Haug, Frigga, et al, *Female Sexualisation: A Collective Work of Memory*. Translated by Erica Carter. Verso Classics, 1987.

Hochschild, Arlie. *The Second Shift*. Avon Books, 1990.

Iborra-Sanchez, Corinne. 'On the wire, Cahiers de littérature orale.' 2 March 2013. journals.openedition.org/clo/980 Accessed 28 Nov. 2018

Kolbenschlag, Madona. *Kiss Sleeping Beauty Goodbye*. Bantam Books, 1981.

Mail Online Reporter. *A Dream Come True!* 17 January 2015. http://www.dailymail.co.uk/news/article-2914269/A-dream-come-true-Photographer-captures-magical-pictures-two-little-girls-dressed-favorite-fairy-tale-characters.html Accessed 1 June 2020.

Orenstein, Catherine. *Little Red Riding Hood Uncloaked: Sex, Morality and the Evolution of a Fairy Tale*. Basic Books, 2002.

Parker, Rozsika. *The Subversive Stitch*. London, Tauris & Co. Ltd, 2010.

Perrault, Charles. 'Cendrillon, ou la petite pantoufle de verre.' *Histoires ou contes du temps passé, avec des moralités: Contes de ma mère l'Oye*. Paris, 1697, pp. 64–71.

Pink, Sarah. *Situating Everyday Life*. Sage Publications Ltd, 2012.

Turney, Joanne. *The Culture of Knitting*. Berg, 2009.

Sexton, Anne. *Transformations*. Mariner Books, 2001.

Warner, Marina. *From the Beast to the Blond*. Vintage, 1995.

—. *Once Upon a Time*. Oxford University Press, 2014.

Weltage, Sigrid Wortman. *Women's Work: Textile Art from the Bauhaus.* Thames & Hudson, 1993.

Zipes, Jack. *Fairy Tales and the Art of Subversion.* 2nd Edition, Routledge, 2006.

CHAPTER TWELVE

'PROM NIGHT: CINDERELLA GETS A GUN'
A STORY AND CREATIVE REFLECTION

LESLEY MCKENNA

Prom Night: Cinderella Gets a Gun

Ella stands in front of the mirror, looking at herself, up and down, up and down. Behind her, Faye's smiling, that hungry, slightly feral smile that always unnerves her, that always manages to flip her stomach with want. It's a smile that says, Hey Ella, don't you look pretty? A smile that says, Hey, Ella, don't that dress suit you just right? It's a smile that says, Hey Ella, didn't I just cover up that black eye and those bruises so good you almost can't see them?

Ella smiles back, and performs a little pirouette, winces as the wrenched muscle in her back pulls. In the mirror she sees her smile drop, replaced by a grimace of pain.

'It's okay,' Faye says, coming up behind her and wrapping her arms around her waist. 'You'll make 'em all dance tonight.' Ella leans back against Faye, closes her eyes, feels soft hands rise up to cup her breasts, sighs. Sighs again, opens her eyes, looks into Faye's, sees the glint of malice there, more feral than ever.

'One more accessory,' Faye says, letting her go. Ella watches her in the mirror as she crosses the room to fetch the finishing touches. Sees the glint of metal flicker silver as two 9mm semi-automatic handguns, and two extra clips-full of bullets are produced. Ella doesn't know how Faye obtained them, or where from, doesn't want to know, but she feels that lurch in her stomach, in her heart, and wonders how she's ever going to use them, even if the people she's punishing deserve it.

'Happy Prom Night,' Faye says, strapping one clip-belt around her own waist, and the other around Ella's—it feels hard, nothing like Ella's soft hands—and slapping a gun into Ella's right palm. 'Happy Prom Night,' Faye repeats. 'You shall go the ball.'

Ella feels tears prick her eyes, because it's not her prom but Faye's and Ella doesn't believe that after tonight, she'll ever go to her own.

'Hey, don't look so sad,' Faye says, seeing the tears in Ella's eyes. 'Tonight you'll shine. Tonight you'll repay everyone who ever hurt you.' A wicked smile. 'You shall go the ball, Ella, and you'll shoot all those bastards down.'

Ella hadn't wanted it to come to this. Of course not. It was easier to let it continue as it was, with her not saying anything, allowing it to happen, because it had always been that way, seemed like. Since she was too little to know any difference. Besides, whatever they'd done, Luke and Johnny, did they deserve to be shot down like the wild dogs they'd shown themselves to be? But Faye had persuaded her otherwise—she could be very persuasive, Faye.

'They hurt you, don't they?' she'd said when this thing—Ella doesn't know what else to call it—with Faye had begun. Said it sweet as pie. 'I wouldn't say it if they didn't hurt you. I love you, more than anyone else loves you. You know that, right?' Faye had looked at her with those mesmerising eyes, and Ella, enchanted, helpless with love, had nodded. 'Them boys think they can do what they like to you.' A narrow look tinged with loathing. 'And they do. And you let them.'

Ella started crying then. Faye was right—she did let them. And who else was going to help her? Not Pa, who'd been pussy-whipped ever since he'd married that bitch Audley, who'd brought those boys into their home after Ma died. Ella had been eight then, hadn't known happiness since. Not until Faye turned up at High School for her final year six months ago, new to town but not new to trouble, and showed her what love was really about. Love meant hot sweet kisses and cold bitter vengeance.

Oh but Faye had a sweet tongue, sweet talking and sweet tasting. A magic tongue that brought her to shimmering ecstasy. Not like the hard penetrating cocks that pierced her and made her bleed. Not like the hard fists that bruised her or the hard hands that slapped her. All under the blind love-struck eyes and deaf ears of Pa and Audley, who were too wrapped up in each other and their own entertainment to bother about a damaged-goods sixteen-year-old girl.

Still, they'd all gotten good at hiding stuff. Ella had learned not to cry, and the boys had learned how to hurt her quietly. Secrets secrets secrets.

All those secrets burning away, incinerating everything good into ash, so there was nothing left.

Faye had stripped all that away with her searching looks, soft hands, sweet tongue and desire for violence. She'd seen all the hurt and loved it away, and with it went the burning secrets, and in blew the truth, cold and ugly and naked as all sin.

The gun feels good in her hands, although she's shaking in a kind of high terror. Faye sees it, just like she sees everything Ella feels, so she comes behind her again, and holds her shaking gun hand with her own.

'Look at how strong you are,' she whispers in Ella's ear, and strokes the muzzle of the gun up and down Ella's cheek, igniting heat in her, a warped excited arousal. 'Look at how much power we have. Power of life and death.'

'Life and death,' Ella repeats through numb lips, and turns in Faye's arms, and numb lips meet hot lips, and it's sweet, sweet as honey, intoxicating as liquor, and bitter as poison.

She'd never believed she could give herself to someone so completely, but Faye was like an answered prayer. Not that Ella believed in prayer anymore, because how many times had she prayed to God that this would all stop. A granted wish, then, a dream come true. Faye's taught Ella to channel pain into hate and now hope that she will be free of it. It's been a hard lesson, but Ella's always been a quick learner, and although the lessons *are* hard, she sees their teachings unfold and foresees a glorious culmination of her suffering and subjugation. Going out in a blaze of glory and gunfire at the world's ending.

'You ready?' Faye asks, still behind her in the mirror, the gun again at Ella's head, softly stroking. Ella feels fire erupt inside her, like a fever. Tonight she'll have her happy ending. She turns again in Faye's arms and chest to chest, aware of how their hearts thunder together, a jackhammering of passion and terror, and she nods.

'Yeah,' she whispers against Faye's mouth. 'Yeah. Ready.' She kisses Faye's lips, tastes honey and poison. 'Thank you. For granting my wish. For making me see. For making me do.'

'It's like putting down rabid dogs,' Faye says, and Ella wonders—has she done this before? Granted other girls' wishes? Or is this some kind of vengeance for Faye too? What has Faye endured, to make her so hot for violence? What's brought her to this desire for murder? Ella knows nothing about Faye, she realises as the kiss deepens. It's like she magically appeared when Ella needed her most. She likes to think this is all for love, because love is all that matters, but deep inside, she knows it's not. Ella recognises darkness when she sees it. Because it lives in her heart and soul, and both are black with despair.

Ella pulls away from Faye, slips on the shoes she brought with money stolen from Audley's purse. Beautiful white satin. Pristine and glistening. She wants to make Faye proud at her prom; and she thinks gain, she'll never have her own. Because tonight the white will turn red, and the world will die.

They wear coats over their dresses and gun belts. It's time to leave Faye's house, empty because Faye's own parents are never there. Too busy to care for their daughter.

'They won't miss me when I'm gone,' Faye says, and Ella looks at her, sees a face dark with fury, and realises for sure that this isn't just about her, it's about Faye's desire to be cared for too. 'Maybe then they'll love me, but it'll be too fucking late.' Now she smiles, and Ella thinks of the snarl of a feral wolf, all teeth and savagery, and understands that Faye's putting herself down too, and her own darkness closes in to reclaim her. Then Faye takes her hand and leads her out into the night, and she knows they're all going to Hell.

It's surprisingly easy to put a bullet through Audley's brain, Ella discovers as she stands in the living room of her home, looking at the carnage before her, carnage she has created. A single bullet between the eyes, a neat little hole that leaks a neat little trickle of blood down her forehead, although the force of the bullet blew out the back of that bitch's head in a mass of blood, bone and brain matter.

'Surprised the vacuous cunt had any brains,' Faye remarks, licking a spot of blood from Ella's face.

Ella barely hears her. It's like her voice is coming from far, far away, because she's staring at the ruin of her father's body lying out on the floor, spilling blood from fatal wounds. When it had come to it, in that split second before thought becomes action, she hadn't wanted to hurt him, let alone kill him. But he'd come for them, of course he had, like a roaring bull, and what choice had there been but to pull the trigger and let fly a flood of bullets. All the time with Faye chanting the magic spell behind her: *Kill. Kill. Kill. Kill him, you silly bitch.* And she had. But tears track down the blood on her face—daddy's blood—and she hiccups a sob. Looks down at her feet and sees the beautiful white shoes spotted crimson.

'You did good,' Faye says, gentle now—she has yet to fire a shot—and after a brief hesitation, Ella lets her hold her, and sobs in her arms. 'You did really good.' A hug rough with bad love. 'They had to go, right?' Ella nods and turns her face away. Yeah. They had to go, and now there's no going back, only forward. Forward to the prom, and to her happily ever after.

After they've washed the blood from their faces—their dresses, they can hide under their coats—and Ella has loaded a new clip into her gun, they leave the murder house. Head on Faye's motorbike through darkened streets hot with summer, Ella holding onto her waist for dear life. Smells come at her through the rushing air. Meat sizzling on barbecues. Fresh mown grass. Night scented flowers. The hot smell of oil and gasoline from the bike. Faint whiff of suntan cream left over from sun-worshippers enjoying the first weekend of summer. But strongest of all, is blood and Faye's excited sweat, and Ella feels herself swell with the promise of more blood to come.

High School glimmers and glitters like the Fairyland Palace it has been transformed into for the Prom Ball. Ella stands outside, staring at the twinkling lights. She can hear music and laughter coming from inside, and her furiously beating heart wrenches in her chest. All her life she has dreamed of this, inspired by fairy tales of princes and princesses and the happy ever after. She wants to say, let's stop all this, Faye. Take me inside and dance with me and whirl me around in my pretty prom dress and red-stained shoes, and be my happy ever after. Let's forget all the pain and hate. Let's forgive and just love each other. But Faye has taught her that love does not conquer all, that hate can't just be switched off, and forgiveness is weak.

They get off the bike and Faye takes Ella's shaking hand, squeezes it. Her eyes glitter and glimmer like black diamonds in the twinkling lights. She looks like something out of a movie, all power and vengeance, and Ella feels her breath hitch in, awed and terrified and excited. They walk toward the Fairyland Palace hand in hand. Stand at the entrance to the Ballroom and the world erupts in a riot of light and laughter and music and dance and romance and colour. Overwhelmed, Ella can only stare and stare, watching the twirling couples dancing together. There's Jaq and Gus, locked in each other's arms and each other's eyes. Going to be married later this year. There's Ana and Driz, a pair of mean girls if there ever was one, dancing together because no boy will look at them. And there's Kit Madden, the most popular boy in school, whirling Ember around, holding her close to him. Later, they'll be announced as Prom King and Prom Queen. Except—Ella swallows—they won't.

And there. And there. Luke and Johnny, all dressed up in tuxes and bow ties, roses in their lapels. Hanging together like they always do, peas in a pod. Handsome both of them, hiding their secrets. They're ogling the girls who sway before them, and Ella wants to shout: don't go near them. They'll hurt you and use you and discard you and make you feel like you're nothing. But that's only her, she guesses, because Luke and Johnny, outwardly charming, always have girls on the go. They often share them, like they share everything else, including her. And in that shining golden moment, she knows she can do what she came here to do.

They don't say anything to each other, Ella and Faye. They walk forward, still holding hands. Ella hears curse words thrown at them as they push through the crowds, but the words don't really register until finally, they're standing in front of the brothers, whose faces turn ugly with derision when they see Ella and Faye, notice they're holding hands. When Faye kisses Ella's lips full on in front of them, they laugh, full of revulsion and contempt.

'Fucking lesbo bitches,' Luke sneers after a moment. 'No wonder you don't come for us.' Johnny looks a little uncomfortable at this. He always was the follower of Luke's lead. 'She's no fucking good for you,' Luke continues, pinning Ella with a snake-stare. He moves forward, takes Ella's free wrist. Twists it hard so the bones grind together, and Ella gasps in pain. 'Can still make you gasp though, Ella,' he observes, and then Johnny gives Faye a little shove, so she stumbles backward into the crowd that's gathering around them, watching the pantomime, and Ella staggers forward, falls into Luke's arms, and Johnny grabs her by the other wrist, and they begin a game of push and pull.

Begin.

'You better stop it now!' A cry from Faye. She's righted herself and drawn her gun. Holds it in both shaking hands, points it at the brothers. A communal gasp goes up from the crowd and, as one, they move backward. Ella's released suddenly, and she crumples awkwardly to the floor as her legs buckle. She feels something twist as her beautiful shoes give way beneath her, and she loses one of them.

'Get up, Ella! Get up, girl,' Faye instructs her. 'Get up and free yourself.'

Ella can't stand. She's pretty sure she's sprained her ankle from the violence of the fall; it's throbbing like a drum; she can feel it swelling. But there's nothing wrong with her arms and she draws the gun from beneath her coat and, sobbing and shaking, aims it at the targets.

'Free yourself!' Faye screams, and Ella's finger tightens on instinct and then there's a flash of hot light and a deafening crack as the first shot is fired. Luke falls to the floor, clutching his gut, and screams erupt around them. Johnny drops beside him, screeching insults and crying for his brother, even as a bullet hits his open mouth and shatters it. Ella drops the gun and curls, foetus-like, around herself, overwhelmed by a sensation of lightness brought on by terror that's almost joy as the world explodes around her. Like she's dancing on air. More cracks fill the air like lightning, like thunderbolts, like magic spells, and the world is a swirling chaos of blood and bullets and screams. The sound of footfalls as the crowd around them disperses. Thuds as more bodies fall. Pulsing of strobe lights. Music still pounding in Ella's ears, gun smoke in her eyes and nose. And Faye's hysterical laughter and incoherent shrieks as she wreaks whatever revenge is playing out in her head, as she smacks Ella's face with her gun, blindsiding her, ripping Ella's from her hand because hers has run out of rounds. Then there's the scream of sirens, overlaid by the toll of the automated clock in the hall sounding midnight.

'Everybody drop!' orders a voice through the madness. 'Everybody on your knees.' But Faye keeps screaming, keeps shooting, until suddenly she's not firing anymore, because she's falling, falling, in slow motion, and blood's pouring from holes riddled in her coat, mingling with the blood of those whose lives she's taken. Ella cries out, stands through the pain in her ankle, blinking through the blood in her eyes, tries to help the only person who's ever tried to help her. Grabs her, holds her. Hears a shout directed at her to drop, to drop now. Too late. A thud in her head brings darkness. And then oblivion.

Minutes later, a police officer makes his way through the crowd, the bodies, the carnage, to the two girls who lay entwined in each other's arms. If it wasn't for the blood and the bullet holes, he thinks as he looks down at them, they'd look like they were asleep. One of the girl's shoes is missing. He sees it sitting a little way away. It's white satin, or was. Now it's crimson. He picks it up, takes it over to the girl who's been felled by the single bullet he fired. Picks up the girl's foot, slides on the shoe, swallowing the hard lump that's suddenly obstructed his throat.

'It fits,' he whispers.

Creative reflection on 'Prom Night: Cinderella Gets a Gun''

ONCE there was a gentleman who married, for his second wife, the proudest and most haughty woman that was ever seen. She had, by a former husband, two daughters of her own humor, who were, indeed, exactly like her in all things. He had likewise, by another wife, a young daughter, but of unparalleled goodness and sweetness of temper, which she took from her mother, who was the best creature in the world. (Opening of 'Cinderella, or the Little Glass Slipper' in Andrew Lang, *The Blue Fairy Book*)

So begins Perrault's classic fairy tale, Cinderella, from which several movies—including Disney's 1950s animated classic, the modern live-action version (Branagh, *Cinderella*)—numerous novels, and short story adaptations have originated. In most of these versions, Cinderella (or Elle, Ella, Ember, and other variations of her name) is a victimised, perfect beauty, unlike her abusers, who are ugly of spirit, of body, or both.

In the quote above, Cinderella is quickly established as being 'of unparalleled goodness and sweetness of temper, which she took from her mother, who was the best creature in the world'. The contrast between the stepmother—'the proudest and most haughty woman that was ever seen' —and the two step-sisters, who were 'exactly like her in all things' (ugliness of personality, rather than physical ugliness, perhaps), and Cinderella herself, is stark, and serves to establish a binary opposition of character, of good and evil, of beauty and ugliness, which continues throughout the text until its ending. Evil is defeated, the stepmother and sisters are forgiven by our ever-perfect heroine, whose unimpeachable goodness is rewarded through marriage and the 'happy-ever-after'. This epitome of perfect womanhood even marries her two (presumably chastened) stepsisters to 'great lords'—effectively rewarding their previously bullying behavior. We don't hear anything more about the stepmother, interestingly.

'Prom Night' was written in an attempt to question and explore the concept of this 'perfect heroine' who forgives all through love, and goes on to live the happily-ever-after 'dream' of marriage that all women are 'supposed' to aspire to. I wanted to shatter these conventions and present, if not a more realistic, then certainly a more nihilistic tale of abuse, victimhood and vengeance. I am a writer of dark fiction, and by its very definition, this kind of fiction is more interested in subverting the happily-ever-after that is peddled to us by the likes of Disney, where the norm— usually white, heteronormative, and patriarchal—is upheld. On a personal basis, I find Cinderella, in its saccharine-sweet incarnation, faintly offensive, both to my personal aesthetic of writing, but also because of the representations of women and relationships they present, and decided to subvert that fairy tale in its wider, perhaps extreme, sense of the word. As Clive Barker says:

> our minds are extraordinary melting pots in which […] nightmares, and dreams, simmer in an ever-richer stew. […] if we once embrace the vision offered in such works, if we once allow the metaphors a home in our psyches, the subversion is under way. We may for the first time see ourselves as a *totality*—valuing our appetite for the forbidden rather than suppressing it, comprehending that our taste for the strange, or the morbid, or the paradoxical, is contrary to what we've been brought up to believe, a sign of our good health. So I say—subvert. And never apologise. (Barker in Bloom 99-100)

If, as writers, we do not question, do not subvert, then we are submitting blindly to authority, and in the case of Cinderella, to a world where to be a 'good' woman means she cannot be active, must always be forgiving, and who must reward her tormentors. In reaction to that, 'Prom Night' was always intended to be, and is at its essence, a horror story. My intention with this story was not only to critique these versions of the tale, but to blow them apart and take them back to their darker roots. These range from the Grimm Brothers' 1812 version, where the step-sisters not only mutilate themselves in order to fit their feet into the slipper, but who also have their eyes pecked out by birds, to the stories of 'Cenerentola' or 'The Cinderella Cat' (Basile); and the Vietnamese 'The Story of Tam and Cam' (Quôc) where the mistreated Tam boils her stepsister alive in a vat of boiling water, serves parts of the body to her abusive stepmother for dinner, whereby the stepmother dies of a broken heart (and probably abject revulsion at effectively cannibalising her own flesh): horror stories in their own right.

In 'Cenerentola', we find the familiar story of the wicked stepmother mistreating Zezolla, the Cinderella character. Her governess, to whom Zezolla is very close, instructs her to murder her stepmother, so she can become her mother (a second stepmother), and the stepmother is killed when Zezolla slams the lid of a large chest on her head while she's searching for a dress. Inevitably, the governess turns out not to be what she seems, and introduces her own six daughters into the family, favouring them and condemning Zezolla to a poor and unhappy life. There follows the familiar story of a ball (feast), a magical dress, a man (this time a King) falling in love with her, and the fitting of a shoe. The story ends in humiliation for the step-sisters and the stepmother. So a happy-ever-after story, in a way, but the original stepmother is murdered by Zezolla, and in this version, there is no fairy godmother, although there is a good fairy (who has no doubt condoned the murder of the step-mother, because Zezolla is not punished for this).

In 'Prom Night', I introduce the character of Faye (a name based on 'fey' for 'fairy'), a bad girl who becomes both governess and fairy godmother/bad fairy, practical in her actions (helping Ella gain vengeance on her tormentors); and metaphorically magical, in that for Ella, she's a wish come true. However, there is no happy ending here for anyone— unless death can be considered a relief, which in many ways throughout the story, it's hinted that it might be. In the eye of the reader, perhaps, Faye holds the power, and Ella remains a victim.

> The Grimm Brothers […] and their spiritual heir Walt Disney, who made the cartoon […] Cinderella (1950) have done more than any other creation to naturalize female—maternal—malignancy in the imaginations of children. (Warner 207)

All power in my piece—(step)maternal or otherwise—is depicted as being malignant. Both the love and hate the two girls share are shown as equally destructive, dangerous, malignant, but alluring and, in the end, irresistible. Faye, as the initial holder of the power, appears to be the instigator of the murders that follow, but Ella, blind with love and loathing, is quick to follow her lead, and takes the power (of the gun) that's offered to her, discharging it at her tormentors (the twin brothers who take the place of the stepsisters).

Continuing with the theme of power, Warner continues: 'Authentic power lies with the bad women, and the plump cosy godmother seems no match for them' (207). In my text there is no 'cosy godmother', and power shifts from the abusive males (her step-brothers, her father—the Patriarchy) to the 'Bad Fairy' figure of Faye, who in turn poisons Ella with her powers of persuasion and words of love—a dark love, true, but more than Ella has been shown in the past. Faye is depicted as a figure of malignancy and, for whatever reasons of her own, she passes it on to Ella, who both fears and embraces it. Is Ella a victim of Faye's power? Well perhaps, but I have attempted to show that she is active too, in that she chooses to accept Faye, rather than reject her dark offering.

Bruno Bettelheim, in his *The Uses of Enchantment* (208), says: 'the misogyny of fairy tales engages women as participants, not just targets.' In 'Prom Night', the misogyny of the male characters, and the internalised misogyny of the stepmother—too blinded by her love for Ella's father to notice (or, more likely, care) that Ella is being abused by her twin sons—is punished by actively murderous women in an orgy of death.

In Stephen King's 1974 novel of the same name, the tormented, telekinetic Carrie (White) is, in King's own words, a Cinderella character: 'Like many of the classics of the field it draws on popular myth—in its case surely a nightmare version of Cinderella's transformation for the ball,' (Flood, *The Guardian*). Carrie White suffers from the isolating effects of maternal abuse through the dubious 'mercy' of her fundamentalist Christian mother. Carrie's telekinetic powers have made her the subject of scrutiny; and worse, her mother decrees that this power comes from the devil. Being a loner, and physically unattractive, Carrie falls victim to relentless bullying from her high school cohort. Finally, she suffers a terrible humiliation at the Prom Ball, and those who have relentlessly teased her (and some who haven't) fall to the murderous effects of her telekinesis. Carrie sets the school hall on fire, locks in her fellow students, leaving them to burn:

> Just below the thrones, a live 220-volt electricity cable was crackling on the floor and beside it, Rhonda Simard was doing a crazed puppet dance in her green tulle formal. Its full skirt suddenly blazed into flame and she fell forward, still jerking.
>   It might have been at that moment that Carrie went over the edge.
> (King, 147)

Similarly, in 'Prom Night' Ella is pushed to listen to the destructive forces outside her (Faye), and inside her (the hurt, abused child), to take vengeance on everyone who's ever hurt her: the faceless stepmother, Audley; a nameless, faceless and traditionally ineffectual father, along with the 'ugly' stepbrothers. And so Ella performs her ultimate act of punishment at the Prom Ball, traditionally a site of celebration, and the site for love at first sight in 'Cinderella', but here, as with Carrie's orgy of destruction, it becomes a bloodbath, a high school shooting, also harming innocent people.

At its core, then, we could argue that Cinderella, in whatever form, is a tale of female violence and an escape from suffering. *Carrie* and 'Prom Night' stick to that premise, and in both, the escape from that suffering is through violent death (Carrie also dies at the end of King's novel), rather than traditional marriage and the received status that imbues upon the female figure.

Marina Warner says that '[f]airy tales like Cinderella bear witness against women. But there are possible reasons […] which mitigate the wrongs they describe, not entirely but in part' (210).

What are the reasons for the violence in 'Prom Night', and can it be mitigated? The abuses and subsequent violence described may be partially explained by the figure of the absent mother (in Ella's case, her natural mother is dead; in Faye's we perceive that her mother is unavailable both emotionally and actually). For Ella, the introduction of an unsympathetic stepmother figure, and the abuse by her step-siblings begins the cycle of violence. If Audley is not actively abusive, then she certainly is passively abusive, because she allows her sons to torture and rape Ella. Bettelheim argues that the 'bad' stepmother, and step-siblings in fairy tales become figures that hurt, abused children in reality can hate without punishment. They can relate to the Lost Child archetype that Cinderella represents. This portrayal of the wicked stepmother echoes through the ages: 'The enmity of stepmothers toward children of earlier unions makes chronicles and stories from all over the world, from the ancient world to the modern day [...]' (Bettleheim quoted in Warner 214), and has been described in sociological terms by Daly and Wilson as The Cinderella Effect. Without going into details of that sociological phenomenon, Audley can certainty be seen to fit into the category of the mother who favours her own children over her stepchild.

The relationship between Ella and Faye caused me some issues. I was never sure how to portray it, whether the two girls should simply be friends, or whether they should be in a same-sex relationship. I dismissed the 'just friends' scenario fairly quickly. For one thing, it seemed unlikely to me that the character of Faye would initiate female friendship. For me, it was as simple as her character just not being the type who cultivates friendships, especially of a slightly younger girl like Ella, whose character is perhaps too withdrawn to attract friendship, although she clearly attracts predators. So in the end, the obviously sexual relationship presented here seemed logical. Faye is a manipulator, and Ella is prey who turns predator under Faye's influence. It may not be obvious, however, given the sexual relationship between Ella and Faye, that their sexual orientation is meant to be ambiguous: are the girls lesbians? Are they even bisexual? For me, their sexuality came out of a shared loathing of what men (in Faye's case, *may*) have done to them. Ella has been so mistreated by her stepbrothers from an early age, that men repel her. As a straight woman, this still caused me misgivings, and this portrayal of a toxic same-sex relationship bothered me a little—do I have the right to portray the relationship in such a dark light? Is this a failing on my part as a writer? Perhaps, and I could tie myself up in knots trying to defend my decision, but ultimately, for me, it wasn't about my not 'having the right', it was about what was inherently 'right' for the story. These two girls turned to each other, and the characters did what they needed to do for the story. In the end, I never envisioned it any other way.

However, during the reading of this piece to an audience, my decision was gently questioned, and although the reply I gave to the questioner seemed to be accepted, I still feel vaguely uncomfortable about it. In 'Queers Destroy Horror! Roundtable Interview' at *Nightmare Magazine*, writers Meghan McCarron, Brit Mandelo, Rahul Kanakia and Carrie Cuinn discuss how being queer has impacted on their writing, and how LGBTQ+ characters continue to be presented as victims or 'evil' in horror stories. It's an interesting piece, and one of the points made by McCarron is how:

> I never, ever, ever, ever want to read a story that ends with one half of a same-sex couple dying, leaving the other tragically alone. Someone has to die at the end of a horror story, is the problem. I submit that gay couples should get a ten year reprieve. In 2025, they can start dying tragically again. (Arkenberg).

McCarron has highlighted an interesting dilemma: in a horror story, someone usually dies at the end, and it's true that same-sex couples suffer, apparently inordinately, from this fate in fiction, but then so do many other non-same sex characters. It is the nature of the horror story. Even bearing this in mind, I decided that death had to be the fate of both Ella and Faye at the end of 'Prom Night'. To reiterate: this is a horror story, and as a writer, I very rarely allow my characters redemptive survival—a nihilistic decision, perhaps—but the traditional trope of good winning out over evil is, for me anyway, outdated and predictable. So, the two girls die, but so, necessarily, do the brothers, along with several secondary characters, whose identities are only hinted at. All their names are taken from previous versions of the Cinderella story to maintain intertextual reference—although this isn't necessarily meant to be understood by the reader.

In regard to the end of what is essentially a linearly structured piece, I wanted to remain true to the glass slipper element of the piece. Ultimately, the fitting of the slipper is what liberates Cinderella, and I spent a lot of time wondering how I could subvert that element of the piece. I made the decision from the start of the writing process that there would be no Prince, no rescuing male figure. But I wanted a reference, and some kind of conclusion. Eventually I decided on white satin shoes to replace the glass slipper, and it doesn't take much of a stretch to understand the final image of blood on white satin to know that this is a reference to Ella's final loss of innocence, as well as the loss of her life.

I could have left it there, but felt it needed the actual fitting of the slipper, and so the point of view needed to change: Ella is dead; her viewpoint is lost. So the brief, but necessary appearance of the police officer came into being. For me, the police officer, although he is too late to save Ella from her own fate—indeed may even have been the one to fire the bullet that killed her (it's not clear in the text or in my own mind, which that is)—cares enough about a fallen girl to replace the blood-flecked shoe on Ella's foot. He utters the words 'It fits' as a conclusion. Those final words could reference at least two things: the obvious fitting of the shoe; but also—perhaps—the only end that this story could have. A fitting end, if you will.

Works cited

Arkenberg, Megan. 'Queers Destroy Horror! Roundtable Interview' at *Nightmare Magazine*. Issue 37. October 2015 http://www.nightmare-magazine.com/nonfiction/queers-destroy-horror-roundtable-interview/ Accessed 1 November 2018.

Bastile, Giambattista, Christopher Stace, translator. *The Tale of Tales* (1694). Cambridge Scholars Publishing, 2018.

Bettelheim, Bruno. *The Uses of Enchantment: The Meaning and Importance of Fairy Tales*. Penguin, 1991.

Bloom, Clive, editor. *Gothic Horror: A Reader's Guide to Poe and Beyond*. Macmillan. 1998.

Branagh, Kenneth, director, *Cinderella*. Disney. 2015.

Daly, Martin, and Margo Wilson. *The Truth about Cinderella: a Darwinian View of Parental Love,* Weidenfeld and Nicolson, 1998.

Grimm, Jacob, and Wilhelm Grimm, *Kinder- Und Haus-Märchen*. 1st ed., vol. 1, Realschulbuchhandlung, 1812.

Flood, Alison. 'How Carrie changed Stephen King's life, and began a generation of horror.' *The Guardian.* 2014. https://www.theguardian.com/books/2014/apr/04/carrie-stephen-king-horror Accessed 18 October 2018.

King, Stephen. *Carrie*. New English Library, 1974.

Lang, Andrew, editor, *The Blue Fairy Book.* Longmans Green and Company, 1889.

Quốc, Minh, Mai Long, illustrator and William Smith, translator, *Tấm and Cám The Ancient Vietnamese Cinderella Story*, East West Discovery Press, 2006.

Sharpe, Betty. *Ember.* Amazon Media. 2007.

Straub, P. 'Ashputtel.' *Black Thorn, White Rose,* edited by Ellen Datlow and Terry Windling. Prime Books, 1994.

Warner, Marina. *From the Beast to the Blonde. On Fairy Tales and Their Tellers.* Vintage, 1995.

WORKS FROM THE CINDERELLA COLLECTION

Items from the Cinderella Collection on display for the conference. Photo by Felix Weedon 2017.

This is a list of books held within the Cinderella collection of books, ephemera and merchandise at the University of Bedfordshire archive, Bedford campus. The titles listed here are in alphabetical order by author (or illustrator, editor, publisher) and divided into chronological sections. The item number within the collection is listed at the end as C#.

1800-1899

Anon, *History of Cinderella*. Otley, Yorkshire. Printed for The Booksellers. J. S. Publishing & Stationery Co Ltd., 1840. C58.

Anon, *The Surprising Adventures of Cinderilla or the History of a Glass Slipper to which is added an Historical Description of the Cat*. Printed by J. Kendrew, Colliergate, 1820, C92.

Bell, Florence and Speed, Lancelot. Illustrator. *Fairy Tale Plays and How to Act Them*. Longman, 1896. C30.

Clarke, C. Allen. *Old Tales for Young Folks*. John Heywood, 1895. C70.

Craik, Dinah Maria Mulock. *Fairy Book: The Best Popular Fairy Stories Selected and Rendered Anew*. Macmillan, 1863. C71.

Crane, Walter. Illustrator. *Cinderella. Walter Crane Picture Books reissue.* John Lane [1897] n.d. C100.

Cruikshank, George. Illustrator. *Interesting Story of Cinderella and her Glass Slipper.* Printed by J. G. Rusher, 1814. C31.

Tuck, Raphael. Publisher. *Cinderella Paper doll with 4 costumes.* Raphael Tuck, 1894. C91.

Warne's National Nursery Library. Comprising Cinderella, The Three Bears, Tom Thumb, Punch and Judy, Jack and the Bean-stalk with forty pages of coloured illustrations. Frederick Warne, 1870. C88.

1900-1949

Adams, Frank. Illustrator. *Cinderella.* Blackie & Sons Ltd. (1910?). C102.

Anon. *Fairyland Doll Dressing Folder. 10 Fairy Story dresses with hats.* Philmar Ltd. 1940. C97.

Attwell, Mabel Lucie. Illustrator. *The Fairy Book.* Thomas Nelson and Sons Ltd., (1920s). C117.

Blackie. Publisher. *Golden Budget of Nursery Stories.* Blackie & Son, 1931. C14.

Blyton, Enid. *How do you do, Mary Mouse.* Brockhampton Press, 1940. C74.

Collin's Bumper Books. *Puck's Cinderella Book.* Collins Clear type press. 1930. C110.

Farjeon, Eleanor and Herbert. *The Glass Slipper.* Allan Wingate (Publishers Limited). 1947. C103.

Franks, Frank E. and Win Taylor. Illustrator. *Cinderella.* John Albinson Ltd., (1927). C115.

Golding, Harry. Editor. Margaret Winifred Tarrant. Illustrator. *Fairy Tales: with 30 colour plates and 18 other illustrations.* Ward, Lock & Co., 1915. C44.

Grimm, Jacob and Wilhelm Grimm. *Grimm's Tales from the 'Kinder- und Haus-Märchen.'* Blackie & Son, 1920. C68.

Hassall, John. Illustrator. *Fairy Tale Pictures 'Won't tear series.'* Blackie & Son. (1930s?). C111.

Kathleen, Lady. Editor. *Cinderella and the Prince: a Fairy Pantomime with Songs and Music. Tales for Little People.* Aldine Publishing Company, 1910. C59.

McCulloch, Derek and Harry Rutherford. Illustrator. *Cinderella.* Sampson Low, Marston, (1940s/1950s). C113.

Nelson. Publisher. *Mother Goose and her Friends in Fairyland.* T. Nelson & Sons, 1920. C47.

Reynolds, Leila. Editor. *Cinderella's Sisters*. A Halle Ltd., 1900. C57.

Sherman, F.J. and Stuart Hardy. Illustrator. *Grimm's Fairy Tales*. John F Shaw & Co Ltd., 1928. C104.

Steedman, Amy and Paul Woodroffe. Illustrator. *Nursery Tales Told to the Children*. T. C. & E. C. Jack, 1908. C80.

Tuck, Raphael. Publisher. *Cinderella*. Raphael Tuck, 1948. C95.

Waltz Song: Cinderella 'Stay in my arms.' Peter Maurice Music Co Ltd., 1938. C96.

1950-1969

Abbott, Eleanor Vera (E.V.A.) Illustrator. *Fairy Tale Doll Dressing and Story Book*. Purnell (1950s?). C112.

Abbott, Eleanor Vera (E.V.A.) Illustrator. *Fairy Tales*. Birn Brothers Ltd., (1950s?). C118.

Birn. Publisher. *Fairy Tale Cartoons*. Birn Brothers Ltd., 1953. C81.

Chivers, Lilian and Henry Barnett. Illustrators. *My First Book of Fairy Tales*. Odhams, 1951. C76.

Collins. Publisher. *Cinderella Panorama Book: Six Magnificent Scenes*. Collins, 1950. C43.

Colum, Padraic and Imero Gobbato. Illustrator. *Girl who Sat by the Ashes*. Macmillan, 1968. C7.

Levy, Muriel and Evelyn Bowmar. Illustrator. *Story of Cinderella*. Willes & Hepworth Ltd. 1955. C79.

McKean. Emma C. *The Animated Cinderella Doll, 7 Beautiful Scenes*. Milton Bradley Company (1957?).

Muir, Percy H. *English Children's Books: 1600 to 1900*. B.T. Batsford Ltd. 1958. C6.

Schermele. Willy. *Cinderella and the Glass Slipper*. Juvenile Productions Ltd., 1953. C109.

Southgate, Vera and Eric Winter. Illustrator. *Cinderella: a Ladybird Easy-Reading Book*. Ladybird book series 606D, 1964. C34.

Walt Disney Company. Publisher. *Cinderella Magic Wand Book*. Dean & Son specially for Stephenson Bros Ltd Bradford. 1950. C82.

1970-1989

Ahlberg, Janet and Allan Ahlberg. Illustrator. *Cinderella Show*. Viking Kestrel, 1986. C49.

Apsley, Brenda. *Cinderella*. World International Publishing Ltd. (1982?). C99.

Arrowsmith, Nancy. *Field Guide to the Little People*. Pan, 1978. C19.

Bamberger, Nicole. *Walt Disney presents Cindrillon*. Hachette, 1982. C119.

Blyth, Alan and Emanuele Luzzati. Illustrator. *Cinderella; La Cenerentola: The Story of Rossini's Opera*. Julia MacRae books a division of Franklin Watts, 1981. C29.

Briggs, Katherine M. *British Folk Tales and Legends: a Sampler*. Granada Publishing Ltd., 1977. C73.

Carruth, Jane and Shirley Tourret. Illustrator. *Cinderella. Purnell Key Classics*. Purnell, 1979. C36.

Clarke, Harry. Illustrator. *Charles Perrault's Classic Fairy Tales*. London. Chancellor Press, 1986. C89.

Cole, Babette. *Prince Cinders*. Puffin, 1989. C10.

Dahl, Roald, and Quentin Blake. Illustrator. *Roald Dahl's Revolting Rhymes*. Harmondsworth Puffin, 1984. C46.

Dowling, Colette. *Cinderella Complex: Women's Hidden Fear of Independence*. Fontana, 1982. C67.

Dundes, Alan. *Cinderella, A Casebook*. University of Wisconsin Press, 1988. C15.

Dutfoy, Serge. Images. Charles Perrault. Author. *Cendrillon*. Editions du chat perché Flammarion. 1977. C48.

Ellis, John Martin. *One Fairy Story Too Many: The Brothers Grimm and their Tales*. University of Chicago Press, 1983. C69.

Evans, C. S. and Arthur Rackham. Illustrator. *Cinderella*. Chancellor Press, printed in Hong Kong, 1987. C86.

Farjeon, Eleanor and Ernest H. Shepard. Illustrator. *Glass Slipper: from the Play of the same name by Eleanor and Herbert Farjeon*. Oxford University Press, 1973. C16.

Fowles, John and Sheilah Beckett. Illustrator. *Cinderella, adapted from Perrault's 'Cendrillon' of 1697*. Jonathan Cape. 1974. C3.

Grimm, Jacob and Pauline Ellison. Illustrator. *Grimm's Fairy Tales*. Routledge and Kegan Paul, 1981. C5

Grimm, Jacob and Wilhelm Grimm, *Cenerentola e altre fiabe*. DeAgostini Ragazzi, 1988. C77.

Merrimack. Publisher. *Cinderella*. Merrimack Publishing Corp. (c1980?). C98.

Murphy, Shirley Rousseau. *Silver Woven in my Hair*. Macdonald and Jane's. 1977. C20.

Perrault, Charles and Errol Le Cain. Illustrator. *Cinderella, or, The Little Glass Slipper*. Harmondsworth Picture Puffin, 1976. C65.

Perrault, Charles. *Cinderella, or, The Little Glass Slipper.* Griffith and Farran, 1977. C75.

Philip, Neil. *Cinderella Story.* Penguin, 1989. C22.

Pienkowski, Jan. Illustrator. Charles Perrault. Author. *Cinderella.* Thomas Y. Crowell Company, 1978. C66.

Sexton, Anne. *Transformations.* Oxford University Press, 1972. C18.

Southgate, Vera and Brian Price-Thomas. Illustrator. *Cinderella: Retold for Easy Reading. Well-Loved Tales.* Ladybird book, 1981. C33.

Spence, Lewis. *British Fairy Origins: The Genesis and Development of Fairy Legends in British Tradition.* Aquarian Press Ltd., 1981. C37.

Tillett, Iris. *Cinderella Army: The Women's Land Army in Norfolk.* Jim Baldwin Publishing, 1988. C64.

Unwin, Stanley and Estelle Ratcliffe. Illustrator. *Fairly Tales.* Caedmon of Whitby, 1985. C21.

Walt Disney Company. *Walt Disney's Cinderella and Her Animal Friends: A Book About Kindness.* Western Publishing Company Inc., 1987. C87.

1990-1999

Anholt, Laurence and Arthur Robins. Illustrator. *Cinderboy.* Orchard books, 1996. C8.

Ballet, Laurence and Ginette Hoffman. Illustrator. *Cendrillon.* Nathan, 1994. C55.

Baxter, Nicola and Jon Davis. Illustrator. *Cinderella. Favourite Tales.* Ladybird book, 1993. C32.

Brown, Debbie. *Debbie Brown's Fairy Tale Cakes.* Hamlyn, 1995. C26.

Buthod-Girard, Ingrid and Carlos Busquets. Illustrator. *Assepoester,* Chevron Hemma, 1995. C84.

Climo, Shirley and Loretta Krupinski. Illustrator. *Irish Cinderlad.* HarperCollins, 1996. C11.

Dakin, Glenn and Rowan Barnes-Murphy. Illustrator. *Cinderella and the Seven Beanstalks.* Brilliant Books Ltd. for Tescos Stores Ltd., 1998. C83.

Daly, Martin and Margo Wilson, *Truth about Cinderella: a Darwinian View of Parental Love.* Weidenfeld and Nicolson, 1998. C54.

Ezell, Lee. *Cinderella Syndrome: Discovering God's Plan When Your Dreams Don't Come True.* Vine Books, 1994. C23.

Garner, James Finn. *Politically Correct Bedtime Stories.* Souvenir Press, 1994. C78.

Grandreams. Publisher. *Cinderella: a Mini Pop-Up Storybook.* Grandreams Ltd., 1995. C72.

Grandreams. Publisher. *Cinderella: Sticker Fun.* Grandreams Ltd., 1994. C1.

Grimm, Wilhelm and Eva Wenzel-Bürge. Illustrator. *Aschenputtel: ein Märchen der Gebrüder Grimm.* Hamburg. Carlsen Verlag, 1995. C50.

Jackson, Ellen and Kevin O'Malley. Illustrator. *Cinder Edna.* Lothrop, Lee & Shephard, 1994. C27.

Jungman, Ann and Russell Ayto. Illustrator. *Cinderella and the Hot Air Balloon.* Francis Lincoln, 1995. C9.

Laslett, Stephanie and Carole Sharpe. Illustrator. *Assepoester.* Hedel. Librero, 1995. C51.

Laslett, Stephanie and Carole Sharpe. Illustrator. *Cinderella.* Parragon, 1994. C52.

Maguire, Gregory. *Confessions of an Ugly Stepsister.* Regan books an imprint of HarperCollins, 1999. C24.

Mazza, Samuele. *Cinderella's Revenge.* Chronicle Books, 1994. C12.

Meddaugh, Susan. *Cinderella's Rat.* Houghton Mifflin, 1997. C63.

O'Loughlin, Aislinn and Marie-Louise Fitzpatrick. Illustrator. *Cinderella's Fella.* Wolfhound Press, 1996. C17.

Perrault, Charles and Francesc Mateu. Illustrator. *Walt Disney: Cendrillon; un livre anime.* Paris, 1995. C62.

Perrault, Charles. *Cendrillon.* France Editions Mango, 1993. C13.

Stockham. Publisher. *Cinderella and the Glass Slipper.* Peter Stockham Associates, (1995?). C90.

Susaeta. Publisher. *Cenicienta.* Susaeta, 1993. C60.

Van Gool, A. Illustrator. *Assepoester.* Mulder & Zoon, 1993. C61.

Wood, Tim, Jenny Wood and Fran Thatcher. Illustrator. *My Fairy Tale Library: Cinderella.* London. Blackie. 1991. C39.

2000-2010

Craft, K. Y. Illustrator. *Cinderella.* SeaStar Books, 2000. C42.

Doherty, Berlie and Jane Ray. Illustrator. *Cinderella.* Walker Books, 2003. C38.

Durant, Alan and Ross Collins Illustrator. *Fairytale Files: Cinderella.* Walker Books, 2008. C56.

Ellwand, David and Christine Tagg. *Cinderlily: a Floral Fairy Tale in Three Acts.* Walker books, 2003. C4.

Fabbri GE & HIT entertainment. Publisher. *Angelina Ballerina's Fairy Tales, Part 1, Cinderella.*, 2003. C108.

Gill-Brown, Vanessa and Mandy Stanley. *Rufferella*. Bloomsbury Children's books, 2000. C28.

Hughes, Shirley. *Ella's Big Chance: a Fairy Tale Retold*. The Bodley Head, 2003. C42.

Ladybird. Publisher. *Disney Princess: Dreamy Dress-up Book*. Ladybird, 2003. C25.

Laslett, Stephanie and Carole Sharpe. Illustrator. *Cinderella*. Parragon. 2001. C53.

Pullman, Philip and Peter Bailey. Illustrator. *I was a rat! Or the Scarlet Slippers*. Corgi Yearling Books, 2001. C45.

Randall, Ronne and Richard Jewitt. Paper Engineering. Francis Thatcher, Illustrator. *Cinderella: a Magic 3-dimensional Fairy-Tale World*. Fernleigh Books, 2006.   C85.

Roberts, Lynn and David Roberts. Illustrator. *Cinderella: an Art Deco Love Story*. Pavilion books, 2001. C2.

Southgate, Vera and Eric Winter. Illustrator. *Well Loved Tales. Cinderella, Personalised Fairy Tales*. Ladybird. Gift republic, 2010. C106.

Southgate, Vera and Paul Finn. Illustrator. *Cinderella*. Ladybird Book, 2005. C35.

Southgate, Vera. *Cinderella*. Ladybird book, 2008. C40.

BIBLIOGRAPHY OF WORKS CITED

Abbott, C. 'Henry Marshall's gag book: pantomime routines for actors in twentieth century repertory theatre.' *Theatre Notebook*, vol. 69, no. 1, 2015, pp. 40-62.

Académie Française. *Le Dictionnaire de L'Académie Françoise, Dédié Au Roi. A–L.*, vol. 1, Jean-Baptise Coignard, 1694.

Adams, D. J. 'The 'Contes de Fées' of Madame d'Aulnoy: Reputation and Re-Evaluation.' *Bulletin of the John Rylands University*, vol. 76, no. 3, 1994, pp. 5–22.

Ahlberg, Janet and Allen Ahlberg. *Cinderella Show*. Viking Kestrel, 1986.

Almodóvar, A. R. *Cuentos al amor de la lumbre*. Alianza Editorial, 1983.

Almodóvar, Pedro, director. *Hable con ella*. El Deseo Producciones, 2003.

Andrews, Eleanor. 'Whither Shall I Wander? Up and Down the Staircase in Film.' *Spaces of the Cinematic Home: Behind the Screen Door,* edited by Eleanor Andrews, Stella Hockenhull and Fran Pheasant-Kelly. Routledge, 2016, pp.137-151.

Anon. 'A Coach for Cinderella' *Harper's Bazaar* 1932 Print.

—. 'A Coach for Cinderella.' *Maclean's Magazine* 1932 p. 51. Print. http://archive.macleans.ca/article/1932/3/15/a-coach-for-cinderella#!&pid=50 Accessed 20 March 2020.

—. 'An Industrial Show and Royalty.' *The Ragged School Union Quarterly,* July 1885, p. 113. *ProQuest.*

—. *Cinderella: A Mini Pop-up Storybook.* 1995.

—. *Cinderella Panorama Book: Six Magnificent Scenes.* Collins, 1950.

—. 'For the Armchair Traveller', *Western Morning News*, 10 May 1950, p. 4.

—. *Golden Budget of Nursery Stories.* Blackie & Sons, 1931.

—. *Mother Goose and Her Friends in Fairyland.* T. Nelson & Sons, 1920.

—. 'Mr Vernon Harcourt on the Marriage of the Princess Louise.' *The Observer.* 16 Oct. 1870, p. 3. *ProQuest Historical Newspapers: The Guardian and the Observer.*

—. 'Pantomimes. Cinderellas with a Difference.' *The Stage*, 30 November 1944.

—. 'Nancy Spain Shows What She Looks Like in Slacks', *Sussex Agricultural Express*, 18 April 1958, p. 9.

—. 'Presentation of the Dahoman Princess to the Queen.' *Morning Post,* 16 Nov. 1850, p. 5. *British Library Newspapers,* http://tinyurl.galegroup.com/tinyurl/6cTai3. Accessed 4 June 2018.

—. 'The Princess Louise.' *The Leeds Mercury,* 29 Dec. 1870, p. 1. *British Library Newspapers Part 1 1800-1900.* Gale Document Number: BB3201654055. Accessed 12 June 2018.

—. 'The Princess Louise as a Needlewoman.' *The London Reader of Literature, Science, Art and General Information,* 25 Dec. 1875, p. 190. *ProQuest*

—. 'The Princess Louise at Deptford.' *The Ragged School Union Quarterly,* April 1886, p. 91. *ProQuest,*

Aranda, Daniel. 'Moral Adjustments to Perrault's Cinderella in French Children's Literature (1850–1900).' *Cinderella Across Cultures: New Directions and Interdisciplinary Perspectives,* edited by Martine-Hennard Dutheil de la Rochère, Gillian Lathey and Monika Woźniak, Wayne State University Press, 2016, pp. 124–40.

Aristegui, Miguel M. 'Dos cineastas se enfrentan a penas de cárcel por rodar un documental sobre un monumento franquista de Pamplona' Eldiario.es, Navarra, 13 Nov. 2018, n.p.

Arrowsmith, Nancy and George Moorse. *Field Guide to the Little People.* Pan, 1977.

Asquith, Anthony and Leslie Howard, directors. *Pygmalion.* Pascal Film Productions, 1938.

Atkinson, Diane. *Rise Up Women! The Remarkable Lives of the Suffragettes.* Bloomsbury, 2018.

Bacchilega, Cristina. *Fairy Tales Transformed? Twenty-First Century Adaptations and the Politics of Wonder.* Wayne State University Press, 2013. Project Muse Ebooks Literature.

Barchilon, Jacques, and Henry Pettit. *The Authentic Mother Goose Fairy Tales and Nursery Rhymes.* Alan Swallow, 1960.

Barsotti, Susanna. 'The Fairy Tale: Recent Interpretations, Female Characters and Contemporary Rewriting. Considerations about an 'Irresistible' Genre.' *Journal of Theories and Research in Education,* vol. 10, no. 2, 2015, pp. 69–80.

Basso, Riccardo. 2016. 'The 20 Best Uses of Mirrors in Cinema History.' *Taste of Cinema.* 13 September. http://www.tasteofcinema.com/2016/the-20-best-uses-of-mirrors-in-cinema-history/ Accessed 9 February 2019

Bassnett, Susan. *Translation Studies.* Revised ed., Routledge, 1991.

Bebić, Domagoj, and Marija Volarevic. 'Do Not Mess with a Meme: The Use of Viral Content in Communicating Politics.' *Communication & Society*, vol. 31, no. 3, 2018, pp. 43–56.

Bell, Florence Lady. *At the Works: Study of a Manufacturing Town [Middlesbrough]*. 1907.

Bell, Florence and Lancelot Speed. *Fairy Tale Plays and How to Act Them*. Longman, 1896.

Benavente, Jacinto. *La Cenicienta, comedia de magia en un prólogo y tres actos dividida en quince cuadros*. Librería de los sucesores de Hernando, 1920.

Besson, Luc, director. *Nikita*. Gaumont, Les Films du Loup, Cecchi Gori Group Tiger Cinematografica, 1990.

Bettelheim, Bruno. *The Uses of Enchantment: The Meaning and Importance of Fairy Tales*. Thames and Hudson, 1976.

—. *The Uses of Enchantment: The Meanings and Importance of Fairy Tales*. Penguin Books, 1991.

Blamires, David. *Telling Tales: The Impact of Germany on English Children's Books 1780–1918*. Open Book, 2009.

—. 'The Early Reception of the Grimms' *Kinder– Und Hausmärchen* in England.' *Bulletin of the John Rylands University Library of Manchester*, vol. 71, no. 3, 1989, pp. 63–77.

Blanchard, Tamsin. *The Shoe: Best Foot Forward*. Carlton Books, 2000.

Block, Geoffrey. '*My Fair Lady*: From *Pygmalion* to *Cinderella*.' *Enchanted Evenings: The Broadway Musical from 'Show Boat' to Sondheim*, edited by Geoffrey Block, Oxford University Press, 1997, pp. 225-244.

—, editor. *Enchanted Evenings: The Broadway Musical from 'Show Boat' to Sondheim*. Oxford University Press, 1997.

Blyth, Alan and Emanuele Luzzati. *Cinderella; La Cenerentola: The Story of Rossini's Opera*. Julia MacRae books, 1981.

Boase-Beier, Jean. 'Poetry Translation.' *The Routledge Handbook of Translation Studies*, edited by Carmen Millán and Francesca Bartrina, Routledge, 2013, pp. 475–487.

Booker, Christopher. *The Seven Basic Plots: Why We Tell Stories*. Continuum 2004.

Bottigheimer, Ruth. 'Cinderella: The People's Princess.' *Cinderella Across Cultures: New Directions and Interdisciplinary Perspectives*, edited by Martine Hennard Dutheil de la Rochère, Gillian Lathey, and Monika Woźniak, Wayne State University Press, 2016, pp. 27-51.

—. *Fairy Tales and Society: Illusion, Allusion, and Paradigm*. University of Pennsylvania Press, 1986.

Boucicault, Dion. *Grimaldi or The Life of an Actress.* [1855] Colin Smythe Ltd., 2010.

Bourne, Michael, choreographer. *Cinderella*, 1997, revised and designed for Sadlers Wells and on tour 2017-2018. Ballet.

Bowen, Elizabeth. 'Dry and Sparkling', *The Tatler and Bystander*, 30 November 1949, pp. 448-449.

Bowen, Elizabeth and Charles Ritchie. *Love's Civil War: letters and diaries from the love affair of a lifetime,* edited by Victoria Glendenning, Simon & Schuster, 2008.

Branagh, Kenneth, director. *Cinderella.* Performance by Kate Blanchett, Lily James: Allison Shearmur Productions, Beagle Pug Films, Genre Films, Disney, 2015.

Briggs, Katharine Mary. *British Folk Tales and Legends: A Sampler.* Paladin, 1977.

Brontë, Charlotte. *Jane Eyre.* [1847] Penguin Classics, 2006.

Brown, Debbie. *Debbie Brown's Fairy Tale Cakes.* Hamlyn, 1995.

Brown, Rita Mae. *Rubyfruit Jungle.* Vintage Classics, 2015.

Bruzzi, Stella. *Undressing Cinema: Clothing and Identity in the Movies.* Routledge, 1997.

Burnett, Frances Hodgson. *Sara Crewe: or, What Happened in Miss Minchin's Boarding School.* 1887. Kindle Edition, Amazon Media, 2012.

Buthod-Girard, Ingrid and Carlos Busquets. *Assepoester.* Hemma, 1995.

Butler, Stephen Henry. 'The Pygmalion Motif and the Crisis of the Creative Process in Modern Fiction.' Unpublished Doctoral thesis. University of Brandeis, 1984.

Caballé, Ana. *El feminismo en España: la lenta conquista de un derecho.* Ediciones Cátedra, 2013.

Callejón, Begoña. *Cenicienta en sangre.* El Gaviero Ediciones, 2010.

Captivating History. *Marie Antoinette: A Captivating Guide to the Last Queen of France Before and During the French Revolution Including Her Relationship with King Louis XVI.* Kindle Edition, Amazon Media, 2018.

Carderera. Mariano. *La ciencia de la mujer al alcance de las niñas.* Imprenta del Colegio de Sordo-Mudos y de Ciegos, 1865.

Carroll, Claudia. *Personally I Blame my Fairy Godmother ... The fairytale ending was just the beginning ...* Avon, 2010.

Cash, Thomas. *Encyclopedia of Body Image and Human Appearance.* Academic Press, 2012.

Castaño Díaz, Carlos Mauricio. 'Defining and Characterizing The Concept of Internet Meme.' *Revista CES Psicología*, vol. 6, no. 1, 2013, pp. 82–104.

Cattrysse, Patrick. 'Cultural Transduction and Adaptation Studies: The Concept of Cultural Proximity.' *Palabra Clave*, vol. 20, no. 3, 2017, pp. 645–62.

—. 'Film (Adaptation) as Translation: Some Methodological Proposals.' *TARGET: International Journal of Translation Studies*, vol. 4, no. 1, 1992, pp. 53–70.

La Cenicienta del Palace. Director, Fernando García de la Vega, performer, Paloma San Basilio, Luis Escobar. 2 Dec. 1985. Musical. Television.

La Cenicienta del Palace. Director and writer, Luis Escobar, writer, director and performer Celia Gámez and Alfonso Godá. Teatro Eslava de Madrid, Madrid. 1 March 1940. Performance.

Centre National de Ressources Textuelles et Lexicales (CNRTL) 2012. https://www.cnrtl.fr/ Accessed 26 March 2020.

Cerrada, Cristina. *Cenicienta en Pensilvania.* DVD Ediciones, 2010.

Chaucer, Geoffrey. *The Canterbury Tales.* c. 1387–1400.

Clarke, Charles Allen. *The Effects of the Factory System.* G. Richards, 1899.

Clarke, Charles Allen. *Old Tales for Young Folks.* John Heywood, 1895.

Clemente, Bernad and Carolina Martínez, directors. *A sus muertos.* Filmoteca de Navarra, 2018.

Climo, Shirley and Loretta Krupinski. *Irish Cinder Lad.* HarperCollins, 1996.

Cole, Babette. *Prince Cinders.* Puffin, 1989.

CollegeHumor. Tinderella: A Modern Fairy Tale. CollegeHumor, 2014.

Collis, Rose. *A Trouser-wearing Character: The Life and Times of Nancy Spain.* Cassell, 1997.

Collodi, Carlo. *The Adventures of Pinocchio.* [1883] Oxford World's Classics, 2009.

Conway, Kyle. 'Cultural Translation, Global Television Studies, and the Circulation of Telenovelas in the United States.' *International Journal of Cultural Studies*, vol. 15, no. 6, Oct. 2012, pp. 583–98.

—. 'Cultural Translation.' *Handbook of Translation Studies*, vol. 3, John Benjamins, 2012.

Cooper, Bradley. *A Star is Born.* Warner Bros. Pictures, Live Nation Productions, Metro-Goldwyn-Mayer, Peters Entertainment, Gerber Pictures, Malpaso Productions, Thunder Road Pictures, 2018.

Craik, Dinah Maria Mulock. *Fairy Book: The Best Popular Fairy Stories*

Selected and Rendered Anew. Macmillan, 1863.

—. *John Halifax, Gentleman.* Copyright ed. edition, vol. 1 & 2, Bernhard Tauchnitz, 1857.

Crispin, Edmund. *The Moving Toyshop.* Penguin Books Ltd., 1946:1960.

Cruikshank, George. *Interesting Story of Cinderella and Her Glass Slipper.* Printed by J.G. Rusher, 1814.

Cullen, Bonnie. 'For Whom the Shoe Fits: Cinderella in the Hands of Victorian Writers and Illustrators.' *The Lion and the Unicorn,* vol. 27, no.1, 2003, pp. 57-82. *Project Muse,* https://muse.jhu.edu/article/39421. Accessed 31 May 2018.

Cukor, George. *A Star is Born.* Transcona Enterprises, 1954.

Cukor, George. *My Fair Lady.* Performance by Rex Harrison and Audrey Hepburn: Warner Bros., 1964.

Dahl, Roald and Quentin Blake. *Revolting Rhymes,* Puffin, 1984.

d'Aulnoy, Marie-Catherine. 'Finette Cendron.' *The Great Fairy Tale Tradition: From Straparola and Basile to the Brothers Grimm,* edited and translated by Jack Zipes, W.W. Norton, 2001, pp. 454–67.

Daly, Martin and Margo Wilson. *The Truth About Cinderella: A Darwinian View of Parental Love.* Weidenfeld and Nicolson, 1998.

Davidson, Hilary. 'Sex and Sin: The Magic of Red Shoes.' *Shoes: A History from Sandals to Sneakers,* edited by Giorgio Riello and Peter McNeil, Berg, 2011, pp. 272–289.

Davies, Stevie. 'Introduction and Notes to Charlotte Brontë's Jane Eyre.' Charlotte Brontë. *Jane Eyre,* [1847] edited by Stevie Davies, Penguin Classics, 2006, pp. xi-xxxiv.

Davis, Jim. 'Introduction' in *Victorian Pantomime: A Collection of Critical Essays,* edited by Jim Davis. Palgrave, 2010, pp. 1-18.

Dayton, Jonathan and Valerie Faris. *Ruby Sparks.* Fox Searchlight Pictures, Bona Fide Productions, DragonCore Studios, 2012.

de Cervantes, Miguel. *Don Quixote.* Francisco de Robles, 1605.

Delarue, Paul. 'From Perrault to Walt Disney: The Slipper of Cinderella.' *Cinderella: A Folklore Casebook,* edited by Alan Dundes, Garland, 1982, p. 110–114.

—. 'The Grandmother's Tale: To Come of Age.' *Little Red Riding Hood Uncloaked: Sex, Morality and the Evolution of a Fairy Tale,* edited by Catherine Orenstein, Basic Books, 2002, pp. 63–84.

Deluzain, H. Edward. 1996. 'Names and Personal Identity.' *Behind the Name.* https://www.behindthename.com/articles/3. Accessed 2 February 2019.

De Pueblo, Moderna. *Idiotizadas.* Editorial Planeta, 2017.

De Santis, Giuseppe. *Roma, Ore 11 / Rome, 11.00*. Titanus, Transcontinental Films, 1952.

Dickie, John. 'How the Muse Defied the Cat', *Sheffield Daily Telegraph*, 6 April 1950, p. 4.

Dillard, Heath. *Daughters of the Reconquest. Women in Castilian Town Society*, 1100–1300. Cambridge University Press, 1984.

Disney, Walt. *Cinderella and Her Animal Friends: A Book About Kindness*. Walt Disney Company, 1987.

—. *Cinderella Magic Wand Book*. Walt Disney Company, 1950.

Dollerup, Cay. 'Translation for Reading Aloud.' *Meta*, vol. 48, no. 1–2, 2003, pp. 81–103.

Dorner, Jane. *Fashion in the Forties and Fifties*. Ian Allan, 1975.

Dowling, Colette. *The Cinderella Complex: Women's Hidden Fear of Independence*. Fontana, 1982.

Dryden, John. *The Preface*. 2nd ed., Jacob Tonson, 1681.

Duffy, Carol Ann. *The World's Wife*. Picador, 1999.

Du Maurier, George. *Trilby*. [1894] Oxford World's Classics, 2009.

Dundes, Alan. '"To Love My Father All": A Psychoanalytic Study of the Folktale Source of King Lear.' *Cinderella: A Casebook*, edited by Alan Dundes, University of Wisconsin Press, 1988, pp. 229-244.

—, editor. *Cinderella: A Casebook*. University of Wisconsin Press, 1988.

Durant, Alan and Ross Collins. *Fairytale Files: Cinderella*. Walker Books, 2008.

Dutheil de la Rochère, Martine Hennard. 'Cinderella's Metamorphoses: A Comparative Study of Two English Translations of Perrault's Tales.' *Przekładaniec: A Journal of Literary Translation*, vol. 22–23, 2009–10, pp. 249–66.

—. 'Introduction: Cinderella across Cultures.' *Cinderella Across Cultures: New Directions and Interdisciplinary Perspectives*, edited by Martine-Hennard Dutheil de la Rochère, Gillian Lathey and Monika Woźniak, Wayne State University Press, 2016, pp. 1–24.

—. *Reading, Translating, Rewriting: Angela Carter's Translational Poetics*. Wayne State University Press, 2013.

Dynel, Marta. ' "I Has Seen Image Macros!" Advice Animals Memes as Visual-Verbal Jokes.' *International Journal of Communication*, vol. 10, 2016, pp. 660–88.

Eknoyan, Garabed. 'A History of Obesity, or How What Was Good Became Ugly and Then Bad.' *Obesity and Chronic Kidney Disease*, vol. 13, no. 4, 2006, pp. 421–427.

Elleström, Lars. 'Adaptations as Intermediality.' *The Oxford Handbook of Adaptation Studies*, edited by Thomas Leitch. Oxford University Press, 2017, pp. 509–26.

—. *Media Transformation: The Transfer of Media Characteristics among Media*. Palgrave MacMillan, 2014.

Ellis, John M. Bill. *One Fairy Story Too Many: The Brothers Grimm and Their Tales*. Chicago University Press, 1983.

Escobar, Luis. *La Cenicienta del Palace*. Unpublished film script, 1940.

Espinosa-Medina, Hernán David, and Enrique Uribe-Jongbloed. ' "Do It, but Do It Dancing!": Television and Format Adaptations in Colombia in the 1980s and Early 1990s.' *New Patterns in Global Television Formats* edited by Karina Aveyard and Albert Moran, Intellect, 2016, pp. 125–39.

—. 'Latin American Contraflow in Global Entertainment Media: Kingdom Rush Series and Zambo Dende as de-Localised Media Products.' *Media International Australia*, 2017, pp. 1–15.

Estow, Clara. 'Women in the Historical Writings of Pedro Lopez de Ayala' *Revista de Estudios Hispánicos,* vol. 11, 1984, pp. 145–52.

Ezell, Lee. *Cinderella Syndrome: Discovering God's Plan When Your Dreams Don't Come True*. Vince Books, 1994.

Farjeon, Eleanor and Ernest H. Shepard. *Glass Slipper: From the Play of the Same Name by Eleanor and Herbert Farjeon*. Oxford University Press, 1973.

Fawcett, Millicent Garrett. *Women's Suffrage: A Short History of A Great Movement*. 1912. Kindle Edition, Endeavour Media, 2018.

Fernández-Lamarque, Maia. 'El bosque, el baile, príncipes y princesas: 'La Bella Durmiente' en *Hable con ella.' L' Érudit franco-espagnol*, vol. 11, 2017, pp. 52–66.

—. *Cinderella in Spain: Variations of the Story as Socio-Ethical Texts*. McFarland Publishers, 2019.

Fernández-Lamarque, María. 'Antonio Robles *La Cenicienta*: A 'Cinderella' Retelling Censored in Franco's Spain' (IRCL) *International Research in Children's Literature,* vol. 7 no. 1, 2014 pp. 78–94 with permission of *Hispania*, The American Association of Teachers of Spanish and Portuguese and John Hopkins University Press.

Fernández-Rodríguez, Carolina. *Las re-escrituras contemporáneas de Cenicienta*. Principado de Asturias. Consejería de Cultura. Universidad de Oviedo, 1997.

—. *La Bella Durmiente a través de la historia*. Universidad de Oviedo, 1998.

Fielding, Sean. 'Shorter Notices', *The Tatler and Bystander.* 19 April 1950, p. 44.

Flanagan, Victoria. *Technology and Identity in Young Adult Fiction: The Posthuman Subject.* Palgrave Macmillan, 2014. Springer Ebook.

Fox, Gemma. *The Cinderella Moment.* HarperCollins Publishers, 2006.

Folguera, Pilar. *El feminismo en España: dos siglos de historia.* Editorial Pablo Iglesias, 2007.

Fortún, Elena. 'Cenicienta' in *Celia lo que dice.* Alianza Editorial, 1928.

Fraser, Antonia. *Marie Antoinette: The Journey.* Weidenfeld and Nicolson, 2001.

Garnett, Henrietta. *Anny: A Life of Anne Thackeray Ritchie.* Chatto and Windus, 2004.

Geronimi, Clyde, and Hamilton Luske, Wilfred Jackson, directors. *Cinderella.* Walt Disney productions, 1950.

Gilbert, Lewis, director. *Educating Rita.* Performance by Michael Caine and Julie Walters: Acorn Pictures, 1983.

Gillespie, Craig, director. *Lars and the Real Girl.* MGM, Sidney Kimmel Entertainment, Lars Productions, 2007.

Glendenning, Victoria. *Elizabeth Bowen: Portrait of a Writer.* Phoenix, 1997.

Gottlieb, Michael, director. *Mannequin.* Gladden Entertainment, 1987.

Goldberg. Harriet. 'Two Parallel Medieval Commonplaces: Antifeminism and Antisemitism in the Medieval.' *Feminist Newsletter,* vol. 7, no. 5 1989.

Gresseth, Gerald K. 'The Pygmalion Tale.' *The Journal of the Pacific Northwest Council of Foreign Languages.* 1981, pp.15-19.

Grimm, Jacob, and Wilhelm Grimm. 'Aschenputtel.' *Kinder und Haus-Märchen gesammelt durch die Brüder Grimm,* 7th edition, volume 1 of 2, Verlag der Dieterichschen Buchhandlung, 1857

—. *The Complete Fairy Tales of the Brothers Grimm.* Translated by Jack Zipes. 1812. University of Princeton Press, 2014.

—. *German Popular Stories, Translated from the Kinder– Und Haus-Märchen.* Translated by Edgar Taylor and David Jardine, vol. 2, James Robins, 1826.

—. *Kinder– Und Haus-Märchen.* 1st ed., vol. 1, Realschulbuchhandlung, 1812.

—. *Kinder– Und Haus-Marchen Gesammelt Durch Die Brüder Grimm.* 2nd ed., vol. 1, G. Reimer, 1819.

—. *Kinder– Und Haus-Märchen: Gesammelt Durch Die Brüder Grimm.* 7th ed., vol. 1–2, Verlag der dieterichschen Buchhandlung, 1857.

—. *Household Tales.* Translated by Margaret Hunt. George Bell, 1884.

Gruner, Elisabeth Rose. 'Cinderella, Marie Antoinette and Sara: Roles and Role Models in *A Little Princess.' The Lion and the Unicorn,* vol. 22, no. 2, 1998, pp. 163-80. *Project Muse,* https://muse.jhu.edu/article/35395. Accessed 1 June 2018.

Guinness, Bryan. *A Fugue of Cinderellas.* Heinemann, 1956.

Hannon, Patricia. '*Corps Cadavres*: Heroes and Heroines in the Tales of Perrault.' *The Great Fairy Tale Tradition: From Straparola and Basile to the Brothers Grimm,* edited by Jack Zipes, W. W. Norton, 2001, pp. 933–57.

Haraway, Donna J. 'A Cyborg Manifesto: Science, Technology, and Socialist Feminism in the Late Twentieth Century.' *Simians, Cyborgs, and Women: The Reinvention of Nature,* Free Association Books, 1991, pp. 149-82.

Hawksley, Lucinda. *The Mystery of Princess Louise: Queen Victoria's Rebellious Daughter.* Vintage, 2013.

Hayton, Natalie. '*Little Red Riding Hood* in the 21st Century: Adaptation, Archetypes, and the Appropriation of a Fairy Tale.' PhD Thesis. De Montfort University, 2013.

Hayward, Susan and Ginette Vincendeau, editors. *French Film: Texts and Contexts.* 2nd ed. Routledge, 2000.

Hayward, Susan. 'Recycled Woman and the Postmodern Aesthetic: Luc Besson's "Nikita" (1990).' *French Film: Texts and Contexts,* edited by Susan Hayward and Ginette Vincendeau. 2nd ed. Routledge, 2000, pp. 297-309.

—. *Luc Besson.* Manchester University Press, 1998.

Heiner, Heidi Anne, editor. *The Fairy Tale Fiction of Anne Isabella Thackeray Ritchie.* Kindle Edition, SurLaLune Press, 2010.

Hibbert, Christopher, editor. *Queen Victoria in Her Letters and Journals.* Sutton Publishing, 1984.

Hitchcock, Alfred. *Vertigo.* Alfred J. Hitchcock Productions, 1958.

Hoffmann, Kathryn A. 'Perrault's "Cendrillon" among the Glass Tales: Crystal Fantasies and Glassworks in Seventeenth-Century France and Italy.' *Cinderella Across Cultures: New Directions and Interdisciplinary Perspectives,* edited by Martine Hennard Dutheil de la Rochère, Gillian Lathey, and Monika Woźniak, Wayne State University Press, 2016, pp. 52-80.

Hughes, John. *Weird Science.* Universal Pictures, 1985.

Hughes, Shirley. *Ella's Big Chance: A Fairy Tale Retold.* The Bodley Head, 2003.

Huntington, Heidi E. 'Subversive Memes: Internet Memes as a Form of Visual Rhetoric.' *Selected Papers of Internet Research*, no. 2009, 2013, pp. 2002–05.

Hutcheon, Linda. *A Theory of Adaptation*. Routledge, 2012.

Innes, Christopher, editor. *The Cambridge Companion to Bernard Shaw.* Cambridge University Press, 1998.

Instituto Nacional de Medicina Legal y Ciencias Forenses. '2017 Forensis: Datos Para La Vida.' *Forensis: Datos Para La Vida*, vol. 19, no. 1, 2018, pp. 255–301.

Iscove, Robert, director. *She's All That*. Miramax, Tapestry Films, FilmColony, All That Productions, 1999.

Izquierdo Arroyo, José María. 'Sobre La Transduccion (Mediaciones Semiológicas).' *Boletín Millares Carlo*, no. 1, 1980, pp. 179–218, http://mdc.ulpgc.es/cdm/ref/collection/bolmc/id/9 Accessed 25 March 2020.

Jackson, Ellen and Kevin O'Malley. *Cinder Edna*. Lee Lothrop & Shephard, 1994.

Jaime, María Felicitas. *Cenicienta en Chueca: mujeres que aman mujeres*. Editorial S.L., 2003.

James, Paula. *Ovid's Myth of Pygmalion on Screen: In Pursuit of the Perfect Woman*. Bloomsbury Academic, 2013.

Jameson, Raymond De Loy. 'Cinderella in China.' *Cinderella: A Casebook*, edited by Alan Dundes. University of Wisconsin Press, 1988, pp. 71-97.

Jenkins, Henry. *Convergence Culture: Where Old and New Media Collide*. New York University Press, 2006.

Jenkins, Henry, Sam Ford and Joshua Green. *Spreadable Media: Creating Value and Meaning in a Network Culture*. New York University Press, 2013.

Johnston, Lucy, and Linda Woolley. *Shoes: A Brief History*. 2nd ed., Victoria and Albert Publications, 2015.

Joshua, Essaka. *Pygmalion and Galatea: The History of a Narrative in English Literature*. Ashgate Publishing Ltd., 2001.

Jungman, Ann and Russell Ayto. *Cinderella and the Hot Air Balloon*. Francis Lincoln, 1995.

Kathleen, Lady. 'Cinderella and the Prince: A Fairy Pantomime with Songs and Music.' *Tales for Little People*, Aldine Publishing, 1910.

Klingberg, Göte. *Children's Fiction in the Hands of the Translators*. Gleerup, 1986.

Laslett, Stephanie and Caroline Sharpe. *Assepoester*. Librero, 1995.

—. *Cinderella*. Parragon, 1994.

—. *Cinderella.* Parragon, 2001.

Lathey, Gillian. *The Role of Translators in Children's Literature: Invisible Storytellers.* Routledge, 2010.

—. 'The Translator as Agent of Change: Robert Samber, Translator of Pornography, Medical Texts, and the First English Version of Perrault's *Cendrillon* (1729).' *Cinderella Across Cultures: New Directions and Interdisciplinary Perspectives,* edited by Martine Hennard Dutheil de la Rochère, Gillian Lathey and Monika Woźniak, Wayne State University Press, 2016.

Law, Helen H. 'The name Galatea in the Pygmalion myth.' *The Classical Journal,* vol. 27, 1932, pp. 337-42.

Lee, Christopher. *The Killing of Cinderella: a Bath Detective Mystery.* Gollancz, 1998.

Longford, Elizabeth, editor. *Darling Loosy: Letters to Princess Louise 1856-1939.* Weidenfeld and Nicholson, 1991.

López Charles, Carlos. 'Transduction between Image and Sound in Compositional Processes.' *Perception,* no. 485, 2008, pp. 1–5.

Luján Pinelo, Aleida. A Theoretical Approach to the Concept of Feminicide/FEMINICIDE. Diss, Director Dr. Peta Hinton, Universiteit Utrecht, The Netherlands Media and Cultural Studies Department, 2015.

Luque-Vera, Nazario. 'La princesa que perdió el pie de su zapatilla.' Comic. *El Víbora,* no. 168. Ediciones La Cúpula, 1993.

MacQueen-Pope, Walter. 'The Story of Pantomime.' *Journal of the Royal Society of Arts,* 105:5002 26 April 1957, pp. 456-458.

McBain, Ed. *Cinderella.* Henry Holt & Co, 1986.

Maguire, Gregory. *Confessions of an Ugly Stepsister.* Regan Books, 1999.

Mallorquí, José. *EL despertar de cenicienta.* Editorial Molino, 1943.

Mangini, Shirley. *Memories of Resistance. Women's Voices from the Spanish Civil War.* Yale University Press, 1995.

Marlow, Joyce, editor. *Votes For Women: The Virago Book of Suffragettes.* Virago, 2008.

Martín Gaite, Carmen. *Los usos amorosos de la posguerra española.* Anagrama, 1986.

—. *Courtship Customs in Postwar Spain.* Translated by Margaret Jones. Bucknell University Press, 2004.

Martínez de Antón, David. *La Teoría de La Transducción Literaria. Hacia Una Teoría Dialógica de La Obra Literaria.* Universidad Autónoma de Madrid, 2015.

Marshall, Gail. *Actresses on the Victorian Stage: Feminine Performance and the Galatea Myth.* Cambridge, 1998.

Marshall, Garry, director. *Pretty Woman*. Performance by Richard Gere and Julia Roberts: Touchstone Pictures, Silver Screen Partners IV, 1990.

Massip, Julia, and Chus Martinez. *Cenicienta tiene un mal sueño*. Illustrated by Marisa Ordoñez. Ajuntament de Barcelona, 2002.

May-Ron, Rona. 'Rejecting the Glass Slipper: The Subversion of Cinderella in Margaret Atwood's *The Edible Woman.*' *Cinderella Across Cultures: New Directions and Interdisciplinary Perspectives*, edited by Martine Hennard Dutheil de la Rochère, Gillian Lathey and Monika Woźniak, Wayne State University Press, 2016, pp. 143–61.

Mazza, Samuele. *Cinderella's Revenge*. Chronicle Books, 1994.

McDowell, Colin. *Shoes: Fashion and Fantasy*. Thames and Hudson, 1989.

Meca, A.; Kneib, T; Gil-Prieto, R; Gil de Miguel, 'Epidemiology of suicide in Spain, 1981–2008: A Spatiotemporal Analysis.' *Public Health,* vol. 127, no. 4, 2013 pp. 380–5.

Méliès, Georges, director. *Cendrillon*. Georges Méliès, Star Film, 1899.

Mestre Juan Carlos, Monedero Juan Carlos. *Te cuento...Cenicienta*. Alkibla, 2015.

Meyer, Marissa. *Cinder*. Square Fish, Feiwel & Friends, 2012.

—. *Cress*. Feiwel & Friends, 2014.

—. *Scarlet*. Square Fish, Feiwel & Friends, 2013.

—. *Winter*. Feiwel & Friends, 2015.

Míguez, María. 'De Blancanieves, Cenicienta y Aurora a Tiana, Rapunzel y Elsa: ¿qué Imagen de La Mujer Transmite Disney?' *Revista Internacional de Comunicación y Desarrollo*, no. 2, 2015, pp. 41–58.

Mills, Margaret A. 'A Cinderella Variant in the Context of a Muslim Women's Ritual.' *Cinderella: A Casebook*, edited by Alan Dundes. University of Wisconsin Press, 1982.

Miller, Beth, editor. 'Sexual Humor in Misogynist Medieval Exempla' *Women in Hispanic Literature: Icons and Fallen Idols*. University of California Press, 1983.

Miller Lewis, Elizabeth. 'Hester Santlow's *Harlequine*: Dance, Dress, Status and Gender on the London Stage, 1706-1734.' *The Clothes that Wear Us: Essays on Dressing and Transgressing in Eighteenth Century Culture*, edited by Jessica Munns and Penny Richards. The University of Delaware Press, 1999, pp. 80-101.

Mitchell, Jennifer. ' "A Girl. A Machine. A Freak": A Consideration of Contemporary Queer Composites.' *Bookbird: A Journal of International Children's Literature*, vol. 52, no. 1, January 2014, pp. 51-62. Project Muse.

Mirrer, Louis. *Women, Jews and Muslims in the Texts of Reconquest Castile.* Ann Arbor University Press, 1996.

Moreno Sardá, Amparo. 'La réplica de las mujeres al franquismo' *El feminismo en España: Dos siglos de historia.* Editorial Pablo Iglesia, 2007.

Morikawa, Hisashi. 'Myths and Legends in Bernard Shaw's Pygmalion.' *Bernard Shaw Studies.* vol. 11, 2010, pp. 1–18.

Mortimer, Carole. *Glass Slippers and Unicorns.* Mills & Boon, 1986.

Mullen, Laura. 'Wearing it Out.' *Footnotes: On Shoes,* edited by Shari Benstock and Suzanne Ferriss, Rutgers University Press, 2001, pp. 282–288.

Mulvey, Laura. 'Visual Pleasure and Narrative Cinema.' *Screen,* vol. 16, no. 3, 1975, pp. 6-18.

Nichols, Charles Washburn. 'Fielding's Satire on Pantomime.' *PMLA,* 46, 4, 1931, pp. 1107-1112, https://www.jstor.org/stable/41366062

Ober de Baubeta, Patricia Anne. 'Fairy-Tale Intertext in Iberian and Latin American Women's Writing' in *Fairy Tale and Feminism: New Approaches,* edited by Donald Hasse. Wayne University Press, 2004.

O'Dea, Jenny A. 'Body Image and Self-Esteem.'*Encyclopedia of Body Image and Human Appearance,* edited by Thomas Cash. Academic Press, 2012, pp.141-147.

Oittinen, Riitta. *Translating for Children.* Taylor and Francis, 2000.

O'Loughlin, Aislinn and Marie-Louise Fitzpatrick. *Cinderella's Fella.* Wolfhound Press, 1996.

Ortiz, Lourdes. 'Cenicienta: Parábola en dos actos.' *Los motivos de Circe.* Ediciones El Dragón, 1988.

O'Sullivan, Emer. 'Children's Literature and Translation.' *The Routledge Handbook of Translation Studies,* edited by Carmen Millán and Francesca Bartrina, Routledge, 2013, pp. 451–63.

—. *Comparative Children's Literature.* Routledge, 2005.

Ovid. *The Metamorphoses.* Translated by Henry T. Riley. Digireads.com, 2017.

Perrault, Charles and Francesc Mateu. *Walt Disney: Cendrillon; Un Livre Anime.* 1995.

Perrault, Charles. 'Cendrillon, ou la Petite Pantoufle de Verre.' *Contes* [1698], edited by Catherine Magnien. Livre de Poche, 1990, pp. 245-53.

—. 'Cinderella or the Glass Slipper.' *Beauties, Beasts, and Enchantment: Classic French Fairy Tales.* Translated and edited by Jack Zipes, Crescent Moon, 2009, pp. 25–30.

—. *Histoires, Ou Contes Du Temps Passé, Avec Des Moralitez*. C. Barbin, 1697.

—. *Histories or Tales of Past Times. With Morals*. Translated by Robert Samber, J. Pote and R. Montagu, 1729.

—. *Tales of Passed Times by Mother Goose. With Morals*. Translated by Robert Samber, 6th ed., J. Melvill, 1764.

—. *The Fairy Tales of Charles Perrault*. Illustrated by Harry Clarke, Introduction by Thomas Bodkin, Harrap, 1922.

—. *The Tales of Mother Goose: Bilingual Edition: English-French,* [1697] Sleeping Cat Press, 2014.

Peters, Sally. 'Shaw's Life: A Feminist in Spite of Himself.' *The Cambridge Companion to George Bernard Shaw*, edited Christopher Innes. Cambridge University Press, 1998, pp. 3-24.

Philip, Neil. *The Cinderella Story*. Penguin, 1989.

Pierson, Frank, director. *A Star is Born*. Barwood Films, First Artists, Winters Hollywood Entertainment Holdings Corporation 1976.

Poesio, Giannandrea. 'Theatre practices and meta-narratives: a reading of the illustrated gestures in the Chludov Psalter.' *Bizantinistica: Rivista di Studi Bizantini e Slavi. Serie Seconda*, Anno XIX, 2018, pp. 250.

Pollack, Sidney, director. *Sabrina*. Constellation Entertainment, Mirage Enterprises, Mont Blanc Entertainment GmbH, Paramount Pictures, Sandollar Productions, Scott Rudin Productions, Worldwide, 1995.

Pop, Doru. 'Mythology Amalgamated. The Transformation of the Mythological and the Re-Appropriation of Myths in Contemporary Cinema.' *Ekphrasis*, no. 2, 2013, pp. 10–25.

Pradas, Monleón and Elena Edith. *In-Out House: Circuitos de género y violencia en la era tecnológica*. Editorial Universitat Politècnica de València, 2012.

Propp, Vladimir. *The Morphology of the Folktale,* edited by Louis A. Wagner and translated by Laurence Scott. 2nd. University of Texas Press, 1998.

Puente, Sonia Núñez. 'Activism Trouble: Transfeminism and Institutional Feminism in Spain.' *Feminist Formations*, vol. 28 no. 2, 2016, pp. 73–93. *ProQuest*, 19 July 2019.

Pullman, Philip. *I Was a Rat! Or the Scarlet Slippers*. Corgi Yearling Books, 2001.

Radford, Jill and Diana E. H. Russell (eds). *Femicide: The Politics of Woman Killing*, Open University Press, 1992.

Randall, Ronne et al. *Cinderella: A Magic 3-Dimensional Fairy-Tale World*. Sterling Publishing, 2006.

Ramírez, Pedro Luis, director. *Cenicienta y Ernesto.* Prod. Cinematográfica S.A, 1957.

Ratcliffe, Marjorie. 'Adulteresses, Mistresses and Prostitutes: Extramarital Relationships in Medieval Castile. *Hispania*, vol. 67, 1984, pp. 346–50

Reinhold, Meyer. 'The Naming of Pygmalion's Animated Statue.' *The Classical Journal,* vol. 66, no. 4, 1971, pp. 316–319.

Reynolds, Leila. 'Cinderella's Sisters.' A. Halle Ltd., 1900.

Richards, Jeffrey. *The Golden Age of Pantomime: Slapstick, Spectacle and Subversion in Victorian England.* I B Taurus & Co Ltd., 2015.

Robles, Antonio. *La Cenicienta.* Editorial Estrella, 1936.

Rodríguez, Delia. *Memecracia: Los Virales Que Nos Gobiernan.* Gestión 2000, 2013.

Rodríguez Marroquín, Ángela María. 'Érase Una Vez Muchas Cenicientas: Cómo Leer El Modelo Femenino Del Siglo Xx Desde Las Películas Norteamericanas de La Cenicienta.' *Memoria y Sociedad,* vol. 16, no. 33, 2012, pp. 84–98.

Roncallo-Dow, Sergio. 'Confused Travolta o El Placer de Lo Simple.' *Palabra Clave—Revista de Comunicación*, vol. 19, no. 1, 2016, pp. 8–14.

Rosenthal, Robert and Lenore Jacobson. *Pygmalion in the Classroom: Teacher Expectation and Pupils' Intellectual Development.* Rinehart and Winston, 1968.

Russell, Diana E. H., and Roberta A. Harmes. *Femicide in Global Perspective.* Teachers College Press, 2001.

Russell, Diana. *Feminicidio: una perspectiva global.* UNAM, Centro de Investigaciones Interdisciplinaria en Ciencias y Humanidades, 2006.

—. *The Origin & Importance of the Term Feminicide.* Video. 1993. http://www.dianarussell.com/videos_and_audio.html Accessed 21 March 2019.

Russell, Willy. *Educating Rita.* Methuen Drama, 2009.

Sallis, Susan. *The Pumpkin Coach.* Corgi Books, 2004.

Sanders, Joe Sutcliff. *Disciplining Girls: Understanding the Origins of the Classic Orphan Girl Story.* John Hopkins University Press, 2011.

Saxon, Wolfgang. 'Hermione Gingold, English actress, dies at 89.' *New York Times.* 25 May 1987. http://www.nytimes.com/1987/05/25/obituaries/hermione-gingold-english-actress-dies-at-89.html Accessed 8 June 2017.

Scanlon, Geraldine. *La polémica feminista en la España contemporánea (1868–1974)* Trans. Rafael Mazarrasa. Ediciones Akal, 1986.

Scott, Martha. 'George Cruikshank at the Osborne Collection.' Online https://torontopubliclibrary.typepad.com/trl/2016/03/curators-choice-george-cruikshank-at-the-osborne-collection.html.   Accessed   26 February 2019.

Scott, Virginia. 'The Infancy of English Pantomime: 1716-1723.' *Educational Theatre Journal.* 24:2, May 1972, pp. 125-134.

Schacker, Jennifer. 'Slaying Blunderboer: Cross-Dressed Heroes, National Identities, and Wartime Pantomime.' *Marvels & Tales,* 27, 1, 2013, pp. 52-64.

Semmelhack, Elizabeth. *Heights of Fashion: A History of the Elevated Shoe.* Periscope, 2008.

—. *Shoes: The Meaning of Style.* Reaktion Books, 2017.

Severn, Bill. *If the Shoe Fits: The Lively Story of Shoes and Shoe Making, from Egyptian Sandals to Astronaut Boots.* David McKay, 1964.

Sexton, Anne. *Transformations.* Oxford University Press, 1972.

Sherman, George, director. *La nueva Cenicienta.* Guión Producciones Cinematográficas, 1965. Film.

Silvy, Camille. 'The African Princess: Sarah Forbes Bonetta.' *Black History Month UK,* 25 Aug. 2015. http://www.blackhistorymonth.org.uk/article/section/real-stories/the-african-princess-sarah-forbes-bonetta/. Accessed 7 June 2018.

Shakespeare, William. *Henry IV: Part I,* edited by Jonathan Bate and Eric Rasmussen, Random House, 2009.

Shakespeare, William. *The Winter's Tale.* [1623] Wordsworth Classics, 1995.

Shaw, George Bernard. *Pygmalion: A Romance in Five Acts.* Prestwick House Inc., 2005.

Shedden-Ralston, William Ralston. 'Cinderella.' *Cinderella: A Casebook,* edited by Alan Dundes. University of Wisconsin Press, 1988, pp. 30-56.

Shelley, Mary. *Frankenstein.* [1818] Wordsworth Editions, 1992.

Sinclair, John. ' "The Hollywood of Latin America", Miami as Regional Center.' *Television & New Media,* 2003.

—. 'Transnationalisation of Television Programming in the Iberoamerican Region.' *MATRIZes,* vol. 8, no. 2, 2014, pp. 63–77.

Sindoni, Maria Grazia. '"The Semantics of Migration". Translation as Transduction: Remaking Meanings Across Modes.' *Hermes —Journal of Language and Communication in Business,* no. 55, 2016, pp. 27–44.

Singer, Irving. *Cinematic Mythmaking: Philosophy in Film.* The MIT Press, 2008.

Southgate, Vera. *Cinderella.* Ladybird Book, 2008.

Southgate, Vera and Paul Finn. *Cinderella.* Ladybird Book, 2005.

Southgate, Vera and Brian Price-Thomas. *Cinderella: Retold for Easy*

Reading. Well-Loved Tales. Ladybird Book, 1981.

Southgate, Vera and Eric Winter. *Cinderella: A Ladybird Easy-Reading Book.* Ladybird Books, 1968.

Spain, Nancy. *Poison in Play.* Hutchinson & Co (Publishers) Ltd., 1945.

—. *Death Before Wicket.* Hutchinson & Co (Publishers) Ltd., 1946.

—. *Murder, Bless It.* Hutchinson & Co (Publishers) Ltd., 1948.

—. *Poison for the Teacher.* Hutchinson & Co (Publishers) Ltd., 1949.

—. *Cinderella Goes to the Morgue.* Thriller Book Club, 1950.

—. *Why I'm Not a Millionaire.* Hutchinson & Co (Publishers) Ltd., 1957.

—. *A Funny Thing Happened on the Way.* Hutchinson & Co (Publishers) Ltd., 1964.

Spence, Lewis. *British Fairy Origins.* Aquarian, 1981.

Stuart, Alex. *A Cruise for Cinderella.* Mills & Boon, 1956.

Styles, Anne. *That Cinderella Feeling.* Scarlett, 1998.

Suárez Solís, Sara. 'Cenicienta 39.' *Ábaco,* no 6. 1989 pp. 114-116. CICEES, http//www.jstor.org/stable/20795710 Accessed 11 Oct. 2017.

Sutherland, Lucie. 'Jeffrey Richards, *The Golden Age of Pantomime* (London: I. B. Tauris, 2014), 438pp.' *Nineteenth Century Theatre and Film*, 42, 1, 2015, pp. 99-102.

Sutton, Martin James. 'The Sin Complex: A Critical Study of English Versions of the Grimms' *Kinder- Und Hausmärchen* in the Nineteenth Century in Comparison with the German Originals.' PhD Thesis. University of Auckland, New Zealand. 1994.

Talairach-Vielmas, Laurence. *Fairy Tales, Natural History and Victorian Culture.* Palgrave Macmillan, 2014.

Tashlin, Frank. *Cinderfella.* Jerry Lewis Productions, 1960.

Thwaite, Ann. *Frances Hodgson Burnett: Beyond the Secret Garden.* The History Press, 2007.

Thussu, Daya Kishan. 'Mapping Global Media Flow and Contra-Flow.' *Media on the Move: Global Flow and Contra-Flow*, edited by Daya Kishan Thussu, Routledge, 2007, pp. 221–38.

Tillett, Iris. *Cinderella Army: The Women's Land Army in Norfolk.* Jim Baldwin Publishing, 1988.

Trevisan, Michele Kapp, Eduardo Biscayno De Prá and Mariana Fagundes Goethel. *Meme: Intertextualidades e Apropriações Na Internet.* Revista Observatório vol 2 no. 1 May 2016, pp. 277–98.

Uribe-Jongbloed, Enrique, et al. 'Cultural Transduction and Intertextuality in Video Games: An Analysis of Three International Case Studies.' *Contemporary Research on Intertextuality in Video Games*, edited by Christophe Duret and Christian-Marie Pons, IGI Glopal, 2016, pp. 143–61.

Uribe-Jongbloed, Enrique, and Hernán David Espinosa-Medina. 'A Clearer Picture: Towards a New Framework for the Study of Cultural Transduction in Audiovisual Market Trades.' *OBSERVATORIO (OBS*)*, vol. 8, no. 1, 2014, pp. 23–48, http://obs.obercom.pt/index.php/obs/article/view/707/642 Accessed 25 March 2020.

—. 'An Introduction to Cultural Transduction.' *Palabra Clave*, vol. 20, no. 3, 2017, pp. 615–21.

Uther, Hans-Jörg. *The Types of International Folktales: A Classification and BibliographyBased on the System of Antti Aarne and Stith Thompson vols. 1, 2 and 3*. FF communications Suomalainen Tiedeakatemia, Academia Scientiarum Fennica, 2004.

Venuti, Lawrence. *The Scandals of Translation: Towards an Ethic of Difference*. Routledge, 1998.

—. editor. *The Translation Studies Reader*. Routledge, 2000.

Vergés Nuria Bosh and Jaume Nualant. 'Feminicides in Area: Interactive Visualizations of Feminicides in the Spanish State.' CIMUAT: Congreso internacional de mujeres, arte y Tecnología, 2010.

Vesonder, Timothy. 'Eliza's Choice: Transformation Myth and the Ending of *Pygmalion*.' *Fabian Feminist: Bernard Shaw and Woman*, edited by Rodelle Weintraub. Pennsylvania State University, 1977, pp. 39-45.

Victoria and Albert Museum. 'A History of Shoes.' *Shoes: Pleasure and Pain*, 2018. https://www.vam.ac.uk/shoestimeline/ Accessed 15 March 2019.

Victoria, Queen. '11 January 1851.' *Queen Victoria's Journals*, http://www.queenvictoriasjournals.org/ Accessed 7 June 2018.

Vincendeau, Ginette. 'Family plots: The Fathers and Daughters of French Cinema.' *Sight and Sound*, vol.1, no.11, 1992, pp. 14-17.

Vitti, Antonio. *Giuseppe De Santis and Postwar Italian Cinema*. University of Toronto Press, 1996.

Vives C., C. Álvarez-Dardet, and P. Caballero. *Violencia del compañero íntimo en España*, Departamento de Salud Pública. Universitat d'Alacant. España. Correspondencia: C. Vives Cases. Departamento de Salud Pública. Edificio de Ciencias Sociales. Campus Sant Vicent del Raspeig. Apdo. 99. 03080 Alicante. España.

Volledorf, Lisa. *Recovering Spain's Feminist Tradition*. Modern Language Association of America, 2001.

Warne, Frederick. *Warne's National Nursery Library; Comprising Cinderella, the Three Bears, Tom Thumb, Punch and Judy, Jack and the Bean-Stalk*. Frederick Warne, 1870.

Warner, Marina. *From the Beast to the Blonde: On Fairy Tales and their Tellers*. Chatto and Windus, 1994.

—. 'Those Brogues: Marina Warner on Her Parents and Other Travellers.' *London Review of Books*, edited by Mary-Kay Wilmers, vol. 38, no. 19, Oct. 2016, pp. 29–32.

Wenzel-Bürger, Eva. *Aschenputtel: Ein Märchen Der Gebrüder Grimm* Carlsen Verlag 1995.

Wartenberg, Thomas E. *Unlikely Couples: Movie Romance as Social Criticism*. Westview Press, 1999.

Weintraub, Rodelle. 'Bernard Shaw's Henry Higgins: A Classic Aspergen.' *English Literature in Transition, 1880 – 1920*, vol. 49, no. 4, 2006, pp. 388-397.

Weintraub, Rodelle. *Fabian Feminist: Bernard Shaw and Woman*. Pennsylvania State University, 1977.

Wellman, William A. and Jack Conway, directors. *A Star is Born.* Selznick International Pictures, 1937.

Weston, Tamara. 'The Problem with Princesses.' *TIME*, 2009, http://entertainment.time.com/2009/12/09/top-10-disney-controversies/slide/the-problem-with-princesses/ Accessed 25 March 2020.

Wiggins, Bradley E., and G. Bret Bowers. 'Memes as Genre: A Structurational Analysis of the Memescape.' *New Media and Society*, vol. 17, no. 11, 2015, pp. 1886–906.

Wilde, Jennifer. *The Slipper.* McGraw-Hill, 1987.

Wilder, Billy, director. *Sabrina.* Paramount Pictures, 1954.

Wittman, Emily. 'Literary Narrative Prose and Translation Studies.' *The Routledge Handbook of Translation Studies*, edited by Carmen Millán and Francesca Bartrina, Routledge, 2013, pp. 438–50.

Woodbridge, Homer. 'William Archer: Prophet of Modern Drama.' *The Sewanee Review.* 44, 2, 1936, pp. 207-221.

Zelnik, Frederic, director. *Mr Cinders*. British International Pictures, 1934.

Zipes, Jack. 'Author Biographies.' *The Great Fairy Tale Tradition: From Straparola and Basile to the Brothers Grimm*, edited by Jack Zipes, W. W. Norton, 2001, pp. 821–42.

—. *Breaking the Magic Spell: Radical Theories of Folk and Fairy Tales: Revised and Expanded Edition.* University Press of Kentucky, 2002.

—. 'Cross–Cultural Connections and the Contamination of the Classical Fairy Tale.' *The Great Fairy Tale Tradition: From Straparola and Basile to the Brothers Grimm*, edited by Jack Zipes, W. W. Norton, 2001, pp. 845–69.

—. *The Enchanted Screen: The Unknown History of Fairy-Tale Films.* Routledge, 2011.

—. *Fairy Tales and the Art of Subversion: The Classical Genre for Children and the Process of Civilization.* Routledge, 1983.

—. *Happily Ever after: Fairy Tales, Children, and the Culture Industry.* Routledge, 1997.

—. editor and translator. *The Great Fairy Tale Tradition: From Straparola and Basile to the Brothers Grimm.* W. W. Norton, 2001.

—. editor. *The Oxford Companion to Fairy Tales: The Western Fairy Tale Tradition from Medieval to Modern.* Oxford University Press, 2000.

—. editor. *Victorian Fairy Tales: The Revolt of the Fairies and Elves.* Routledge, 1987.

INDEX